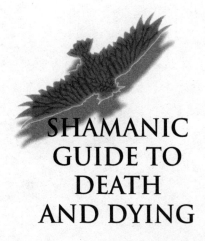

SHAMANIC GUIDE TO DEATH AND DYING

Take a journey beyond this reality . . .

. . . as a shamanic deathwalker gives you a firsthand account of her many journeys to the Lands of the Dead. This book is written for anyone interested in death and dying, as well as those who are interested in shamanism.

An ancient mystical path, shamanism uses altered states of consciousness to gain insight, effect healing, and act as a bridge between realities. A shamanic deathwalker is responsible for guiding us through our journeys to the next world.

Author Kristin Madden tells how she and other deathwalkers assist the dying, the departed, and those loved ones who remain on the physical plane. She also explores:

- Why many people may experience an increase in psychic abilities and paranormal encounters when a loved one passes on

- What effect a stroke or coma has on one's soul, and what you can do to help someone in this condition

- What actually happens on the spirit level at the moment of death

- How to reconnect with departed loved ones, and your own spirit guides

- How you can assist a pet or animal through their passage

Death and birth are considered "gateways" between the physical and spirit worlds. *Shamanic Guide to Death and Dying* is your complete guide for the journeys between worlds.

About the Author

Kristin Madden (New Mexico) is a licensed Avatar Master; a Druid and tutor in the Order of Bards, Ovates, and Druids; and a former environmental chemist. In addition to being a writer, she is a wildlife rehabilitator and raptor researcher. Raised in a shamanic home, Kristin is herself a "deathwalker." She is a frequent contributor to *Circle Network News* and the *Avatar Journal*.

To Write to the Author

If you wish to contact the author or would like more information about this book, please write to the author in care of Llewellyn Worldwide and we will forward your request. Both the author and publisher appreciate hearing from you and learning of your enjoyment of this book and how it has helped you. Llewellyn Worldwide cannot guarantee that every letter written to the author can be answered, but all will be forwarded. Please write to:

Kristin Madden
℅ Llewellyn Worldwide
P.O. Box 64383, Dept. K494-4
St. Paul, MN 55164-0383, U.S.A.

Please enclose a self-addressed stamped envelope for reply, or $1.00 to cover costs. If outside U.S.A., enclose international postal reply coupon.

KRISTIN MADDEN

SHAMANIC GUIDE TO DEATH AND DYING

INCLUDES MEDITATIONS & RITUALS

1999
Llewellyn Publications
St. Paul, Minnesota 55164-0383
U.S.A.

FIRST EDITION
First Printing, 1999

The following is reprinted with permission: Simon & Schuster from *Parallel Universes: The Search for Other Worlds* by Fred Alan Wolfe. ©1988 by Youniverse. *Eye of the Centaur,* by Barbara Hand Clow. © 1986, Bear & Co, Santa Fe, NM; *The Teachings of Don Carlos,* by Victor Sanchez. © 1995, Bear & Co, Santa Fe, NM; *Ecstasy is a New Frequency,* by Chris Griscom. © 1987, Bear & Co, Santa Fe, NM; *Far Journeys* by Robert A. Monroe: Doubleday, a division of Bantam Doubleday Dell Publishing Group, Inc.; *Ultimate Journey* by Robert A. Monroe: Doubleday, a division of Bantam Doubleday Dell Publishing Group, Inc.; Dr. Maureen B. Roberts ©1998. *Soul-Making and Soul-Retrieval: Creative Bridges Between Shamanism and Depth Psychology* (work-in-progress). Quotes from chapter "Embracing the Fragmented Self;" Eliade, Mircea, *Shamanism: Archaic Techniques of Ecstasy,* ©1972 by Princeton University Press. Reprinted by permission of Princeton University Press.; Collinder, Bjorn; *The Lapps.* ©1972 by Princeton University Press. Reprinted by permission of Princeton University Press; *Dr. Pitcairn's Complete Guide to Natural Health for Dogs & Cats,* © 1982 by Richard H. Pitcairn & Susan Pitcairn. Permission granted by Rodale Press, Inc. Emmaus, PA 18098; *The Tao of Physics* by Fritjof Capra, ©1975, 1983, 1991. Reprinted by arrangement by Shambala Publications Inc., Boston; *Man and His Symbols,* by Carl G. Jung, Ferguson Publishing Company, Chicago.

Cover design: William Merlin Cannon
Book design and editing: Michael Maupin

Library of Congress Cataloging-in-Publication Data
Madden, Kristin, 1964 –
    Shamanic guide to death and dying : includes meditations & rituals / Kristin Madden. — 1st ed.
        p.   cm.
    Includes bibliographical references and index.
    ISBN 1-56718-494-4
    1. Death—religious aspects. 2. Shamanism—Miscellanea. I. Title.
    BL504.M25 1999
    291.2'3—dc21   99-047186

Llewellyn Publications
A Division of Llewellyn Worldwide, Ltd.
P.O. Box 64383, Dept. K494-4
St. Paul, MN 55164-0383, U.S.A.
www.llewellyn.com

♻ Printed in the United States of America on recycled paper.

For Karl and Dave, with all my love

....

Dedicated to Stewart Farrar
and the Order of Bards, Ovates, and Druids

CONTENTS

CONTENTS

EXERCISES, MEDITATIONS, CEREMONIES, AND JOURNEYS

ACKNOWLEDGMENTS

There are so many people who have contributed to the creation of this book, on both sides of the Veil, that it would be impossible to list them all. I have been blessed with a lifetime of wonderful teachers in all forms and I thank each of you for your part in who I am.

First and foremost, I want to thank my husband for his unswerving patience and support, and for reading countless revisions of the same chapters over and over. Dave, my best friend, your love makes all things possible and wonderful.

My mother, of course, is mostly responsible for how I grew up and the wild experiences I was exposed to. She was the first deathwalker I knew and her shamanic and psychic abilities still amaze me. Without the unconditional support of my Mom and Woz (my Dad), and their willingness to be explorers, I probably would have grown up to be a "normal" American—and I wouldn't have been nearly as happy.

I send heartfelt thanks to all my friends of the original Shaman-Circle. Our discussions around the cyber-fire were invaluable in helping me learn to communicate my thoughts and experiences. Your support and contributions to the *Shamanic Guide to Death and Dying* made it a better book.

Love and thanks go out to Stewart Farrar. Without his advice and encouragement, I may not have had the motivation to start writing. This, and the fact that he has always reminded me of my grandfather, are why this book is also dedicated to him.

My deepest appreciation goes out to all the authors, writers, and speakers who have given me their support, advice, and encouragement along the way. Thank you to Maya Heath, Janet and Stewart Farrar, Gavin Bone, Oz Andersen, Trish Telesco, Niall Robin Lockhart (Nicholas Mann), Maya Sutton, Philip and Stephanie Carr-Gomm, and all the people the Monroe Institute.

I can honestly say that without Avatar, this book might not be a reality and my life would be vastly different. I lovingly thank the people at Star's Edge International for their work and for their unconditional support of my creations.

I offer blessings of honor and gratitude to all my spirit guides, especially Grand-mother Spider, who wove me into this project and didn't give me much choice about backing out. I know written thanks are not necessary, but it is important for me to acknowledge this Other realm of support.

Barbara Clow, of Bear & Company, deserves my thanks for her honesty and for working with me for several months. Although Bear & Company did not choose to publish this book, it would not be the book it is without the input of Ms. Clow.

I gratefully acknowledge Llewellyn and their entire staff, especially Ann Kerns, Nancy J. Mostad, and Michael Maupin, for their support and assistance throughout the process. They took a chance on a first-time author and have dealt with me in a straightforward and honest manner. I offer my gratitude and respect to Bill Cannon who was in charge of the design of this cover. How you managed to capture so much in such a beautiful cover is beyond me. Llewellyn has earned my utmost respect and appreciation.

PREFACE

This book is written for anyone who is interested in death and dying, as well as those who are interested in shamanism. As a result, I have attempted to communicate these ideas and experiences in terms that the general metaphysical population can understand. I have also made suggestions based on an understanding that not all reading this book are about to embark upon a strictly shamanic path.

Although the *Shamanic Guide to Death and Dying* contains a good amount of traditional shamanic information, it is written from a modern shamanic viewpoint. Those of us walking a shamanic path in modern society are called to work with people of many diverse backgrounds and religions. We serve these communities best by expanding our own experience and understanding beyond the limitations of any one tradition. Modern shamans incorporate any methods they feel are necessary and beneficial for themselves and their communities. As a result, you will find several non-"shamanic" elements in these pages.

I do offer some basic exercises and ceremonies that are based on traditional indigenous ceremonies. I make no apologies for this. I am not teaching any specific tradition, nor am I divulging anything that has not already been incorporated into general metaphysical society. The point is that people are and will continue to use these elements. If we are totally honest, none of our ancestral traditions are as they originated with the first People. As the human race has migrated and wandered, we have mixed with and assimilated elements from many different peoples. My goal is to teach the sacredness inherent in these ceremonies and guide readers in using these elements with honor and respect.

Throughout this book, I make use of the word departed in place of the words dead or deceased. I do this specifically to stress the understanding that these beings have not "died." I also want to distinguish the death of the physical body from more damaging (to the whole being) deaths, such as those associated with soul-fragmentation and emotional or mental deaths. These departed individuals have undergone a natural, yet incredible transformation and continue to live on in another state of energy. This is something all of us have experienced and will certainly experience again. When we regain our abilities to remain open to these Other worlds, we will recognize that this is not unknown to us. Far from being the end of someone, it is the reintegration of our complete beings.

I also make use of the word "shaman" throughout this book, mainly for ease of use, to denote anyone that follows a shamanic path and uses that path to work for the benefit of his or her community. While the vast majority of these individuals are more likely shamanic practitioners than shamans, and many may simply choose to use shamanic methods to complement their own special path, it would be far too cumbersome to attempt to address each of these possibilities within these pages.

Furthermore, I have chosen to capitalize and italicize certain words in this book that are not generally printed this way. Some of these are written this way to indicate their sacredness. For example the Bear is a holy animal to the Saami, and as such, is capitalized in that discussion. Other words such as *knowing* and Other, as in alternate (or Other) realities, are written this way to denote their special implications in this book. Most of these words are used in common language with far less vital and specific meanings.

In order to stress the importance of opening to personal intuition and creativity, I have not gone into elaborate detail in the exercises and ceremonies outlined in this book. Although a few include specific prayers, they are all intended to be guides and references. It is my hope that my words will spur the reader's own inner voice to create truly meaningful rituals. Therefore, I encourage you to use the basic outlines, even use my words if you choose, but feel free to add or alter whatever seems to resonate best within you.

And finally, I should note that most of the exercises in this book are written as guided meditations. While there is a certain degree of freedom in those labeled as "journeys" and much of the imagery is more traditionally "shamanic," it is impossible to write an outline for a true shamanic journey. The journey can be suggested, a goal can be offered, and a way can be presented, but the true shamanic journey has a way of taking on a life of its own. This is the difficulty facing those of us writing with a shamanic focus.

My goal is to offer a place to begin; a road for you to start down. Initially, many of you may need to follow a guided meditation. In modern society, many of us are drilled to disbelieve Otherworldly experiences and mistrust our own intuition. Before we can consciously return to the true journey, we may need to use imagination or guidance. This is nothing to be ashamed of. If your mind wanders or if you just don't feel you are deep enough or really out-of-body, just be with what happens without judgment. Things will change as you progress and open to your spirit guides.

Chapter 1

INTRODUCTION
TO SHAMANISM

Shamanism has become very trendy in the last few years. Hundreds, perhaps thousands, of people sign up each week to journey to drums and connect with their spirit guides. Books are selling off bookshelves and there are entire on-line message boards, newsgroups, and chat rooms devoted to the discussion of shamanism. But how many of us really know what shamanism is? What is the role of a shaman in society? How does one become a shaman? And what does shamanism have to do with death and dying?

The answers to these questions will vary according to the individual and the culture. Since modern shamans recognize that the only constant is change, shamanism is a continually changing path. Although there usually are traditional methods associated with shamanic workings, shamans must be able to evolve along with their changing societies if they are to continue to effectively serve those societies. Shamans are responsible to their communities as healers, seers, and guides. Therefore, it is counterproductive for shamans to rigidly hang on to old beliefs and methods while our societies continue to change.

This is not to say that old necessarily means obsolete. Quite the contrary; those of us who walk a shamanic path have great respect for the wisdom of elders and the guidance and protection of our ancestors. In fact, most modern shamans still use time-honored techniques for inducing shamanic states of consciousness, for divination, and for healing. We honor ancient ways and build on them, incorporating new worldviews and techniques to better serve our communities.

There are a number of modern individuals who are working shamanically without making the connection between what they do and shamanism. These are people who work with their dreams and out-of-body experiences to channel energies of growth and healing to their communities. They are those individuals who have answered the Call of the spirits, even though it means facing their fears and embracing the unknown. For example, Robert Monroe, founder of the Monroe Institute that developed the Hemi-Sync technology, was a revolutionary shaman.

Robert Monroe was a successful businessman who, in 1958, began to experience spontaneous out-of-body journeys. It is specifically this type of journey that distinguishes the shaman from other mystics. Monroe studied these travels and recorded them in three books. He went beyond belief systems, worked with guides from other realities, and assisted the dead to the next world.

Monroe underwent a complete psycho-spiritual change, a type of shamanic initiation, and dedicated his life to bringing his knowledge and technology to the public. The Hemi-Sync technology developed by the Monroe Institute is an incredibly effective means of inducing shamanic states of consciousness.

Monroe never saw himself as a shaman and, to my knowledge, he has never been called one. But in my opinion, he was one in every sense of the word. He traveled the Other worlds and served his community as only he could, with the assistance of his spirit guides. In this way, Monroe brought healing and guidance during and beyond life to many that could not have accepted a shamanic worldview.

As I will discuss in a later chapter, it is essential today to be able to move beyond our egos and release limiting beliefs in order to frame healing and guidance in terms that those in need can accept. Shamanic workings move us beyond the limitations of personal identity and ego. Through our Otherworld journeys, particularly to the Lands of the Dead, we gain a much more expanded, less personal view of life and reality. A shaman cannot work effectively from within the confines of the ego and personality.

For example, the Hindu view of death would most likely be of little comfort to a Catholic, just as the analogies used by someone from Siberia would probably not make much sense to someone from Tahiti. We need to allow healing energy to flow, unrestricted by personal or cultural beliefs, and we must be able to communicate in such a way that we are of greatest benefit to all.

Traditional shamans assisted their communities from within a specific and frequently ancient culture. However, in many countries today, the lines between cultures are often much less defined. With the advent of global media, including the use of the Internet and satellite dishes, many other cultures are having a significant impact on the majority of people on the planet. No longer are most of us isolated and limited to the traditions of our ancestors. Many of us are finding that our paths differ greatly from those of our parents or our grandparents.

Many of us living in the modern world do not live in the land of our ancestors. Our heritage is often made up of many different nationalities. I find that those beginning a shamanic path often do not know where they fit in or what path to follow. This is one reason why Michael Harner's workshops have gained so much popularity. He focuses on the core elements of shamanism and does not teach any specific tradition. In this way, participants are not doing anything too foreign to them, nor do they are infringing on any culture's traditions.

There has been a great deal of controversy in recent years about indigenous "wannabes," particularly in North America, Scandinavia, and Australia. This is a difficult situation in that many indigenous cultures have become rather trendy in their homelands and "outsiders" have begun to mimic some of these traditions.

Many native peoples fear further degradation of their traditions by false seekers or by those who learn just enough to get by, then move on to become teachers on their own. Some indigenous peoples still react with anger because their ancestors were persecuted by the majority culture. A large number of these non-native people who are practicing traditions from indigenous cultures are doing so out of honest respect. These outsiders seem to have an innate affinity for the People and their spirituality.

I do not advocate total dissemination of indigenous traditions. However, I do believe the time has come to put the past behind us. In order to create a better common reality, we must evolve as One People. There are a large number of people on the planet today who have incarnated with a true connection to the land of their birth and its Spirits. There are also a significant number of people who, through spontaneous memories or regressions, remember their own past-lives in these native cultures.

Are we to turn true seekers away because of what their ancestors may or may not have done to ours? If we honestly believe our indigenous viewpoints can help to restore balance on this Earth, is it not our responsibility to do so? Complete secrecy and isolation no longer serve the best interests of our local and global communities.

On the other hand, the prospective student of shamanism must be cautioned that this is not an easy path. It is not a path of white light and glory. Many indigenous peoples reject outside seekers due to their lack of dedication and endurance. There are very real psycho-spiritual dangers and significant responsibilities inherent in the shamanic path. This is a path of courage, self-knowledge, and complete honesty.

So what, exactly, is shamanism? It is an ancient mystical path that uses altered states of consciousness to gain insight, effect healing, and act as a bridge between realities. These altered states of consciousness are also known as shamanic states of consciousness, trance states, and ecstatic states. While many other spiritual and magical practitioners use altered states, not all are shamans.

Mircea Eliade is considered by many to be *the* authority on shamanic studies. He was the first to make a comprehensive study of shamanism across the globe. Although his work is derived from an anthropological research point of view, it does serve as a good basis for understanding the subject.

Eliade distinguished shamans from other psychics, healers, and seers; what he called ecstatics. The difference is that the shaman is believed to actually leave his or her body and travel to Other worlds during the shamanic journey. The shaman is able to retain full awareness and control while functioning in these Other worlds and has the ability to use what he has learned in these Other realms for the benefit of those of us in this reality. This is the shamanic journey that has gained so much recent attention.

Classical shamanic and religious thought generally divides the universe into three worlds. Within these three worlds, many other realms are often delineated according to various cultures. These tend to be areas, or levels, of the three major worlds. For example, David Spaan lists over 100 different names for the Celtic Otherworlds. However, these can be broken down into three main overlapping worlds, the Middleworld, the Lowerworld, and the Upperworld.[1]

The world we inhabit during ordinary consciousness is known as the Middleworld. To many, this is the *real* world. In this reality, time appears to be a linear phenomenon, which is separate from space. Our physical bodies usually function according to Newtonian physics and we inhabit them as ego-personalities.

This is the world we all know and feel relatively comfortable in. However, in shamanic states of consciousness, there are no time or space limitations in the Middleworld, nor is it quite as solid as we like to believe. During a shamanic journey, we are able to travel wherever and whenever we choose. This is the basis for distant healing, telepathy, and past-life regression.

Many shamans are believed to be able to alter their physical shape (shapeshift) and physically travel about in the Middleworld, defying Newtonian physics. There are countless tales of shamans of the Saami people, more commonly known as Lapps or Laplanders, knowing what was happening at a distance and returning from a shamanic journey with tangible objects.[2] My great-aunt loved to talk of our ancestor who physically flew with her reindeer and sled, over a flood in Saamiland (Lapland) to get help for her community.

Australian shamans of the Chepara tribe were said to dive into the ground at one point and come out wherever they chose, often quite a distance from their starting points.[3] There are many stories and legends of shamans taking animal form to travel about this world and Others. I even knew a man who was able to alter his physical appearance, without the use of anything external, to the point that he was utterly unrecognizable to anyone.

Whether you choose to believe that these shamans actually bend the laws of physics, or are able to alter energy fields enough to appear that they defy physical laws, is really unimportant. The point is that these are individuals who have cleared their personal limitations to the extent that they are able to effect significant control over our experience of this reality. Furthermore, through their abilities to navigate Other worlds they are able to serve their communities to the greatest benefit of all.

The Lowerworld (or Underworld) is commonly viewed as the place where our ancestors and power animals reside. It is here that our spirit guides often manifest to us as those species of animals with which we associate specific energies and lessons. This is often the first place participants will go in local journeying classes at metaphysical shops and conferences. Some people believe it is easier to travel to as a first journey due to its associations with the Earth and the ancestors, although I have not found this to be necessarily true.

The Lowerworld tends to be the place where we are closer to the Earth and Her creatures. I have also found it to correlate with the lower chakras. Many cultures and individuals experience the lower chakras as being associated with animal instincts and feeling. The lower chakras are also the means through which we ground ourselves into physical form and to the Earth when we incarnate as infants.

This is often a place of resting and new beginnings. As such, many believe this is where souls go immediately after death and immediately before rebirth. To the Saami, this is *Jabmeaimo*, the Lands of the Dead where the ancestors continue to live their lives in a parallel world until they are ready to reincarnate to this world. To the Celts, this is Annwn where we go immediately after death to await rebirth.

The Upperworld is usually associated with celestial or humanoid spirit guides and immortal beings. Precognitive dreams are often viewed as having their origins in the Upperworld. This is where we contact our higher minds and universal energies, as opposed to Earth energies.

I have also found the Upperworld to be associated with the upper chakras; again this is largely dependent upon your beliefs. The higher chakras are generally believed to be the mental and spiritual centers. These are those areas where we can activate our telepathic abilities and *see*. The higher chakras are also where we first enter incarnation and where many people believe we leave the body from, whether at physical death or during out-of-body experiences.

Many cultures believe that the dead rise to a celestial or mountainous Upperworld. Since the advent of Christianity, those who have lived a "good" life are often believed to rise to a heavenly place of rest. This is interesting in that many pre-Christian beliefs held that life begins in a Lowerworld and progresses toward a more evolved Upperworld. For example, according to Welsh druidic tradition, all life begins in the Cauldron of Annwn, which is a Lowerworld at the center of the rings of incarnation. Throughout the process of growth and rebirth, we move toward the Upperworld Gwynvyd.

While these are the common associations with these worlds, the individual experience can vary. As Dr. Maureen B. Roberts, a Jungian and shamanic therapist in Australia writes, "I find that journeying to the celestial Overworld fires my ideas and ability to focus thought with the cool clarity of stellar contemplativeness, while my journeying to the Underworld fires—often through encountering fire—my instinctual passions and sheer, unreflective, animal exuberance for life."

Many people experience different animal guides in the Upperworld, or different versions of the same Lowerworld guides. For example, one person may experience her bird guides mainly in the Upperworld, while all other animal guides contact her through the Lowerworld. Someone else may find his faery allies in the Upperworld and his more physical guides in the Lowerworld.

In a shamanic journeying workshop I offered in the American Southwest, one participant found she had a spirit Bear guide in both worlds. However, the Upperworld Bear was pure white and had a different *feel* than the brown Bear from the Lowerworld. This illustrates my point that, although there are common associations, the individual experience of the shamanic Otherworlds is highly personal.

Keep in mind that this is all in terms of classical shamanic beliefs. According to the new physics, what we believe to be physical reality is not the totality of reality, but rather our rational construction of it. Scientists have been forced by their own findings to acknowledge what mystics and shamans have understood for thousands of years: that our rational minds are incapable of truly comprehending the totality of our reality. Therefore, these Otherworlds we travel through during the shamanic journey and after physical death manifest to us through our personal symbolism in whatever manner is easiest for our consciousness to handle.

Our experience of reality is defined by our personal and cultural beliefs. Through this filter of beliefs, we interpret our experiences and translate them into a communicable form comprised of the symbols of language and images. Since the realm of shamanic journeying and spirit guides is beyond our everyday reality, we interpret what we see based on what we know.

Just as a child learns the "labels" of this reality through the eyes and ears of her family and culture, we all label our shamanic encounters with the symbols we are familiar with. How often have you experienced a dream or a shamanic journey that was too weird for words? You may have found it nearly impossible to describe. It was so foreign to your rational mind that there were no known symbols available for translation.

In his Otherworldly travels with don Juan Matus, Carlos Castenada encountered worlds in which he had no frame of reference to interpret what he saw. *In The Fire From Within,* he wrote that his rational mind could not handle the rush of Otherworldly perceptions he encountered and immediately shut down.[4] In a sense, shamans must lose their minds in order to maintain their sanity. We move beyond thinking and translation to a point of pure, direct experience.

Similarly, I experienced a loss of reference points for this reality after a process during the Avatar course. I had become so expanded beyond my personal identity that when I decided to reenter this reality, my mind was blank. I remember sitting up and looking at a painting on the wall across from me. It seemed to be an abstract mass of color with no meaningful form. I watched in wonder as my identification with this reality returned. I felt myself slowly becoming more defined and "conscious." Suddenly, I realized this was a painting of a simple flower! It was so clear to me from within this perspective.

Albert Einstein was the first to realize the importance of perspective in our interpretation of this reality. His special theory of relativity describes the way that the relative elements of our physical reality appear to vary, depending upon the point of view of the observer. Rather than being a theory of how everything is relative, as most people assume, Einstein really describes how appearances and measurements are relative.

This theory relates to the state of motion of observers relative to each other. A bus, passing us by as we sit on a bench, may appear to be ten feet long. To an observer in a car, speeding past the bus at the same time, it may appear to be only eight feet long. Of course, this car would have to be going exceptionally fast. Similarly as velocity increases, clocks begin to run more slowly until at the speed of light they stop running altogether.

What does all this have to do with shamanism? At face value, probably not much. But most modern and traditional metaphysical thought proposes that the different planes of existence, or realities, are separated only by their vibrational frequency. Just as ice becomes water and then water vapor as its molecules speed up with heat, many people believe that the physical world of matter moves more slowly than the spiritual worlds, in the sense of energy.

Therefore, it is possible that from our slower frame of reference in the physical body, these other realities appear different to us than they do to a being on a higher plane of existence (higher frequency of motion). It is also possible that in order to communicate with us in this denser reality, these other lifeforms must slow their energy down to a point within our perceptive abilities, appearing to us as something other than what they truly are. It is further possible that our three-dimensional perception limits our abilities to distinguish interdimensional beings, unless we move beyond the limitations of the physical body into a shamanic experience.

The Eastern idea of this world being comprised of *maya*, or illusion, is apt although not entirely accurate. We possess three-dimensional perception while inhabiting a four-dimensional world. What we see as a chair or a tree or a person is a limited interpretation of the totality of what this represents.

Although this is not entirely illusion, it is not the big picture. For example, a two-dimensional being inhabiting a three-dimensional world can only be aware of the length and width of the world. For this being, there is no space. Everything lies along the same plane of existence, there is no up or down. Anything that may be above or below this plane in a three-dimensional world does not exist for a two-dimensional being.

There is another relatively new theory proposing a holographic universe. According to this theory, our perception only allows us to view one small portion of the total hologram. Depending on one's perspective, very different universes may be experienced. Therefore anything we perceive with our limited focus is certain to be a mere point in a much larger holographic entity, or world.

In similar fashion, our view of shamanic guides and power animals is merely the representation of the total energy that is embodied by that symbol. Our guides manifest to us in whatever form is best suited to our personal and cultural reality constructs. Our power animals are not generally physical animals of any particular species, but a certain species may represent the greater group soul and/or a particular set of energies and lessons for us.

A shaman is often distinguished by an ability to travel to the Lands of the Dead and return unharmed. It is this aspect of shamanism that is the focus of this book. As shamans and deathwalkers, we have walked these roads ourselves many times, most notably during shamanic initiations. We have often come face to face with our own mortality and the death of the ego. We have emerged from these encounters as stronger, more complete beings.

This is one reason why shamans are known as the Wounded Healers. The archetype of the Wounded Healer is illustrated by the Greek myth of Chiron the Centaur. In the most common version of his story, Chiron attended a dinner given by the Centaurs for Hercules. Over dinner, a fight broke out and Chiron was wounded by a poisoned arrow. As the child of a god, Chiron was immortal, so this wound did not kill him. However, it did create an unhealable wound that plagued him until he traded his immortality to Perseus and finally died. Chiron eventually became a master physician, a teacher, a prophet, and a musician. It is significant that in his own search for personal healing his ability to teach and heal others was increased.

We can look to a related myth and its association with the principle of homeopathic healing. Apparently, Chiron gave Peleus, father of Achilles, an ashen spear on his wedding day. It was this spear, thrown by Achilles, that wounded Telephus. This was another wound that would not heal.

Telephus went to the oracle of Apollo and was told that the wound could only be healed by its cause. Achilles healed Telephus by scraping off the rust of his spear blade. This is applicable to shamanism in that he who has been wounded and healed is the most capable of effecting healing. Hence the related homeopathic premise of "like curing like."

In order to work effectively for others, we must first heal ourselves. I was struck on a recent flight by the wisdom inherent in the flight attendant's direction to place our own oxygen masks first, before attempting to place that of another. If we do not first take care of ourselves, we both may suffocate. This correlates to the rest of our life experience.

The shamanic path is one of tremendous personal work and responsibility. We work continually to heal ourselves, bring ourselves into balance, and clear our limitations. It is essential that a shaman be able to face, accept, and fully integrate all aspects of Self, particularly the shadow side.

The shadow side is a part of every human's *Self*. It is stored within our minds and bodies, and it contains all the characteristics and experiences that we keep hidden from society. Our shadows are all those things we don't want to admit, even to ourselves. This is where our fears, angers, weaknesses, and embarrassments lie.

When repressed and denied, our shadow side causes us to create external situations that mirror these secrets. The more we try to avoid them, the larger they become and the more often they will smack us in our faces. These external situations are usually experienced as suffering and hardship, but in truth, they can be tremendous opportunities for personal growth and self-knowledge. These are the projected manifestations of our own issues, externalized so that we might have a less personal look at them and, hopefully, learn from them.

In order for a shaman to help anyone, particularly the dying and the departed, it is necessary that she continue to work with her shadow side. Shadow aspects that have not been examined will often present themselves during shamanic journeys. As these aspects continue to be repressed and avoided, they grow and gain more power over us. When we encounter them during the shamanic journey or through dreaming, they can be truly terrifying. They have a way of manifesting as frightening experiences, violent deities, and monstrous images.

Many of those who come to a shaman for help also reflect issues and lessons that are pertinent to his life at that time. In this way, he attracts and creates situations that provide him with the opportunities to clear these issues by allowing him an external view of them. Of course, it is not always easy to admit that these individuals are one's own reflection, but that resistance is just the ego rearing its ugly head. This reflection is one way in which the shamanic path leads to continual growth and learning, once one gets beyond the ego-identity.

In the process of moving through such experiences and integrating our own shadows, we become stronger and more balanced. We are able to better understand another's need for healing and have answered the Call to give back as we have received. As a friend of mine used to say, we become the light rather than the light bulb, meaning that we allow our personality to step aside and channel universal Medicine through us.

Shamanism is not a religion in the usual sense of this word, although it has been a part of most ancient and indigenous religions. Shamans are seen as the spiritual guides and guardians of the community, a role that often carries over into religious duties. Shamans work for themselves and their communities through the shamanic journey and with the assistance of various spirit allies, or guides.

10

Although it is a common belief that we all have some form of guardian spirit, the allies of the shaman are specific to the work at hand. A shaman may have many spirit helpers. Some act as messengers, some aid the shaman during journeys, some enable the shaman to embody necessary energies in various realities, and all act as teachers for the shaman.

The helping spirits of the Saami shaman, or *noiade,* are a select group especially effective in journeying and protection. The Reindeer, Bear, Owl, Eagle, Snake, and Wolf bring incredible power to the noiade. The Saami believe that there are times of the year when the impact of this power can actually be felt on the land of the polar regions.

As Ted Andrews acknowledges in *Animal-Speak,* spirit beings in innumerable forms permeate our ancient myths and scriptures.[5] There is indeed a universal belief in supernatural beings that aid us in some way. These spirit guides can be with us throughout our entire lives; or they may come to us when we are in need of their specific energies and leave when we no longer need them. Many people have reported new guides or different aspects of old guides appearing during specific life situations.

For example, when my husband and I were thinking about having a child, I encountered geese, doves, and pigeons everywhere. In fact, the female pigeon I had been feeding for three years had her young next to our balcony. I accepted the energies and company of all these birds. I respected them as messengers and honored them in various ways. We invoked their energies and invited them into our lives through ritual. I drew a goose from one of my divination card decks and kept this card on my altar to use as a focus and an honoring of her presence. Each of these birds has been associated with fertility and parenthood throughout the ages.

One afternoon during this time, my mother and I came upon a Canadian goose, dead on the side of the road. She had been hit by a car and was left there, alone and ignored. Much to our husbands' displeasure, we picked her up and brought her home. As my husband and I buried her on my parents' land, we used some of her feathers and performed an appropriate rite of passage. Two honking geese flew over as we concluded the rite. Within a month, I was pregnant.

Most indigenous shamanic cultures have seen birds as messengers of Spirit. I know several modern shamans who share the Owl as a messenger of death. In my family, a death is always indicated either by the sight or sound of an owl. This can precede the death, but most often the Owl appears at the time of death. One example of the pre-death appearance of the Owl happened the day before my grandfather died.

My grandfather had been in the hospital for some time before his death as the result of a stroke. He developed sepsis after the insertion of a food peg and became very ill, very quickly. I knew his time was limited and I divided my time between my home in Connecticut and his hospital in Pennsylvania.

It was obvious to us that he was more and more in touch with the Other side. We were almost certain we lost him at one point. His room was filled with departed loved ones and he was aware only of their presence in his room. He began to sing in his native language and we felt him slipping away. Although he did make it through that night, we realized that his time with us was very short.

On a beautiful Friday in April, I was hiking with my dog in Connecticut on our usual trail. On a whim, we took a side trail that we had never been down before. I have found that following these whims usually takes me directly into the path of communication from my spirit guides. This particular trail opened up onto a wide grassy meadow surrounded by huge oaks and evergreens.

As I entered the meadow, I saw the largest Great Horned Owl that I had ever seen. He was sitting on a low oak branch and was larger than my Chow-Akita dog. The energy of the meadow was unusually intense for that area of the forest. The air seemed to crackle with physically tangible energy. It felt to me to be sacred space, outside of this reality almost on the verge of the Veil between the worlds.

The Owl turned and stared directly at me. He connected with me powerfully yet worldessly. As he looked into my eyes, we merged for a moment and my rational mind went blank. Then he flew low over the meadow before disappearing into the woods. I had received a Great Horned Owl in a journey several years earlier to act as my guide. At this point, I knew I had been given an explicit and powerful portent.

I recognized that this was a message concerning my grandfather, so we quickly returned to the car. The hooting of that Owl followed us the entire hike out. That evening we drove back down to Pennsylvania to say goodbye to my grandfather. I arrived after visiting hours and snuck upstairs, as usual, to see him. He knew his time had come. He said goodbye and told me to go home and get some sleep. He died very early the following morning.

Ted Andrews also describes Owl as a messenger from beyond the Veil in *Animal-Speak*. He writes that a good friend of his gifted him with some Owl teachings. He became very emotional during these teachings as he was confronted with images of death and funerals. He knew without question that his father would pass away in the near future.[6]

As shamans, we recognize the messages present in the natural world. We pay attention and remain open to All Our Relations. There is a tremendous amount of learning to be had, if we just choose to acknowledge it. Divination through the actions of animals (especially birds), clouds, and rocks, is common among shamanic cultures. The shaman walks her path in gratitude and respect for the varying roles of other beings in the great Web of Life. In return, the Earth and Her creatures teach and care for us all.

The role of the shaman in society is discussed everywhere these days. Are we responsible only to ourselves, and possibly our families, or is there a larger responsibility inherent in walking a shamanic path? Most of us would agree that by accepting the role of shaman we become responsible for a larger circle of beings. Many would say we accept responsibility for All Life.

Shamans recognize that all things are interconnected and walk their paths with respect for the Web of Life. It is clear to shamanic peoples that our every action affects the reality of all other creatures. It is for this reason that we also consider the effect of our actions on our children's children's children, or on the seventh generation, before taking any significant action. Many modern physicists now believe the physical world is really a web of relationships. The meaning of each element is to be found in its relationship to the whole.

This means that not only do none of us exist independent of anything or anyone else, but the meaning of our individual and collective existence is to be found in our relationships to All Life. Since quantum mechanics has found that the physical world we all depend upon is not as substantial as we believe, this web of relationships would seem to apply to more than just this physical reality we all know and love so well.

The question of how one becomes a shaman can be just as controversial as the question of who really is a shaman. Many people believe that anyone who has been Called to a shamanic vocation, journeys out-of-body, and works to benefit herself and her community is a shaman. Some people make no distinction between a shaman and a shamanic practitioner. In this case, the practitioner being one who learns of shamanism from books or classes and uses the shamanic journey but does not fill all the requirements to be considered a shaman.

There are those who believe only those raised and trained in a shamanic culture can be real shamans. I would agree that only these individuals can be considered traditional shamans, but that raises the question of what exactly "tradition" is. And that opens a whole other can of worms.

The title of *Shaman* seems to have become something of a status symbol these days. In truth, few shamans broadcast their vocation, preferring to be of service in subtle or private ways. As a result of this recent trendiness, many people who have been Called and accepted by the spirits are afraid to "come out" as shamans for two reasons.

The main reason is that there are a fair amount of, what has been called the "IRAB" shamans, sorcerers, high priests, and high priestesses.[7] These are those individuals who have read a book or two (I Read A Book), possibly attended a public workshop, and without any real personal work or experience have set themselves up as great magico-spiritual leaders. True shamans do not seek glory, nor do they do what they do for social reasons. They respect and understand the work and responsibility involved in a shamanic path.

The other main reason is an offshoot of this first issue. A person coming out and telling others he is a shaman is instantly vulnerable to criticism and derision. Modern shamans face the "prove-it-to-me" syndrome. Everyone suddenly wants to see his credentials; his résumé, if you will.

There are plenty of groups and individuals today who teach others to use the shamanic journey for their own personal development. Most of them have truly honorable intentions and many possess a considerable amount of talent and experience. There are also groups that offer to train shamans through certification programs. For a number of reasons, the general shamanic community receives these certification programs with mixed feelings.

Traditionally, one becomes a shaman in one of two ways. He is either chosen by the spirits themselves or he voluntarily pursues the shamanic vocation. In many cultures, the voluntary shaman is regarded as inferior to one degree or another when compared to the shaman who has received a direct Calling from Spirit. This is often because of a lack of natural ability or acceptance by the spirits.

I will offer no opinions here as to degrees of power and ability in anyone. I have met people in basic journeying workshops who were tremendously talented and others who were raised in shamanic families who were limited in their abilities *in this area*. However, the point is well taken that a shaman school is somehow selling out to our societal need for pieces of paper to prove we are worthy. Shamanism is beyond the limitations of our consciousness and this physical reality. A direct experience of the Source of all Life and the Otherworlds cannot be verified by an academic-type degree.

On the other hand, I have met many people who call themselves shamans to any that will listen. Everywhere they go, they make a big deal out of the fact that they are Shamans and they will discuss their great knowledge at length to complete strangers. I have heard this described as analogous to saying one is a doctor after just completing high school or college biology. In light of this, I do understand the desire to provide monitored and structured training. Those who emerge from training programs such as these have necessarily completed a good deal of shamanic work and have been trained to provide various counseling services.

While a shaman must be able to face up to any challenge, this type of notoriety produced by the IRAB phenomenon is counterproductive to the work. While there is certainly a difference between self-knowledge and self-delusion, this situation is indicative of ego-interference, not a shamanic Calling. It is for this reason that many modern shamans fulfill their roles in secret.

In the opinion of many shamanic communities, there are two main elements to being a shaman. The first is obviously a Calling or an acceptance by the spirits. The second element is service to one's family and community, in addition to one's self. This is a significant element. While all of us have the ability to journey and to use the shamanic journey for our own personal development, the shaman is required by her vocation to hone and use her abilities to benefit her community and any in need.

One of the most vital and traditional ways in which the shaman fulfills this element of service is through the role of deathwalker, also known as the psychopomp. This means that the shaman is frequently responsible for assisting the dead beyond this existence into their next world. A psychopompic journey is one that leads a shaman from this world into the Lands of the Dead and back. The shaman is uniquely suited to this role due to his knowledge of and ease in travelling the Other worlds, particularly those of the dead.

The shaman often first encounters the Lands of the Dead in the shamanic initiation. This is generally considered to be the beginning of one's personal shamanic path. The shamanic initiation is usually a life-changing direct experience of the source of all power. It often manifests as a psychospiritual crisis of death and rebirth, which is classically experienced as a dismemberment or ingestion by spirit guides.

The Yakut people of North-central Asia describe how evil spirits carry off the future shaman's soul and shut it up in the Underworld. These spirits cut off his head and cut him into small pieces while he watches from his dismembered head. These small pieces are then given to the spirits of various diseases. Only by passing through this experience is the new shaman given the power to cure.[8]

Here again, we see the image of the Wounded Healer. This is a fairly typical dismemberment experience and illustrates the importance placed on the need for an experiential understanding of woundedness in the shamanic vocation. After all, how many of us have not wondered, as we sit sick and waiting in a room, if our doctor truly understands what it is like to be in our position?

I have experienced two relatively common alternatives to the classical dismemberment experience. Both involve a merging of shaman and guide. In this way, shaman and guide become as One. From that point on, the shaman is able to fully embody and channel the wisdom of that guide whenever necessary.

15

I experienced one particularly intense journey following a deathwalk, some of which was reminiscent of the classic ingestion experience. A large white reindeer met me at an Upperworld entry point, following the deathwalk. He looked at me so pointedly, I felt I was given an order to mount him. As I started toward him, I felt myself pulled in through his eyes. I experienced the dissolution of my human form as my energy filled his form. As I passed into him, I saw though his eyes; breathed through his lungs. I felt physically as though I had the body of a reindeer, although I was aware that we shared this body. I was obviously the guest, as he had full control of the body. I surrendered to his guidance and watched as we flew over oceans and land until we landed on a snow-covered expanse.

Later on, the Sun drew me out of the reindeer, again through his eyes and into a ray of sunlight. I was formless and made of pure light as I traveled out over the ocean again. I descended with incredible speed as the Sun deposited me into a fish that was quickly swatted out of the water and swallowed by a polar bear. From his belly, I spread out to become the whole bear. This differed from the reindeer experience in that I was aware of having been chewed and eaten. In the state I was in, it was not an entirely horrific experience, although I must admit it was certainly not pleasant. From the mass of chewed being (no longer defined solely as Kristin) in his belly, I felt my awareness spread outward until I encompassed his entire body.

Again, I felt as though I possessed the body of a bear but with shared awareness. I felt the musculature of the bear and the four-legged gait. However, it was similar to a child learning to dance on her father's feet. She is dancing, but is supported and guided by a more experienced being. Although Bear has walked with me since childhood, I have never so completely felt the power and strength of Bear, as I did during our walk along the tundra.

Afterward, the white reindeer joined us and we settled down to watch the aurora borealis together. While we sat there, I felt a kinship between the three of us as though we were all one organic unit. We were more connected than family, yet we each possessed our own unique individuality. More than that, we shared a common awareness that continues to this day.

In many cultures, there is an associated ritual performed by the teaching shaman(s) for the initiate. This ritual frequently mimics a death experience or religious ritual for the dead. Among the Menomini tribe of North America, a future shaman is ritualistically stoned to death with magical objects, then is resurrected by the initiating shaman.[9] This not only forces the future shaman into the realm of the dead as a test, but it also is a symbolic ceremony of the death of the shaman's previous personality and his rebirth as a new being, a shaman.

As one's shamanic development progresses, her experience in travelling the Other worlds builds. She is occasionally called upon to travel to the Lands of the Dead in order to retrieve lost souls or soul fragments and to perform the deathwalk. Death becomes an integral part of reality; a change in status rather than a mystery to be feared.

According to Carlos Castenada, don Juan Matus counsels us to use Death as an advisor.[10] Death is an inevitable part of life. While we are in this life, it is vital to live it with this in mind. Don Juan suggests that we bring awareness of our death into focus when our egos begin to assert themselves and we feel self-important, over-whelmed, or victimized.

This awareness allows us to align ourselves with life by determining how we would react to any given situation if we knew death was imminent. Would the same things that really get to us and throw us off balance be as important if we only had a moment to live this life? Maybe they would and maybe they wouldn't, but the point is that by using our death in this way, rather than denying it exists, gives us power and focus. It helps us to maintain balance and prevents our egos from getting the better of us.

One does not need to be a shaman to benefit from shamanic wisdom or to use the shamanic journey. My Saami ancestors believed that everyone journeys, whether in trance or while they are asleep. Most modern metaphysical experiences seem to support this belief. Participants in public journeying and guided meditation classes often report tremendous personal insight and healing as the result of a weekend, or even a two-hour workshop.

I have personally offered various shamanic workshops for many years now, including the basic journeying workshops. Each time I offer a new workshop I am amazed at the rich symbolism and guidance received by participants. Even those who have arrived as serious skeptics have left with valuable personal experiences of their own inner workings. I am continually surprised at our abilities to return from our journeys with pertinent and healing symbols for ourselves and for others.

It is what one on a shamanic path can do during the journey that distinguishes her travels from that of the rest of the community. A shaman develops a control and familiarity with these Other realms that enables her to use them to aid herself and her community. She is able to retrieve valuable information from beyond our three-dimensional consciousness, translate it into language, and apply it for the benefit of all.

I believe that much of the recent interest in shamanism is due to our collective need to connect with the Earth and other lifeforms. We recognize on a deep level that we have isolated ourselves too far from that great Web. Jung said that "as scientific understanding has grown, so our world has become dehumanized. Man feels himself isolated in the cosmos, because he is no longer involved in nature and has lost his emotional 'unconscious identity' with natural phenomena . . . His contact with nature has gone, and with it has gone the profound emotional energy that this symbolic connection supplied."[11] Our hearts and souls seem to be crying out for the freedom to reconnect with other realities and to find balance within this reality. Shamanism is one path that can enable us to do just that.

Endnotes

1 Conway, *By Oak, Ash, & Thorn*, pp. 85–99.
2 Collinder, *The Lapps*, p. 214.
3 Harner, *Way of the Shaman*, p. 25.
4 Castenada, *The Fire From Within*, p. 291.
5 Andrews, *Animal-Speak*, p. 7.
6 Ibid., p.13.
7 Farrar, *Writer on a Broomstick*, 1995.
8 Eliade, *Archaic Techniques of Ecstasy*, pp. 36–37.
9 Ibid., p. 55.
10 Sanchez, *The Teachings of Don Carlos*, p. 104.
11 Jung, *Man and his Symbols*, p. 85.

Chapter 2

GATEWAYS

Most spiritual and religious traditions recognize death as a Door or Gateway for the departed. When we die, we pass through the gates of death into the next world. What is not commonly understood is that death can also open a Gateway for those still living. Frequently, people close to the departed, particularly parents and children, experience an increase in psychic abilities and paranormal encounters immediately following the death. For those with some familiarity with other realms, this may be an acceptable or even welcome phenomenon.

Unfortunately, many people react with fear and denial. These tend to be those individuals with a worldview that either precludes the existence of Other worlds or one that assigns an evilness and danger to any connections through the Veil. Frequently these people are afraid to even mention their experiences to anyone for fear they will be carted off to the nearest psychiatrist for medication and therapy. They push on, wondering if they are losing their minds and not knowing what to do about it.

This Gateway opens as a result of our lingering connections with those who have departed. These are often seen as ties and cords binding two people together. While we live, we establish energy connections to other people as the result of our relationships. These are the "ties that bind" and we experience a sharing and mixing of our individual energies through these connections.

These cords are seen as a reaching out and merging of both people's energy fields. Within this reaching out is a more defined cord of energy that generally connects to the individual at a specific energy center, or chakra. This chakra is indicative of the spiritual level and personal issues or lessons that are present in this relationship.

The longer and deeper these relationships, the more energy cords exist and the stronger these cords tend to be. These bonds do not disappear with the death of the physical body. It is due to these connections that we finish each other's sentences during life; and it is through these connections that we continue to experience psychic communication with the departed after death. The more strong cords exist between us, the more connected we are to the Other side when that loved one passes over.

As the energy of our loved ones changes through their Otherworld experience, we also become more expanded and aware of these worlds due to the sharing and mixing of energy produced by these connections. The experience of departed loved ones can significantly affect our own energy fields as we receive this influx of Otherworldly energies. We can feel as though we have "one foot in each world." The being with one foot in each world, hopping back and forth between the two, is a common shamanic image.

This energy change can be so intense as to catalyze a major kundalini rising in the individual remaining in our reality. Kundalini is that spiritual energy that is generally dormant in all living beings. Kundalini resides at the base of the spine. It is often seen as a coiled-up and usually sleeping serpent. It is my belief that the kundalini rising is the catalyst for the shamanic Calling and initiation experience.

According to yogic traditions, the awakened kundalini serpent rises up through the spinal column, energizing the chakras until it reaches the head. Once that occurs, the individual then experiences samadhi or Oneness with God. If one is not properly prepared, the rising of the kundalini can produce some frightening experiences as it plows through our blocked energy centers.

Often the opening of the Gateway to death produces terrifying experiences that are due to a premature release of shadow aspects associated with the clearing of blocked energy centers. As the rising kundalini pushes its way through one's blocked energy centers, it brings walled-off memories and fears to the surface. Consequently, the individual's consciousness necessarily becomes aware of them. Since we have refused to own responsibility for these aspects, they are projected onto the outside world. During an opening of the Gates, they generally manifest as frightening paranormal encounters.

When this occurs, we can experience our deepest fears as real, external situations. The spirits are giving us a tremendous opportunity to clear these issues and move forth as stronger, more balanced beings. Many people experience the presence of threatening spirits and possession. I have one friend who experienced both possession and an inability to re-enter her body during dream journeying. When she experienced difficulty returning to her body, she feared that she had died and was stuck between worlds. This woman was terrified both of death and of losing control over her reality. Interestingly enough, she experienced both of these scenarios during a kundalini rising associated with the death of a friend.

These energy connections also play a significant role in the tremendous psychic connection between parent and child that goes beyond the instinctual and emotional. This connection is often seen as an umbilical cord of energy, which develops during pregnancy. It is a similar connection to the cords we form in any relationship but tends to be much deeper and stronger. It connects mother and child, and usually develops quickly between father and child.

As a result of this energy umbilical cord, the process of pregnancy and birth can open a Gateway similar to that of the death experience. Pregnant women and new parents frequently experience heightened psychic sensitivity, which can manifest as precognitive dreams and an increased awareness of paranormal activity in the home. In many ways, death is a birthing of our complete and reintegrated spiritual beings from the limitations of this reality.

Barbara Brennan describes this energy umbilical cord in terms of the development of the human energy field. She states that, although it exists throughout life, it is strongest at birth, becoming less pronounced as the child grows. This energy umbilical cord is the means by which children remain psychically in contact with their parents during their lives.[12]

When our children are very young, a significant amount of our energy flows into them through this cord. This energy is used to bolster and contribute to the healthy development of their energy systems, as well as for protection from external influences. This is one reason why it is vital that we maintain a healthy and honest psychic atmosphere in the home of a young child. As they grow and their own energy systems stabilize, they no longer need such an intense connection to their parents, and the cord becomes less pronounced.

Although this cord may become less obvious as we grow up, it does remain after the death of either parent or child. This is often the means by which an after-death connection is attempted. One of the ties that deathwalkers frequently see binding the departed spirit to our reality is this energy umbilical cord.

Through these cords, our departed loved ones strongly feel our resistance and pain. Their lingering associations with previous incarnations often compel them to stay and attempt to fulfill a sense of loyalty and responsibility. When the emotional attachment to this bond is released, the cord no longer anchors the departed to our reality. The departed soul is then able to fully move on to other realms. The cord at that point appears more as a thin line, which continues until the physical death of both individuals. Through this line, a connection is nearly always possible. The only exception I have found is when the departed has re-entered an incarnation, although this does not always prevent a lingering connection.

For those readers who are not experienced with the shamanic journey but would like to be able to communicate with a parent or child who has passed over, I would recommend the following exercises. Keep in mind that a true shamanic journey cannot be led. Even your experience of the exercises in this book may take on a life of their own. This is nothing to fear. Just follow your own intuition where it takes you. Anyone who is experienced with journeying should be able to connect with departed loved ones using normal journeying techniques, much the same way we connect with other ancestors.

Journeying Exercise
For Connecting with a Departed Loved One

To be done with a shamanic journeying drumming audiotape if a drummer is not available to be present to drum for you.

Clear your own energy field, and the area you will be performing this exercise, using any of the purification ceremonies from chapter three, before turning on or starting the drumming.

Allow the drumming to carry you into an altered state of consciousness. Feel the drumming. Ride the rhythm down, deeper into your center with the intent to contact your departed loved one.

Now see a cord of energy emerging from your heart center. Be aware of the appearance of this cord. This cord goes out into the multiverse (our reality and all Other worlds) and eventually connects you to this loved one. Allow the drumming to focus your complete attention on this cord. The cord becomes a tunnel that carries you to your loved one.

Follow this cord. Be aware of the appearance and feeling of the cord as a tunnel. Suddenly, you are face to face with your loved one. This tunnel is no longer apparent, and the cord connects you both at your heart centers.

Send your love through this cord to your loved one. Tell him or her all you have wanted to communicate. As you speak this, send it also through this cord.

Accept whatever response you receive, even if you are not aware of any response at this time. Go with whatever occurs to you. (*long pause*)

Now, say goodbye to your loved one and prepare to return to your body. (*pause*) Hear the call of the drum, beckoning you back. Follow this sound as the cord once again becomes a tunnel. Be aware of the appearance and feeling of the cord as a tunnel. Allow the drum to carry you back. (*pause*)

You are once again fully within your own body. You remain aware of this cord emerging from your heart center. Know that you can always re-establish contact through this cord and you may receive communication from your loved one, but you are in full control of your journeying at all times.

Turn off, or stop the drumming, and smudge yourself once more.

Dreaming Exercise
For Connecting with a Departed Loved One

Just before falling asleep, on the verge of sleep but still aware of this world, visualize a beautiful cord of energy connecting you to your loved one. Be aware of the colors of this cord and the areas where this cord attaches to each of you.

Send your love to this being through this connection and ask them to visit you in a dream that night.

With focus and intent, tell yourself you will remember this dream when you awaken. Then allow yourself to drift off to sleep.

It is a good idea to keep a pad of paper and pen next to your bed. People often awaken immediately after the dream meeting and will usually lose the memory if they fall back to sleep without recording it.

Initially, some people may have difficulty with dreaming exercises. Many of us do not remember our dreams and if we do, we generally believe they are nothing more than the psyche replaying or working out events from this reality. We don't remember how to bring them back into our waking lives, so we can't. As a result, dreams are frequently filtered out of waking consciousness automatically.

We all have the ability to eliminate this filter. The blocks to dreaming are learned. We were not born with them. These are the same blocks that prevent most people in modern society from consciously using the shamanic journey. The dreaming body is the free soul. It is this energy body that we take with us when we journey out-of-body. Therefore, dreaming is often shamanic journeying. They are one and the same. The only difference is that during dreaming the physical body is in its daily period of hibernation, allowing the free soul to wander at will, without the need for trance induction.

If your initial attempts at dreaming do not appear to be very productive, I strongly recommend sticking with it. In addition to your dreaming exercises, work with the breathing exercises given in chapter five. Additional practice with the shamanic journey while you are awake is another excellent tool for learning control over dreaming.

Keeping a dreaming journal is also very beneficial. In this initial journal, you may prefer to record any sensations or experiences that are associated with your dream exercises. Many people experience feelings of motion or vibration associated with lucid dreaming and astral travel. When you notice a pattern beginning to emerge through your exercises, use that to develop dreaming techniques specific to you. Keep in mind, that we are relearning a skill that was lost many years ago. With practice, it will return.

I would not recommend that anyone practice this frequently or with a large number of departed spirits, unless you are prepared to accept the possibility that these Gates will remain open. This opening to the Other side can mean the beginning of a psychic or shamanic vocation. On the other hand, for those who are unaware of what is occurring or who reject the shamanic Call, it may result in nightmares, unexplainable encounters or abilities, and even spontaneous and unwelcome possessions. As they say, be careful what you ask for, you just might get it.

The first time my mother was visited by a departed spirit from outside our family, she rejected the contact. This was not a member of our extended family and she wanted neither additional responsibility nor additional paranormal encounters at that time. This was soon after her mother had died and she had enough departed spirits to deal with as it was. The "visitor" was the recently departed father of a close friend of hers from work. He had been unable to reach his son and somehow found his way to her. As I said before, the spirits seem to instinctively know who can hear them.

My mother *saw* this man come through the window in our upstairs sunroom. After attempting to ignore his presence and shut herself off from communication, she felt him forcibly enter her body. The next thing she knew, she was speaking with his voice. It was clearly an older masculine voice, and did not even remotely resemble her voice. She was both frightened and angry.

She went in to work the following day and told her friend about what had happened. She made it clear that she wanted no further contact with his father and insisted that he start to listen for communications from his father. That very night, he had a dream in which his father came to say goodbye to him. No one had any further contacts with his father. It would appear that, having finally reached his son, the father was able to get on with his nonphysical life.

As I indicated above, those who possess shamanic talents are often Called as the result of a death experience. A number of those participating in a shamanism-related Internet newsgroup recently reported a personal near-death experience as the initiatory event that led to them following the shamanic path. The shamanic Call has traditionally taken the form of a deathly illness, which seems to be the physical manifestation of an initiation by the spirits themselves. This illness is the physical manifestation of the shamanic initiation, which is accompanied by a spontaneous kundalini rising.

My own experience of this initiatory illness occurred when I experienced a series of extremely high fevers when I was about five years old. Although I had experienced psychic tendencies before this point, I became extremely sensitive afterward. I remember the fevers as times when I was in Other worlds where very different events were occurring. I felt as though my body and soul were a battleground upon which some type of war was being fought. I even vividly remember the sound of cannons and sight of people and animals fighting.

The kundalini progressed through my body, producing extreme heat manifesting as high fevers. As it rose, my conscious mind experienced the release of blocks and repressed experiences from this life and others. The wars were some of my greatest fears at that time and were also symbolic of my own internal struggle between subconscious issues and conscious judgments.

I called repeatedly for my mother, unaware that she was right there holding me throughout most of it. In my experience, I was truly alone. As I emerged from the fevers, I became aware of an enormous spirit Bear, stationed at the foot of my bed. I was initially very afraid of him and his huge size, but he led me back through the carnage of the war and helped me to reintegrate my being in a more balanced way.

Bear has been with me ever since and has been a constant guide and guardian throughout good times and bad. Within a year of these fevers, my grandmother died, our home went wild with additional paranormal activity, and my training in this reality and Others began.

My friend West Hardin relates a similar story. As a child, he had an extremely high fever that kept him bedridden for a week. Although his mother was not at all metaphysically inclined, she followed her instincts one day while shopping and brought him home an alabaster whale. West kept this whale with him the entire night and was healed the very next day. He believes this was a turning point for him and was the beginning of his shamanic awakening. He notes that Whale has been a lifelong guide to him.

It is interesting that in both these cases, a shamanic vocation was initiated not only by a potentially life-threatening illness but also by fevers, which took us outside ourselves and into an awareness of Other worlds. The ability to produce heat is common to shamans all over the world. This is a result of the individual ability to control or effect one's personal kundalini through shamanic states of consciousness. The fevers that are experienced by so many shamans and seers as part of the initiatory illness are the beginning of this and seem to be required for the physical body to develop this ability.

The presence of a lifelong spirit guide appearing just before recovery is significant in our lives. These spirit allies guided us back from the Other worlds and our own possible deaths. With their assistance and protection, we first learned to navigate the roads of the Other worlds, particularly that of the dead. These guides have continued to walk with us as teachers and guardians since that day. Furthermore, after this experience we were each significantly more open to other spirit guides and alternate realities.

While a personal near-death experience or serious illness is a classical initiatory event, a large number of other people have experienced the actualization of their shamanic potential through the death of a loved one. The ensuing Otherworldly connections manifest as another type of shamanic Call. Since there is no escape from these abilities or from the associated encounters, one must choose to accept the mantle of shaman in order to remain sane and healthy. For my mother, it began with the death of her grandfather when she was approximately five years old.

My mother has little memory before the death of her grandfather, but she began having spontaneous journeys out-of-body soon after his death. Often, these journeys would occur during everyday consciousness. During her "spells," she felt she was pulled from her body. Everything would change color and she would lose awareness of this reality as she was sucked through the Otherworldly tunnels.

Her departed grandfather would frequently call to her from the woods surrounding their house. Whenever she *heard* him, she would run out to the woods to meet him. They would walk together, talking about many things while he comforted her in her grief. This was a great consolation to her, to know that she could still communicate with this man who had been so close to her. Throughout these visits, her shamanic potential was catalyzed. From that point on, she was particularly attuned to Other worlds. She knew instantly whenever a family member died and she alerted the family.

As I said, there are those for whom this is a welcome experience. These are frequently those individuals who have not accumulated a significant amount of indoctrination and limiting belief systems. Since children have less defined belief systems than adults, they are often more open to the Other side. They frequently have no difficulty with a visit from a departed loved one. In many cases, these visits ease their grief. In fact, many children find such comfort in these contacts that they will try to talk about these experiences with their families.

When I was a child, I had a friend who lost his beloved dog under the wheels of a truck. Even then, I seemed to be responsible for handling the dead. Although I was only about eight years old, I was asked to retrieve the dog's body from the road and I buried him. I was very aware of the dog's spirit still hanging around our World. As I surrounded his grave with a circle of rocks, I prayed that he might be taken quickly and easily Home.

Every night for well over a year after this dog's death, my friend would pet him goodnight before falling asleep. He swore the dog licked his hand in the middle of the night when he had nightmares, enabling him to relax and go back to sleep without fear. He was absolutely convinced that his dog had come back to be with him and he tried to convince his parents of this. I clearly recall seeing the dog following him around in spirit and backed him up whenever he talked about it. His parents decided we both had very vivid imaginations.

While most adults will not permit themselves to experience this type of contact, children usually find these visits very comforting. They tend to adjust more easily to the loss of a loved one when they are allowed to believe in these experiences. The world is not such a frightening place if we experience life as continuing after the death of the physical body.

In shamanic societies, the dead are not gone from our lives. They continue to play an integral role in the community and we experience a continual interchange with them. We feel more like they have moved to a far away place, rather than that they have died. Shamanic people recognize that the departed continue to affect our reality.

The ancestors not only often choose and train new shamans, but they protect children and animals. In many societies, they are also believed to be able to cause illness and suffering. I see remnants of this understanding in the Christian belief that particularly pious people or family members may become protective angels or saints after death. In shamanic cultures, one's community is made up of beings in two worlds: this World and the World of the Dead.

Unfortunately, most adults do not believe in paranormal encounters, particularly contact from beyond the Veil. As a result, they do not view these experiences as a good adjustment. In an attempt to get them to face the "truth," children are frequently told that the contact is just wishful thinking or their imagination. I have never understood why it is acceptable for children to believe in Santa Claus and the tooth fairy, but not in their "invisible" friends or in visits from departed loved ones.

Children and adults alike can gain tremendous comfort and healing through the acceptance of this gift of communication. The recently departed also benefit greatly from the ability to communicate with loved ones on our side of the Veil. Not only are the departed able to successfully pass on their messages of love, but their still-physical loved ones are able to say goodbye. Once this is accomplished, they can all get on with their respective lives knowing with certainty that life and love continue after physical death.

In any event, the Gateway does not usually remain open for the general population. It often begins and ends with the attempt of the departed to say goodbye or to ensure that those left behind are all right. Fear and denial on the part of the living work to shut the Gates in most cases. While this may be desirable for many, a great deal of healing and closure can be effected on both sides of the Veil if this communication is accepted.

When my grandmother died, she first came to my mother in dreams. All she really wanted was for my mother to let her family and friends know she was well and was still alive in the Other world. It was very important to her that they be comforted by this communication. Unfortunately, some of those she wanted to help by this message denied that such communication could be possible. One woman in particular had adopted a devoutly religious belief system. She refused to listen to any of that "rubbish." She was angered and frightened by the mere mention of messages from beyond the grave, believing it to be either a cruel game or the work of the Devil.

This is a common reaction in our society to any type of communication from beyond this life. We have become so mechanistic and materialistic, that the possibility of nontangible life threatens our entire reality constructs. How can we control it, if it is beyond physical laws? This is not measurable by scientists and they have dictated how we view our world. If this were to be true, it would require a complete re-evaluation of what we believe to be real. The possibility is absolutely terrifying to many people, although few would admit to fear.

There are those with latent psychic and shamanic talents who are blasted out of their present belief systems about the nature of reality by the Otherworldly connections made as the result of the death of one close to them. They can no longer deny the presence of nonphysical beings and alternate realities. They do not believe, yet this is exactly what they are experiencing. What is worse, they have nowhere to turn to discuss this without being viewed as mentally unstable. Far too often, these individuals end up on medication or in mainstream therapies that cannot possibly help them.

Many people who have been raised in modern mainstream society are convinced that the onset of paranormal activity and psychic abilities means one thing only: they are mentally ill. In mainstream society, psychics are generally seen as jokes; they are not taken seriously by the majority culture. If they were, there would not be an abundance of psychic hotlines—for entertainment purposes only—to tell people when they will get rich and fall in love with the perfect person.

Shamans are rarely discussed in "polite company" and many mainstream people don't even know what shamanism is. Someone that my husband worked with at one point came in to work one day, chasing after my husband because she had seen my name on a sign-up sheet for a shamanism workshop. She had no idea what shamanism was and was naturally curious what I was doing. Her openness to the idea made things much simpler for everyone. But in general, normal, modern people just don't become shamans or psychics. Therefore, any indication of psychic or shamanic abilities showing up in a normally functioning mainstream adult is cause for serious concern.

Joseph Campbell wrote that the shaman is one who has an "overwhelming psychological experience," similar to a schizophrenic breakdown. This experience turns the shaman inward to the unconscious, which opens wide and engulfs the shaman.[13] This is similar to my description of how we face our shadows and how these buried aspects are made manifest by the opening of Otherworldly Gates. The unconscious is no longer a safe storage area for unsavory aspects of Self. The unconscious is suddenly accessible, actually more like unavoidable, to the shaman. What differentiates the shaman from the mentally ill person is how the individual handles this phenomenon.

My friend Dr. Maureen B. Roberts, a Jungian and shamanic psychotherapist in Australia, has worked extensively with schizophrenic patients. She has found many similarities between the schizophrenic and the shaman. In fact, she believes that the main difference between the two is the ability of the shaman to integrate these experiences and become both a healer and a highly productive member of the community. She writes that in shamanic states of consciousness "the ego is not submerged but rather deliberately and temporarily displaced, destabilized, or disempowered . . . for the purpose of trance-journeying. The schizophrenic's loss of ego, however, does not parallel the mature and responsible shaman's subsequent healing vocation . . . "[14]

30

It has been my experience that many schizophrenics are honestly in tune with alternate realities. However, the schizophrenic is incapable of consciously choosing which reality to experience at any given time. Furthermore, unlike the shaman, the schizophrenic is unable to focus on one reality at a time, nor can he or she determine which experience goes with which reality. They have significant bleed-through between realities and are forced to wander helplessly among realities, similar to the Alzheimer's patient.

Stanislav Grof relates similar findings to Dr. Roberts' in his book, *Beyond the Brain: Birth, Death, and Transcendence in Psychotherapy*. He notes that cultures in which shamans are recognized and revered do not name just anyone with unusual behavior as a shaman. He writes that "genuine shamans have had powerful, unusual experiences and have managed to integrate them in a creative and productive way." He writes that the genuine shaman exhibits "superior functioning and 'higher sanity.'"[15]

Indigenous cultures and dualistic therapies make a significant distinction between the mentally ill and the shaman.[16] Although Western anthropologists once associated the shamanic vocation with epilepsy, schizophrenia, and hysteria, most modern researchers find quite the opposite. If shamans were to exhibit mental illness, they would be labeled as such rather than being respected and honored by their communities.[17]

In fact, shamanic cultures have always been well aware of mental illness. The shaman is responsible for healing the mind as well as the body and spirit of indigenous peoples. All of these bodies are viewed as being interrelated. What affects one body, affects all. There are specific and powerful methods for dealing with mental illness among shamanic cultures. Those members of the community who are in need of these methods are not revered, but recognized as sick and suffering people.

Schizophrenics are known to see and hear other beings that are not "really" there. They detect "nonexistent" smells and experience a multitude of other hallucinations. Physicist Fred Alan Wolf writes that these schizophrenic experiences may not be mere hallucinations. These individuals may be capable of a distorted perception of other realities, potentially parallel worlds.[18]

Several modern physicists have adopted parallel universe theories in order to explain the bizarre findings of relativity theory and quantum physics. In fact, parallel universe theory is not entirely new. It actually first began in the 1950s but did not initially gain a good deal of supporters. However, the recent incomprehensible—even for most physicists—theoretical and experimental findings of relativity theory and quantum mechanics have spurred a new and more popular interest in these theories because these findings cannot begin to be understood within our current limited beliefs about reality.[19]

For example, the generally assumed model of the atom was once the solar system image of a nucleus–Sun with the electron–planets circling it in defined orbits. The atomic model is more commonly viewed today as the electron cloud theory. This newer model states the electrons exist within a cloud of probability around the nucleus, rather than in any specific position.

This newer atomic model is taken one step further by parallel-worlds theorists. They propose that the electron *does* exist as a single particle all the time, not as a wave or cloud of probability. However, each position the electron takes does not exist within our one universe. The electron occupies a single position in an infinite number of overlapping universes, or parallel worlds. What we see as the electron cloud is, in effect, the overlap of all these parallel worlds.[20] Quantum physics really does have its own set of rules. Amazingly enough, these rules correlate rather well with the shamanic experience.

This would lead me to believe that if our subatomic structures exist within interconnected and overlapping worlds, then we, as total beings, must also. This certainly appears to be the next logical step. If we view our energy bodies as quantum objects, then it is not so difficult to believe that through the manipulation of these bodies (our free or journeying souls) we are able to increase our focus on these other worlds, thereby making them real to us.

As I said, the main difference between the schizophrenic and the shaman is the ability of the shaman to control her reality focus and to recognize which experience belongs to which world. The shaman knows the roads between worlds extremely well and is able to choose what world to experience at will. Furthermore, she is so competent in her extraworldly travels that she is able to switch realities at will in search of guidance and information, then return and apply what she has learned.

The shaman stands apart because she has more direct experience with the Source of All Life and all its manifestations. She possesses the capability to effectively perceive, integrate, and use these manifestations for the highest benefit of herself and her community. Yes, she is different from the majority of a society that views her experiences with fear, but she is far from mentally unstable. In fact, when shamans learn to control these abilities and heal themselves they become highly functioning members of society, much like the prophet-shamans of the Dyak people in Borneo, who have been noted for their superior mental abilities. These Dyak shamans are honored for possessing an intellectual capacity well above that of the general population. They are the poets and prophets, as well as the healers and keepers, of rites and legends.[21]

In any event, it does appear that once we have passed through the Gateway, there is no going back to 'normal' life. Our reality is permanently altered, whether we like it or not. Once through that Door, we know without question that we are not alone in one single universe. It is suddenly crystal clear that we share a *multiverse* with an infinite number of other beings. We can try to fight it for a while, but that only makes it more difficult. For those individuals that can't close the Gates or don't want to, the key is to learn to accept and control these experiences.

Although this book is written from the shamanic perspective, I am well aware that not all readers would choose a strictly shamanic course of action. There are a number of alternate paths that can aid the seeker in integrating these new realities. Throughout this book, I attempt to discuss and describe these issues in such a way as to make them understandable for all readers. (All contact addresses are listed in the back of this book, on page 237.)

I highly recommend the Monroe Institute audiotapes and residence programs. The Monroe Institute began in 1974. It is named after Robert A. Monroe, who I described in chapter one as a revolutionary shaman. The Institute emerged as the result of a research group started by Monroe that was exploring out-of-body experiences and the self-control of human consciousness. They developed the Hemi-Sync technology, which aligns or synchronizes the hemispheres of the human brain. In other words, upon hearing the Hemi-Sync sound patterns, the two sides of our brains begin to function as a concerted whole. In my experience, this significantly promotes shamanic states of consciousness and allows these experiences to be more easily integrated with our rational minds.

According to the Monroe Institute, Hemi-Sync makes it possible for the individual to focus the resources of mind, brain, and body for an almost limitless range of purposes. I have found this to be absolutely true. The Monroe Institute offers a variety of tapes for specific goals, many of which put you in touch with spiritual guidance or your Higher Self. They also offer the Gateway program, for the exploration of your own consciousness; and the Lifeline program, which guides you in gaining familiarity with the realms inhabited by those in transition to or after physical death.

I began experimenting with various Hemi-Sync tapes around 1990. Since that time, I have experienced tremendous results, which seem to get deeper and more intense with use. I have found them to be extremely effective in inducing trance, relaxing and healing the body, and eliminating the effects of stress. I have experienced several significant and very intense shamanic journeys (including the deathwalk) while using these tapes for trance facilitation.

The benefit here for the deathwalker is not only that the Monroe Institute has direct experience in the exploration of Other worlds including the realms beyond physical life, but also that these tapes can be used in the privacy of your own home. They are not loud, as drumming can be, nor are they "just too weird" for most people. Families with some tolerance for the New Age will often not think twice about some new meditation tape.

The Silva Method course is a wonderful experience in developing control and accuracy as well as learning new ways to gain any help and healing you may need. Silva is usually a week-long course in learning to use your mind more effectively. Silva also guides you in constructing an internal forum from which to interact with your guides (they refer to them as counselors) and to perform any type of work you choose to do. This is a comfortable and safe space, where you can access your own Self and gain assistance from your counselors and your higher mind. One significant benefit of Silva for those on a shamanic path is their emphasis on working with guides and their focus on improving memory both in everyday reality and in altered states of consciousness.

In 1944, José Silva began exploring human consciousness for himself and his family. Silva International has done a tremendous amount of research into the human brain and mind. Similar to the Monroe Institute, they teach people to use both sides of their brains and alter their brain-wave frequencies (induce trance levels) at will. Silva International also uses sound to facilitate the induction of trance states. As with the Monroe Institute tapes, the Silva International tapes are perfect for the individual who prefers or requires privacy and quiet in their explorations of reality.

I first took the children's version of the Silva course in 1972, immediately after my mother took the adult course. Although these are essentially the same course, one is geared more towards a child's understanding and attention span. I have reviewed the course countless times since then and have attended all of the Silva graduate courses. Each time, I have learned something new, experienced healing, received answers to questions I was seeking, and was better able to heal others at long-distance.

The Avatar course offers the best tools I have experienced for eliminating limiting beliefs and creating a preferred reality. Although I have only been involved with

Avatar since 1995, I have experienced incredible insights and life changes as a result. In fact, I was so impressed with Avatar's effectiveness that I went on to become licensed to deliver the basic Avatar course. According to the Avatar Journal, Avatar is "a powerful and speedily effective course based on the simple truth that your beliefs will cause you to create or attract situations and events that you experience as your life." The basic Avatar course is a seven-to-nine day experiential process of personal exploration.

I have recommended the Avatar course for many people interested in following a shamanic path and for those who are trying to gain control of their reality after the death of a loved one has opened up those gates to them. However, I do not recommend mixing techniques. The Avatar processes are specifically designed and work beautifully in and of themselves, as do shamanic methods for their particular purposes.

Although Avatar is not a shamanic process, it is a wonderful tool for the shaman through its effectiveness in eliminating limiting beliefs and creating preferred beliefs. This is especially beneficial for the modern shaman who has not been raised with a shamanic mindset. Modern individuals tend to have a significant amount of indoctrinated beliefs that can limit the achievement of one's full shamanic potential. Avatar also enables one to face and successfully clear the shadow side, much like the soul-retrieval process does.

These limiting beliefs that we experience as fear, disbelief, and anger are much of what make up our shadow sides. In chapter one, I discussed the importance of assimilating our shadows and continuing to work with them on the path toward self-knowledge. Through the Avatar processes, we are able to uncover limiting beliefs that we may not have previously been aware of, and eliminate them, if we choose. Avatar is about putting yourself back in the driver's seat; it's about self-understanding, expansion, and empowerment.

While there are many beneficial physical systems (Tai Chi, Stav, and Stadhagaldr to name a few), kundalini yoga is especially effective in learning discipline and gaining control of your own energy fields. As Ravi Singh wrote, kundalini yoga uses the flow and frequency of our spiritual energy.[22] In this way, kundalini yoga can affect us on every level of being and has the potential to dramatically impact our personal potential.

As I have said, the opening of these Gateways to Other realities is often the result of, or the catalyst for, a spontaneous kundalini rising. And, if the kundalini rises before the individual is prepared for it, it can have devastating physical, mental, and emotional effects. The frightening manifestations of the projected shadow side can have the power to create significant soul fragmentation, in addition to extreme mental duress and potentially life-threatening physical stress.

Often when we are spontaneously exposed to alternate realities and/or the effects of kundalini, our body's energy systems go berserk. We feel out of control because we *are* out of control. Since our energy is so scattered, we are unable to focus our attentions on any one reality. Therefore, we are unable to control our experiences. Through kundalini yoga, we can develop the necessary focus and control to deal with these situations.

The practice of kundalini yoga, sometimes called the "Mother of All Yogas," is an active discipline which also incorporates *pranayama*, the conscious control of the breathing. The experience of kundalini yoga is one of balance, discipline, and control. There are sequences designed to act on specific physical, mental, and emotional issues through the manipulation of your personal spiritual and physical energy. These processes can have dramatic effects on one's personal potential in all areas of life.

Finally, pranayama is an essential part of most spiritual-magical traditions, although this is not always the term used. Pranayama is most commonly viewed as the science or manipulation of breath. According to Swami Rama, pranayama literally means the energy of manifestation or expansion; the vital energy of the universe.[23] We all know that breathing is essential to life, but few people are aware of the importance of breath on our emotions, our health, and our reactions.

Most metaphysical teachings show that our mind, body, and spirit are interrelated. We learn, from people such as Barbara Brennan and Caroline Myss, that our energy bodies have a direct impact on our physical bodies and vice versa. Prana, meaning the flow of energy of the universe, is the link between body and mind. This flow of energy is vital to health and life. Prana moves through the breath. As Alan Hymes, M.D., writes: "The effects of breathing extend to the workings of the heart and lungs as well as to subtle physiological interactions such as the molecular processes through which the body's energy production is maintained."[24]

We can see the impact of the body on the breath, and the breath on the body, during an emotional outburst. When we are frightened or very upset, we begin to breathe more quickly and from the chest. Unfortunately, chest breathing is quite common during normal functioning in our society. The shallowness of chest breathing reduces our oxygen intake and fatigues the body-mind. This effectively puts our body and mind in a state of constant anxiety and stress.

On the other hand, when we are calm and centered, such as we are when meditating, our breathing is significantly different. During these times, our breath fills us from the diaphragm through to our shoulders. We breathe slowly and deeply. It is no surprise that when we want someone to calm down, we inevitably tell him to "take a deep breath" and relax.

As Swami Rama describes, the "science of pranayama is thus intimately connected with the autonomic nervous system and brings its functioning under conscious control through the functioning of the lungs."[25] This is the one exception to that rule we were all taught in high school biology: that the autonomic nervous system processes are involuntary. This is also where a student of shamanism, or anyone who is dealing with wide-open Gateways to Other worlds, derives the greatest benefits.

Through the conscious variation of inhalation and exhalation, and through maintaining diaphragmatic breathing during everyday life, we can regulate our responses to these Otherworldly encounters. Rather than instantly being thrown into a "fight-or-flight" fear response, which can paralyze the mind and spirit, we have the ability to step back from the situation. Through the simple control of the breath, we can remain calm and centered, then view things from a much more confident and expanded perspective. This also enables us to enter trance states at will, and with full control. I highly recommend the breathing exercises in chapter five for anyone experiencing open Gateways to Other realities.

Unfortunately, few of these aforementioned systems in and of themselves can reassure us with the fact that we are not alone in these experiences. Although there are a great number of wonderful people practicing and teaching these methods, a relatively small number, with the exception of the Monroe Institute, have personal experience with the Gateways that we experience after the physical death of a loved one. Even among Monroe Institute participants, a relative few experience a true shamanic Call.

As a result, it can be of tremendous benefit to have some type of support system. Unfortunately in today's society, few people are equipped to understand or even accept the onset of paranormal activity, whether it occurs as the result of a death or not. Most mainstream families react with fear and concern, pushing the individual toward traditional therapies. Although there are a great number of metaphysical teachers today, few of them have the training or experience to be of much help in learning how to handle this.

While this may sound discouraging, there is a brighter side. Although local metaphysical teachers may not have an experiential understanding of what you are going through, they can be a great help in connecting you with a support system. Often, these people can recommend applicable books and may be aware of study groups for these books. They may know of other people who are experiencing similar circumstances. They may even know of some experienced shamans or psychics who may be able to help you through this phenomenon.

Keep in mind when contacting anyone for help that, while they may be wonderful guides, you must do the work yourself. In order to effectively work as a shaman, one must clear and integrate the shadow side. I believe that part of the reason for this is that self-knowledge and self-acceptance are the keys to personal control in other realities. If we allow ourselves to be frightened or deluded by our own *stuff*, we can easily get lost or fragmented.

One strong caution: be wary of any teacher who says they can cure you or fix it for you. Be equally cautious of anyone who asks you to become dependent upon them or do anything that does not feel right for you. The shamanic path is not about hierarchy and a priest or priesthood that interprets the will and words of a deity for us. It is about direct personal experience and walking the path on our own.

A local metaphysical teacher or workshop leader may also be the right person for you at the time to spark you to new understandings simply through conversation. Sometimes being able to talk about it without fear of ridicule can make a huge improvement in our abilities to cope. Even if this person has no personal frame of reference from which to understand our experiences, just the ability to share with someone who is interested and willing to learn with us can be the support we need to handle it on our own.

I have found that even through casual conversation, someone will say something that stirs a memory or a new recognition for me. Especially when speaking with a person who tends toward psychic sensitivity, these moments of clarity are frequently spurred by input from spiritual guidance. My mother, in particular, will say things that she has no idea why she said them or where they came from. They are very often exactly what we needed to hear at the time.

I have been told that I have a tendency to do the same thing for others and I am generally aware when I am acting as a mouthpiece for higher guidance. It feels as though I have stepped aside and opened up. I feel almost as a witness within my body, watching or listening as the words flow through.

When looking for a support system, there are a number of places you can go to find like-minded people. Again, I would try your local metaphysical centers. Most of them offer workshops and lectures on a variety of topics. Even local colleges have been known to offer drumming, yoga, and meditation classes where you may find others looking for a support system. My mother met a most wonderful friend and guide at a community college yoga class, at a time when she was in real need. I have found it to be true that the teacher will arrive when the student is ready.

In every area where I have lived, I have discovered several wonderful publications that contain calendars of upcoming events. *Circle Network News* has a national calendar that also lists the big neo-pagan festivals across the country. These can be excellent forums for networking with people from all over the United States and beyond,

37

who have varying interests and levels of experience. There are a number of wonderful teachers leading these classes who would be happy to speak with any in need.

Cyberspace is the up-and-coming network forum for everything you can imagine. For about a year, I counseled a woman online who had been dealing with a considerable amount of psychic activity and abilities that were frightening to her. Her family could not understand what was wrong with her and just wanted it all to go away. She lives in a small mainstream religious community and had nowhere to turn. Fortunately she had a computer.

This woman went looking in the message boards on one of the Internet providers and found something I had posted on a related message board. Something about my message reached her and made her feel that I might be able to help. She contacted me for advice and we communicated via e-mail for about a year. I introduced her to others online who have an experiential understanding of what she is going through. Through her participation in our private e-mail list, she was able to make some sense of what was happening to her. She also received some extremely helpful advice from the others on the list. She has said a number of times that it makes all the difference in the world just to know she is not crazy and is not alone.

There are Internet newsgroups (e-mail lists) that focus on shamanism and just about anything else you could want. There are message boards on most online service providers devoted to shamanism, metaphysics, death, psychic abilities, and paranormal experiences. Many metaphysical and pagan communities have e-mail lists or Web-rings of local Web sites for others in the community to connect with each other and discuss issues of interest to the community. If you have a computer, go exploring.

You are quite likely to find just what and who you need to help you maintain your sanity. While it is certainly wise to be cautious initially when sharing your deepest self with anyone, most people I know have had very positive experiences online. Many of us have even met some very good friends via the Internet. It is also quite possible that you will connect with modern shamans or experienced practitioners who can advise you in integrating these experiences. If nothing else, you are certain to find people who care and genuinely want to help, even if all they can do is listen.

In the meantime, there are things you can do to get a handle on what is happening. First and foremost, don't panic. Fear is the ultimate paralyzer and, if allowed to gain control of you, will make everything appear worse than it really is. Fear is notorious for inhibiting growth on all levels. Although change truly is the only constant in the multiverse, most people seem to resist it and find it frightening.

Harry Palmer, author of the Avatar materials writes, "an initial unreality (disorder) occurs when one creates a new reality that violates the limits of the host reality.

Persevering through this unreality is essential to expansion and growth."[26] When we expand our experience and beliefs to include these shamanic Other worlds, we create a new personal reality. This "unreality" can be likened to the various growing pains we all endure as we grow through childhood and the teenage years. The "initial unreality" is often a period of chaos or disturbance that must be passed through in order to fully integrate the total self.

Keep in mind that you do have guides and guardians on these other levels that will help you. These are beings that love you unconditionally and have chosen to work with you specifically to assist your own spiritual growth, even if you are not consciously aware of them. Also, understand that these other realities and entities are not unknown to you, your conscious rational mind just does not often remember them in everyday consciousness.

From a shamanic point of view, the first order of business is to get in touch with our personal spirit guides and enlist their active help in our transition. Whether we use a guided visualization tape, meditate on our guides, or attend a class such as basic shamanic journeying or the Silva Method, it is vital that we make the connection with guides and guardians. It makes no difference if they are viewed as our Higher Selves, angels, power animals, or universal archetypes; they can be invaluable in our development and our handling of this type of phenomenon.

How we receive these communications from spirit guides is equally unimportant. We each get it in our own ways. For some people, these connections manifest as a *knowing*, like a memory or a thought that comes out of nowhere. Some people actually see or hear their guides in everyday awareness; some see them in meditations or while dreaming.

While I highly recommend the exercises in chapter three for getting in touch with spirit guides in a shamanic journey context, dreaming is another excellent way to begin to work with your guides. For Carlos Castenada's mentor, don Juan Matus "*dreaming* is the best avenue to power . . . returning us to the unknown and mysterious side of our awareness."[27] According to Victor Sanchez, don Juan speaks of *dreaming* as an art, helping us to unite our total being.[28]

In other words, dreaming is a natural means for us to develop awareness of who we are beyond the limitations of this reality and our rational minds. All things are possible in dreams because the filters of the ego and the analytical mind are turned off. Through dreaming, we can easily establish interdimensional communication and accomplish a re-integration of our total selves.

Many people today prepare for lucid dreaming in ways very similar to those first described by Carlos Castenada in *Journey to Ixtlan*. According to Castenada, don

Juan directed students to give themselves an order just before falling asleep, to look at their hands while dreaming. Once this is accomplished, most people will work on finding other objects in dreaming, sustaining dream images, and learning to move about at will. This process is an effective one and guides the individual in developing control over the free soul, that we take with us out-of-body during both dreams and shamanic journeys. We can use a variation on this method for our purposes here.

Lucid Dreaming Exercise
For Contacting One's Spirit Guides

With practice, it may be varied for any purpose.

Begin at that threshold of consciousness immediately before falling asleep. Experience what this place feels like.

When you have a good feeling of it (and before falling asleep), tell yourself firmly and with focused intent, that you will meet with your spirit guides in a dream and you will remember it.

If you are able to before falling asleep, call on your spirit guides and ask them to meet with you. If nothing happens that night, be patient. We have years of dismissing dreams and filtering them out of our consciousness to overcome here. With practice, it *will* happen.

Once you have successfully met with your spirit guides in a dream, continue to just meet with them for two more nights. When you are able to remember this for three nights, move on to speaking with them during dreaming. Decide ahead of time what you want to say. Before falling asleep, instruct yourself to meet with your guides and say what you have prepared.

When you feel comfortable with dreaming, begin to work with consciously moving about in the dream. Experiment with altering your size or shape. Try going to specific places in our reality and see if you can verify what you see.

Keep a pen and paper next to your bed. You may awaken immediately after the dream, at which point you should write everything down then in case you lose it when you fall back asleep. I would also suggest writing it down if you remember it upon awakening in the morning.

There are many people who will assume this exercise has not worked because they do not remember awakening in the night and they remember nothing in the morning. Quite often, they will encounter something during the day that sparks a memory of the dream. This can take on some rather interesting forms. Sometimes a television show or even a billboard along the side of the road will spark the memory of the dream experience. For this reason, you might also want to carry a notebook and pen with you during the course of your day.

One point I always stress when working with anyone is to set realistic goals. Start small and work your way up. Attempting too much too soon is only setting yourself up for potential disappointment. I find quite often that when people attempt to go too fast, their failure to accomplish what they wanted will reinforce beliefs that they can't succeed. They inevitably get frustrated and occasionally give up.

The motivations for attempting fantastic goals immediately need to be examined. While there are innumerable reasons for this, they must be recognized and cleared if any real progress is to be made. As I have indicated before, the shamanic path is not one for social status or personal glory. Attempting to force your own shamanic development is just as foolish as placing a preschooler in college or sending a novice skier down an Olympic run.

Having said that, I recommend starting out with just a meeting between you and your spirit guides. If anything else happens, that is wonderful, if not, that is wonderful too. When you begin to speak with your guides, thank them for their guidance in your life and ask them to help you now. It helps to be respectful and specific. If you want the right books to fall of the shelf next to you in a bookstore, ask away. It works! If you want to only deal with these types of experiences in dreams until you feel more comfortable, or if you want a physical support system, let them know.

Once you have established a conscious connection with your spirit guides, things are likely to progress fairly rapidly. Your dreaming will take on new significance as you learn to distinguish which dreams are just dreams and which are true journeys. Life itself will seem new to you as you recognize the opportunities for growth in each experience and find teachers in every encounter.

Many people will ask for a teacher, some are even specific enough to ask for a physical teacher. While there is a good chance one will show up, they may not show up when you want them to and if they do show up, they may not be quite what you expect. It is important to accept what comes up as the most beneficial teacher or guide for you at that point in your life. This is true whether you encounter a cock-roach, a telephone pole, or the person who abused you as a child.

For example, we have a dear family friend who met his teacher and mentor during dreaming. This mentor was a yogi from India who taught our friend a great deal. Then one day, this yogi told our friend during dreaming that he would be arriving on a specific flight at a certain East Coast airport and would be staying with him for a while. Incredible as it sounds, when our friend went to the airport, there was his "dream" teacher in the flesh.

If a physical human teacher does not present herself, it may be that you require training and guidance directly from the spirits first. To be honest, most shamans will tell you that the greatest teachings come from Spirit. In many indigenous cultures, the shaman was believed to be chosen and trained by the spirits alone. While we do learn through reading and hearing the experiences of others, all true learning comes from personal experience.

Harry Palmer, author of the Avatar materials, describes this difference in learning in terms of "word lessons" and "world lessons." A "word lesson" is something we are told. It is usually another's experience or another's description of still another person's experience. A "world lesson" is an understanding, which has been gained through our own experience. A teacher may be able to suggest or guide, but they cannot give you an experiential understanding of or an ability to function in these Other worlds. That you must do on your own.

Although modern mainstream society may greatly misunderstand the effects of open Gateways after death experiences, it is not uncommon. In fact, most shamanic and indigenous communities revere this phenomenon as a sacred gift. Those who possess the abilities to consciously communicate beyond the Veil are respected and valued members of the community.

When faced with these open Gateways, it may help to think of all this in terms of the birth and infancy experience. Both death and birth are potential catalysts for the opening of these Gateways. Both the elderly and the newborn are closer and more naturally connected to Other worlds. As infants, our abilities are limited. Although physical development is rapid, it is not always easy. Just as we fear the unfamiliarity of Other worlds, a being entering this world and a new body after the freedom of noncorporeal life may feel similarly frightened or frustrated as they realize they are unable to communicate and move about as they wish.

But we all grow up and learn to function with relative ease in this reality. So too, do those of us experiencing a conscious connection to Other worlds, whether as the result of a death or not. We also grow up and remember to function easily and effectively in Other realities.

To the disappointment of many people, there is no magic pill that can sweep us through youth and adolescence without any growing pains. This is equally true for the shamanic path. It must be fully experienced in order for us to learn and grow through it.

The best thing one can do when confronted with the opening of shamanic and psychic Gateways is to be flexible, particularly in one's beliefs. If you can expand your perspective to the point that you can enjoy the ride for the tremendous growth opportunity it is for your complete spiritual being, you are on your way to a relatively easy transformation. While the road may be challenging at times, it is always rewarding. Once we do grow through this, we realize the potential of our total beings. Then finally, we feel complete and at peace.

Endnotes

12   Brennan, *Hands of Light*, p. 64.
13   Campbell, *The Power of Myth*, p. 85.
14   Roberts, "Soul-Making and Soul-Retrieval" chapter of *Embracing the Fragmented Self*, work-in-progress.
15   Grof, *Beyond the Brain: Birth, Death, and Transcendence in Psychotherapy*, pp. 299–300.
16   According to *Psychotherapy East and West*, pp. 12–15; 29-32: dualistic therapy as opposed to the reductionist mainstream psychoanalysis can be found in ancient Western esoteric philosophies, Sankhya philosophy codified by Patanjali, and Taoism. Carl Jung is the best known of the modern dualists.
17   Eliade, *Archaic Techniques of Ecstasy*, p. 31.
18   Wolf, *Parallel Universes*, p. 20.
19   Ibid., p. 20.
20   Ibid., pp. 43–46.
21   Eliade, *Archaic Techniques of Ecstasy*, p. 31.
22   Singh, *Kundalini Yoga for Strength, Success, and Spirit*, p. 1.
23   Rama, Hymes, & Ballentine, *The Science of Breath*, p. 91.
24   Ibid., pp. 25–26.
25   Ibid., p. 95.
26   Palmer, *Living Deliberately*, p. 91.
27   Sanchez, *The Teachings of Don Carlos*, p. 177. Don Juan Matus was the mentor of Carlos Castenada.
28   Ibid., p. 177.

Chapter 3

TRANSITION

Those in the period of transition through physical death often need special assistance from the shaman. In many ways, the process of dying and knowing one is at the end of this life is more difficult than a sudden death, at least on this side of the Veil. While this individual has the opportunity to say goodbye and tie up loose ends, they also have a lot of time for fear and regrets. Many times these people are also dealing with pain and limited physical capabilities. The shaman must be able to find a way to prepare them for physical death while working to heal body, mind, and spirit.

This transitional period before the actual death of the physical body can have tremendous impact on the spirit in passing. Unfinished business can hold the spirit in the body, making the eventual passing more difficult, both on the loved ones remaining and the one passing over. As I said in chapter two, the bonds we have to loved ones can be powerful ties binding us to this world. They are also potent conduits, through which a significant amount of both conscious and unconscious communication can pass.

When there are blocks, whether unfinished business or a refusal to let go, on either side of these connections, it is felt by both individuals. This can make the transition into death difficult, and even traumatic. It has been known to prevent a being from passing over when they should, due to feelings of guilt, loneliness, or responsibility.

A shamanic associate of mine, whom I will call Russ, has been working for over ten years as a health professional with those who are dying and have recently departed. He worked with a woman in early 1995 who refused to leave her body because she feared for her daughter's emotional well-being. This woman was impatient to meet her death but deeply felt her daughter's resistance to losing her. She believed that her parenting responsibility took precedence over her own death. She held on long after she needed to, in the face of pain and ill health, because of this strong bond with her daughter.

In this case, Russ was called as shaman for both mother and daughter. Not only was he responsible for assisting the mother through her death on a shamanic level, but he acted as counselor and healer of spirit for both of them. The mother requested that Russ speak with her daughter about death and help her to accept her mother's need to pass on.

Although it was necessary for Russ to frame his communications with the daughter in terms she could understand and accept—and not shamanic terms—Russ was able to help the daughter see that her mother was suffering terribly. He listened with compassion to the daughter's fears even as he pointed out that her refusal to let her mother go was causing her even more distress.

Through the creative use of storytelling and compassion, Russ was finally able to convince the daughter that her mother was ready and deserved to die freely. Once the daughter released her need to have her mother present in this reality at any cost, her mother was able to accept her own release from her body and passed peacefully beyond the Veil.

My own grandmother is another example of the spirit's choice to prolong physical death out of a feeling of responsibility to family. She was very ill for many years after giving birth to my aunt and was instructed by her doctor not to have any more children. When she insisted on carrying my mother, she suffered kidney damage and several other medical complications. She struggled through, wanting to see her children, and then her grandchildren, grow up.

When she suffered her first stroke, she told my mother that everyone could take care of themselves now. She said it was finally all right for her to leave her body for good. Eight days later, she had a severe stroke and died very soon afterward. She had consciously chosen to remain in her body until she felt it was OK for her to go. She put off her final passage from physical life until she was sure her family would be all right.

This is one of the most common concerns of the dying. During physical life, we become so focused on nurturing and on our responsibilities to our families, that we are unable to simply release these needs. We worry whether our families will be able to pay the bills, whether our children will feel abandoned, and whether our spouses will be able to carry on without us. Attachments to loved ones, particularly children and spouses, are usually the strongest cords binding the passing spirit to this world.

Many elderly people recognize that their departed spouses stay with them after their passing. Usually other family members chalk this up to senility or wishful thinking. My great-aunt Hulda said goodnight to her departed husband each night from his death until hers. He was with her often during the day and was always there to kiss her goodnight. She was fortunate to be aware of this while she lived. As I describe in a later chapter, when she made her final passage from this realm, her husband was right there with her.

Although chapter seven focuses specifically on the responsibility of the shaman to loved ones remaining in physical life, this is worth discussing here due to its effects on everyone concerned. How effectively we are able to facilitate release and acceptance by loved ones has a direct impact on the spirit in transition, as illustrated by the example above.

Accomplishing this release and acceptance is often a difficult task. It is frequently easier to catalyze this in a newly departed spirit than in either those remaining in the physical or those in the transition to their own deaths. Most of us who are solidly planted in this reality are not open enough to Other realms to conceive of what the newly departed experience. For most of us death is still a big unknown. We don't remember experiencing the continuity of life without a body. All we can say for sure is that when the body dies, that person is gone from us.

It is here that the need to frame our responses in terms of the worldview of the individual becomes extremely important. To tell someone with a mainstream belief system that her loved one will probably pass into a belief system territory for a while, or that if she doesn't let them go, they may remain stuck between worlds, would be more damaging than saying nothing. For similar reasons, it is equally important to communicate with the dying from within their individual worldviews.

How does one go about effecting healing and encouraging acceptance among those with different belief systems, or among those who just can't let go? It takes creativity, flexibility, and the ability to move beyond our own egos and personal beliefs. It may also require learning a bit about the other person's worldview.

The truth is that the modern shaman must be able to understand and communicate between varying belief systems. No longer is everyone in our communities of responsibility part of one shamanic culture. Shamans and shamanic practitioners are often called to heal and guide people with radically different views from our own. Unless we develop the ability to move beyond our personal beliefs, we cannot be effective when working with these people.

If necessary, we can work from within the belief system of the individual in need, to create a change in their energy. Our goal here is to create an uplifting, healing, and expansive energetic atmosphere. We do not attempt to change their beliefs, nor do we try to force them to confront anything. We merely assist them through their respective issues while helping them complete unfinished business.

We gently guide both loved ones and those in transition to release denial and resistance as well as to understand and accept death as a natural, unavoidable part of life. This is what the Cycles of Life meditation in chapter four is designed to do. Without death, there would be no rebirth. Without winter, there would be no spring; without night, no sunrise.

This is an important concept to recognize for those of us in modern society. As I said before, in traditional shamanic societies the departed are acknowledged as a part of the community. These are beings who have completed a transformation in status, but they are understood to be present and to continue to affect our reality in many ways. Furthermore, the departed are known to return to the world of the living, frequently within the same family.

This is an accepted and integral part of shamanic belief systems. Unlike those in "modern" societies, rebirth is not a question, nor is it a great, hopeful idea. It is a fact. We do not fear death because it is a natural transition. We know without question that we will continue to live on and will quite likely return to this world in a new body to continue our path of evolution.

This clarity and connection has been lost as science and religion have progressed through our societies. People nearing death fear the unknown. Death, to them, is unknown because they have forgotten their natural place in the flow of energy and cycles of life. They just don't have that certainty of belief that death is not the end.

Those in the transition to physical death are often so close to the Other side that much of this communication can be accomplished on a spirit level. However, these people do still occupy a physical body. Until they actually take their final journey from this life, that part of them cannot be ignored.

I have known people who use the spiritual or magical aspects of life to avoid directly dealing with others face-to-face. Often they will hide behind ritual and meditation out of fear. They feel unprepared to deal with another's anger or dis-agreement. Often, they do not want to risk losing approval of friends or their public image so they attempt to solve everything on a spiritual or magical level.

While I can understand the feelings involved here, I feel I must stress the lack of honesty and courage that these actions result from. It can be difficult to openly dis-agree or stand up in the face of potential ridicule or hostility, but hiding behind our spirituality does nothing for our soul growth and degrades our spirituality. From then on, one's chosen path becomes a crutch and a barrier to spiritual growth.

One way in which we may engage the rational mind of the dying and encourage the opening to natural creativity is to get the individual in transition involved in the planning of her memorial or death ritual. Involving her in the process, or even encouraging her to take charge of the planning, allows this individual a sense of con-trol over something concrete. This can be extremely beneficial in bolstering a sense of self-esteem and confidence. It can also be very comforting to some people to have this completed and to know that there will be a service that holds meaning for them.

49

I will discuss the importance of creating rituals that speak to our souls in more detail in chapters four and seven. Assisting the dying in ensuring that their rituals resonate well within them can contribute to the ability of each individual to accept the reality of his own death with ease. The death ritual becomes a gentle send-off that catalyzes the release of old emotions and beliefs and prepares the individual to meet the Creator. Of course, this can only take place if he has attained a certain level of acceptance regarding physical death.

If an individual is a devout follower of a specific religion, it is essential that we work with members of the clergy of that religion when planning any death ritual. If this religion precludes any outside involvement, it does not mean we necessarily need to stand by and do nothing. We merely shift our actions and take on a concerned family member/friend role—in this reality.

We offer comfort and love while making ourselves available to listen or help out as needed. We remain open to spirit guidance and allow their words to come through when offered. We act as a clear channel of unconditional love and healing energy whenever we are in the dying individual's space. At the same time, we work in private and subtle ways to create emotional and spiritual healing.

Once I assisted a woman through the death of her father. He had been ill for several years and by that time, his doctors indicated he had less than three months to live. This woman, whom I will call Shirley, is Wiccan. Her father was Christ-ian. Although he knew a little of what she was "into," he did not want to know too much.

I suggested to Shirley that her father's transition into physical death was not the time to either attempt to force him to accept her beliefs or to try to indoctrinate him with a new belief system. At that point in his life, he needed the safety and familiarity of beliefs he had held for a lifetime. To try to shake the foundations of his view of reality and the Afterlife at this point would only create fear and stress for him. He would be made to feel even more lost and helpless at the time when he was most vulnerable. Even if his personal beliefs were not shaken, he would most likely be angry and shut off from his daughter when he needed the love and support of his loved ones most. He might have become unable to receive any energy from her as a result.

This turned out to be a very important step for Shirley as a person and as a Wiccan. In working through her own shadows and resistance to her father's beliefs, she found even greater peace and power in her chosen path. She found that her relationship with the God and Goddess was deepened and strengthened once she was truly able to release all of that stuff.

Once Shirley was able to move past her insistence that her beliefs were the right ones, she was able to reconnect with the beauty and truths at the core of her father's beliefs, particularly since she was raised Christian. I recommended that she honor her father as a fellow spiritual being and respect his chosen path. While it was a path she rejected in favor of one that felt more correct for her, Christianity was what he chose as the best for him in this incarnation. And it worked for him.

I counseled Shirley to help her father say his goodbyes and focus of the joys of his life while working within the Christian worldview (or in a nonreligious worldview) to create acceptable ways for him to welcome his passing. In the end, she and her father were closer than they had been in years. They rediscovered that beliefs really are the only things separating us, and that true love is beyond all of that.

From within the beliefs of any person, there are usually ways to shift the focus from fear and loss to acceptance and satisfaction with the life just completed. Even the atheist can be directed toward the joys and accomplishments of their life and the recognition that their energy will now be joined with that of the universe.

As we all know from high school physics, energy can neither be created nor destroyed. Einstein's special theory of relativity combined mass and energy, and their respective laws of conservation. According to the law of conservation of mass-energy, the total amount of mass-energy in the universe does not change. Mass may be converted into energy, and energy may be converted into mass, but the total amount of mass-energy in the universe remains stable. Therefore, if we choose to view this from a purely mechanistic point of view: when we die and our bodies decay, they do not just disappear. They are converted into the energy that continues to create the world.

Each of our bodies contains a surprising amount of potential energy as shown by Einstein's general theory of relativity. This is the well-known $E=mc^2$. What this means is that the energy contained in a piece of matter is equal to the mass of that matter multiplied by the speed of light squared. Therefore, every particle of matter, no matter how small, has within it an enormous amount of concentrated energy. When we die and our bodies decompose, this concentrated energy is released into the totality of the universe. Even on a purely physical level, we really do become One with the universe.

One of the biggest blocks to an easy passing, even for those who do not believe in a Great Spirit or an Afterlife, is fear. Robert Monroe wrote that "Fear is the great barrier to human growth."[29] It is essential that we face our fears and move through them or they will forever control us. The facing of fear is part of facing the shadow side, as discussed in chapter one. Fear can paralyze the body, mind, and spirit. Fear, in and of itself, can create blocks, which may cause the spirit to remain stuck between worlds. Fear can be so traumatic that it can shatter the spirit, requiring significant soul-retrieval before any healing can occur.

Unless fear is accepted and cleared, the individual in transition through death will not be able to let go of this life. They will frequently carry this fear with them beyond the body. This is often the reason why some spirits remain bound to the people or places they knew in their previous incarnations. These beings resist death so much as a result of their fear that they often deny to themselves (and to anyone else they may come in contact with) that they are physically dead.

The fear of death is something we can only overcome for ourselves. No one can do this for us, no matter how much they love us and no matter how much they are willing to shoulder for us. There are any number of beliefs at the core of our fears and they will vary according to the individual. However, the most common of these beliefs is that death is an unknown. We believe that we cannot really be sure what will happen since we do not remember ever experiencing death before, nor can we be certain we will not be utterly alone once death takes us.

Having said this, there are things we can do to make death more of a "known" for both the living and the dying. We can read experiential accounts of after-death or near-death experiences along with the individual in transition. We can use variations on the journeying and dreaming exercises in this book. Once you gain some familiarity with these exercises, it should be a simple matter to vary them for your specific purposes. One of the simplest ways to make death more familiar and welcoming is to use guided meditation.

Even most organized religions today are accepting of guided meditations. Modern people use them for a multitude of reasons. Below, I have outlined a wonderful

51

meditation for anyone nearing physical death or anyone who experiences a fear of death. I would recommend leading anyone in need through this meditation several times. Like all others outlined here, this meditation may be used with anyone, even those experiencing Alzheimer's disease, coma, or the heavily medicated.

Guided Meditation
Moving Past the Fear of Death

Count down from ten to one, stopping periodically to remind this person that she is getting deeper and more relaxed. It may help to have her visualize walking down a step with each descending number.

At the count of one, you will be perfectly relaxed; you will feel calm, confident, and safe. At the count of one say: "You are now perfectly relaxed. You feel calm, confident, and safe.

"You are walking down a forest path. It is a well-worn trail, with wild flowers growing along its edges. Beside you runs a clear stream. Listen to the sounds of the stream *(slight pause)*, the singing of birds *(slight pause)*, and the rustle of small animals in the forest. *(pause)* Hear the crunch of your feet on the path. *(pause)* With each step, allow something you fear or regret to come to your mind. *(pause)* Do not judge these things. Just acknowledge them and allow your mind to move on to the next thing. *(long pause)* Continue to allow these things to come up and fade away. *(long pause)*

"Now you are approaching a bridge which takes the path over the stream. *(pause)* As you cross the stream, stop to watch the water below. *(pause)* See these fears and regrets pass you by from under the bridge, as the stream carries them away. *(pause)* Watch without judgment as the current sweeps them away downstream. *(long pause)*

"Take a deep breath and continue on the path as it leads you up a hill. *(pause)* You are approaching an opening in the side of the hill. *(pause)* As you enter it, you realize it is a large, bright cave. *(pause)* You follow the well-worn path into the cave, knowing it is safe and comfortable. *(pause)*

"Soon you come to a door off the main path. *(pause)* Open the door and enter the chamber beyond. Inside you are met by someone or something you have left unfinished in this life; some situation you feel the need to complete. *(pause)* Say or do whatever is necessary to create a satisfactory outcome for you. *(pause)* See this situation complete in a manner most beneficial to all concerned. *(long pause)* When you are satisfied with this situation, return to the main corridor of the cave and continue on the path."

Repeat this step as many times as you feel necessary. If possible, have the individual give you some type of signal when there are no more doors to unfinished business left, or when they want to move on.

"As you walk through the corridor, notice that scenes of the joys, love and accomplishments of your life appear on the walls. *(pause)* Take a good look at each of these scenes and rejoice in this life. *(pause)* Continue to see these scenes illuminate the walls."

Repeat this step as many times as you feel necessary. If possible, have the individual give you some type of signal when they want to move on.

"Ahead of you, there is a brighter light. As you approach this light, the corridor opens up into a huge room. *(pause)* As you enter this room, you are greeted by all your loved ones who share this life with you. *(pause)* Greet each of them, stopping to embrace those you want to. *(pause)* Tell each of them how you feel about them. Let them know the things you always wanted to say but never did. Listen to their words of love for you. *(very long pause)* Allow yourself to feel the love and unconditional support in this room. *(long pause)*

"You hear your name called from a brilliantly lit doorway at the other end of the room. Say goodbye to those who have gathered here to support you and pass through this doorway. *(pause)* As you pass through the door, you are enveloped in the most complete sense of unconditional love imaginable. You feel totally safe and comfortable. It is a feeling of Home. *(pause)* You are greeted by loved ones from beyond this life. *(pause)* Some of these are loved ones who have passed over from physical life. Some of these may be people or animals you do not recognize, but they know and love you. They welcome you and tell you how much they love you. *(pause)* Bask in this feeling of love and support. *(pause)*

"These beings lead you to an open doorway. Beyond the doorway you see your physical life and body. *(pause)* Listen as they tell you that you are free to return to your body as you choose. When you are ready to join them, they will be here waiting for you. *(pause)* Know that you are never really alone and that no matter what happens, you will always be able to return to this place of love and comfort."

Let this person know you are leaving her here so that she may take her time and fully enjoy his experience. Make it clear to her that if and when she decides to return to her body, she will return easily and quickly with full memory of the wonders of this place.

With a few alterations in language, this meditation is appropriate for most people over the age of twelve. However, it is a long meditation and may not be the best thing for younger children or certain people. We may not want to think about it, but the truth is that children die too. And many children die of prolonged, difficult conditions that allow them plenty of time to ponder and fear what happens when the body finally gives out. The exercises for connecting with spirit guides combined with breathing exercises and lots of love and attention are best for younger children in this situation.

Keep in mind that the shaman, like everyone, is many things to many people. A shaman is guide and guardian as well as counselor and healer. My shamanic associates and I often jokingly call each other chameleons, because of our abilities to shift identities and methods depending on the situation. There will be times when the best thing we can do in this reality is to just sit by and listen with appreciation to whatever the dying person has to say. Many times, this is all it takes to work through an issue and clear it. We allow those in the transition through physical death their dignity, power, and free will at all times. It is also essential for us to maintain open communication with our spirit guides throughout this process.

Remaining open to guidance can only occur once we are able to move beyond our ego-identities. The ego is the creation of the rational mind. It contains all our fears and beliefs, which together make up our current identity. One cannot work shamanically from this place. As Harry Palmer writes, "Beliefs have the capacity to stimulate impressions, to filter impressions, or to react with other creations."[30]

When attempting to work from within this creation, which is the ego-identity, we are subject to our beliefs. As we receive communication from the Other side, we define it based on these beliefs. We cannot get a clear and accurate experience in this way, because it has been limited and defined by our identities. Shamanic work takes us beyond these limitations. It allows us to fully experience all worlds and all communications so that we may clearly manifest them in this reality.

Palmer goes on to write, "Believing defines realities, experiencing dissolves realities."[31] Shamanism is an experiential path that takes us beyond the limitations of defined realities so that we may most effectively work to benefit ourselves and our communities. Working from within the ego limits us to the knowledge of our rational minds and subjects us to the effects of our own beliefs and reactions.

When we open ourselves to guidance from Spirit, we accept the inflow of universal wisdom. We allow our identities to step aside as we receive communication from many places, including the spirit guides of the individual in transition. We must learn to trust this communication; to "trust our instincts" as we say in my family. All of us in my family have paid the price for analyzing away a direct communication from the Other side. This can be as simple as an urge to bring along the diaper bag on a short walk to something as serious as choosing not to take an airplane flight that later crashes.

If there were one recommendation I could make to those beginning the shamanic path, or any other spiritual path, it would be this: trust yourself and your spirit guides. Do not allow your analytical mind to overshadow your heart, but also do not allow your emotions to control you. When we open to the universe and to the Earth, we are filled with balanced energy. As long as we allow this to flow freely through us, we receive unlimited wisdom and power. Especially in the case of those individuals experiencing a death transition, all the answers you need are available to you if you remain open.

When working with those experiencing this transition to physical death, it is very important that we maintain our personal shamanic work. There have been plenty of individuals who have neglected their own work and allowed themselves to get caught up in the issues of the dying. I have one acquaintance, whom I will call Mike, that has a tendency to do this time after time.

For a period of about six months, Mike completely put off his own personal journeying and any personal work with his spirit guides while focusing all his energy on a young boy who was dying. Mike allowed himself to become so enmeshed in this situation that he began experiencing the boy's physical symptoms. Mike became utterly drained of energy and was forced to stay away from the boy in order to regain control.

I know many people who find this amusing or cool when it happens to them in minor ways. I knew a man once who loved to tell everyone how he just picked up everyone's stuff. He found it humorous that he would get someone else's headache. While I can appreciate the novelty and the clear proof that our energy systems and physical bodies can receive this type of input, we must grow past this. To become a psychic sponge benefits no one and can be very detrimental to one's well being.

55

Once again, we are responsible for ensuring that we are healed and fully prepared before attempting any healing work for others. While shamanic and other healing vocations can be fun, they are not games. Working with someone's energy fields without being completely ready to handle this, is unethical and potentially dangerous for all involved. Anyone who is unable to avoid soaking up other's psychic influences without the ability to ground and clear these influences is better suited to another vocation.

A less extreme example of the importance of personal work through this process is my own. My step-grandmother, Kathleen, died in 1990 after a long battle with Alzheimer's disease. She was institutionalized near the end during the time when my husband and I were preparing for our wedding. We drove the hour and a half every weekend to visit. First, we would spend time with my grandfather at his home, then we would visit Kathleen in the hospital.

Each time we saw her, Kathleen seemed to forget even more. Sometimes she would not know us, other times she would ask why we had not visited for so long. It was both heartbreaking and frustrating for everyone involved. One weekend, two weeks before our wedding, we decided to skip our visit to the hospital. We had spent all day with my grandfather, after a very long week of work, and we were exhausted. We assumed we could just see her the following weekend and she wouldn't even know the difference. Kathleen died two days later.

I experienced terrible feelings of guilt as a result of having skipped our visit that weekend. I felt extremely selfish and could not believe I had not *known* that her death would come so soon. Had I not kept up with my own personal work, these feelings would have prevented me from assisting the rest of the family through this time. A shadow would have hung over our wedding and honeymoon, which took place so soon after her death. I would have carried this baseless guilt that served no purpose, and it would have controlled me.

Through personal journeying and work with my spirit guides, I was able to face these feelings and move through them. This was a wonderful learning experience for me. Rather than continuing to create the wound of "not being there," I was able to assist both Kathleen and my family in the best possible ways.

I consciously choose to carry this experience as a reminder to live life to its fullest and to treat others as though I may never see them again. As don Juan Matus counseled Carlos Castenada, I use Death as my ally, or my advisor. I do not hold back my feelings with those I love. When someone needs me, I am there if I can be. If I honestly can't, I have no regrets. Through continuing our personal work, we are also able to maintain the necessary emotional detachment to the outcome and we quickly recognize when we need to make a change in our responses.

While the shamanic journey and work with spirit guides is an exceptionally powerful way to clear issues like these, it can take a good deal of experience and a willingness to be very vulnerable to yourself. For those who prefer, or need, a more structured means to the shadow side, I have detailed a guided meditation below.

Guided Meditation
Through the Shadow

Please allow plenty of undisturbed time in a safe, comfortable space whenever you perform this meditation. Designed for use with a shamanic drumming tape, which is optional.

Allow the drumming to carry you down, deep within yourself. Follow the sound of the drum as it resonates with your own energy. Ride this tunnel of sound into the center of your being.

Deep within your center, you see a dark doorway. Ride the sound of the drum through this doorway and into the deep darkness beyond. Become aware of your spirit guides surrounding you as you move deep into the darkness.

You are comfortable within the protection of your guides. You know this is merely the darkness of your own self and it cannot harm you, unless you give it the power to do so.

As you follow the sound of the drum, images come forth out of the darkness and pass by you. Recognize these as images and symbols of your own beliefs and experiences. Watch them without judgment as you move beyond them. Soon all you see is the darkness.

Now, you find you are standing on solid ground. Your guides are right there with you standing in absolute darkness. Call forth one image from the darkness. Ask that this be an image that holds a minor amount of discomfort for you and allow it to present itself to you.

Look deeply within this image. See it for what it really is, at its core. What does this image have to say to you? What can you learn from its presence in your life? Why have you hidden it away in the darkness? Be aware of any communication from your guides during this process.

Now reach out and embrace this image. Acknowledge this as a part of you that has been denied. Feel yourself become more complete as you integrate this experience. Now take a deep breath and blow all the feelings and judgments you have attached to this thing into a bubble of shadow. Take another deep breath and feel them leave your body as you blow them out into the bubble.

The bubble is filling with light. It is expanding and transforming these attachments. It fills to overflowing with light and pops, releasing these transformed energies back into your center. These are enlightened energies that are now free of their bonds. You may now choose to use this energy as you wish.

Continue this process with gradually more uncomfortable images (you may need to repeat this process with some images more than once).

Now, look around you. Notice that this place is not so dark anymore. These shadows of experience and belief are merely shadows. It is only your perception of them that shrouds them in darkness. All those parts of you that have been denied are not bad or evil, they just are and they have much to teach you. You are strong enough to integrate them into your whole balanced being.

Be aware of any further communication from your guides. Feel the transformation of this process fully. Be aware of a new sense of strength and wholeness.

Now become more aware of the sound of the drum calling you back to your center. Follow the rhythm up through your center, back to your physical body. Thank your guides for their continued guidance and protection and return to normal awareness.

Some modern shamanic practitioners have told me they don't feel they have the right to make the choice of leaving or staying for those who are dying. This is absolutely true. The choice is up to the individual in transition. We offer unconditional healing, support, and guidance. We work to connect the dying with their spirit guides. We remain open on all levels, if and when these people choose to call on us for assistance. The rest is up to them. At no point should we attempt to interrupt the normal death cycle, except in very specific and extreme cases.

Such cases may include situations of terminal illness accompanied by extreme physical or mental pain and difficulty. I must strongly stress here that these situations are rare and the decision to pass over is still up to the dying individual. In no way do we ever press our beliefs or feelings of when and how a passing should occur upon an individual in transition.

While this chapter is not intended to be a healing manual, it is important to discuss the various factors affecting the ability of the dying to ready themselves for their passing. Certain medications and conditions such as Alzheimer's can impair the normal functioning of the rational mind. Various technologies and physical ailments can interfere with communication and the functioning of the energy bodies. These factors will influence how we handle our work with the dying in ordinary reality and during the shamanic journey. The deathwalk itself can be affected by these variables as well.

Often the life-prolonging technology that has become standard procedure in hospitals can interrupt the normal death cycle. Although these technologies save millions of lives, more and more people are asking at what cost do they do so. There are those individuals who would have passed easily and with dignity out of physical life, if allowed to. Most of these people are given neither the choice nor the right to die. We hook them up to machines that breathe for them, keep their hearts pumping, clear their kidneys, and perform a multitude of other physical tasks to keep the body alive.

While I am certainly not against all medical intervention, I believe that the vast majority of these situations occur as a result of our societal terror of death. The body is the only tangible reality we know. Anything else is still that big Unknown, and is therefore something to be feared. The unfortunate result of much of this refusal to allow death to happen organically and in its own time can be severely detrimental to the spirit of the dying individual.

Don is a shamanic associate of mine, who has been working in the health-care field and aiding people in their deathwalks for twenty years. As a licensed health-care administrator specializing in elderly care, Don is faced with death on a daily basis. He has found that the soul can become fragmented as a result of this medical intervention. Many of us, who work shamanically with the dying, have found fragmentation of those in transition as a result of trauma, fear, and certain disorders.

Anything that threatens the self or interferes with the normal functioning of the ego and the mind has the potential to traumatize the individual. This fragmentation is a defense mechanism of the body-mind. Just as an animal will sometimes attempt to chew off a foot or leg that is caught in a trap in order to escape, the rational mind can effectively eliminate from normal consciousness any parts that are affected by trauma through splitting the spirit. This is often done in an effort to escape the memory of that experience and the associated feelings of fear and helplessness. Those parts that are now deemed too threatening to the self are shut down or permitted to get lost.

Don has recently been working with his aunt who has Alzheimer's in addition to other medical problems. As many of us who have worked with Alzheimer's patients find, her soul is very fragmented. Don has found that she stays in her body out of fear, even though parts of her have already passed over. She is terrified of death and has given her family instructions to do whatever is needed to keep her alive or resuscitate her.

Through my discussions with other shamans and healers who have encountered Alzheimer's, I have found some striking similarities in patient responses on a spiritual level. As a result of the impaired functioning of the rational mind and the subsequent fear and embarrassment, these individuals tend to both shut down certain chakras along with aspects of their spirits and to frequently wander about the shamanic Other worlds.

In shutting down various parts of themselves, these people effectively split the soul. This can be likened to the splitting of a personality due to trauma, as is seen in multiple personality disorder. The spirit will actually fragment. Some parts will be closed off and locked away deep in the shadow side. These are often stored in the denser energy of the physical body so as to make it less accessible to conscious awareness. This can be indicated by closed or blocked chakras, although major chakra issues are not always the cause of blocked energy flow.

Care must be taken during any healing involving the flow of energy through the body. This is particularly important when dealing with a dying person or one with a degenerative condition such as Alzheimer's. Blasting one's way through a blockage can produce even more detrimental effects, including more fragmentation. Even gently opening the flow can be useless if the individual is unprepared to maintain this flow. Unless the issue that created the blockage is not fully cleared, it can be expected to recur.

As I said, individuals with conditions like Alzheimer's are also prone to shamanic wandering. Their hold on our space-time continuum begins to slip as does their focus on the physical body. These individuals are not truly delusional in their memories and their recognition of reality. Their episodes frequently indicate where they are on an energetic and spiritual level. As they associate less and less with their current physical point in space-time, they will begin to communicate what they are experiencing. These episodes can be seen as a type of uncontrolled journeying, usually taking place within the Middleworld.

This wandering has an interesting side effect. Often, these patients will experience what we term hallucinations. Patients who are unable to control their shamanic wandering may often wander into Other worlds as well. They may return with wild stories of strange beings or places. They may also show signs of a split reality awareness, leading them to confuse realities and describe the appearance of "unreal" objects in our reality.

A friend recently brought his father to our house after a cross-country driving vacation. His father had been experiencing waking nightmares and confusion during the trip. His father, whom I will call Tony, was wide awake at night and appeared to be having some disturbing hallucinations. He was not aware of this reality but was physically acting out what he experienced in Other worlds.

Each time this happened, Tony's hallucinations seemed to coincide with the area in which they were staying. For example, while visiting some of the local Pueblos, Tony was lost among Native American people, dressed in traditional, ancient clothing. He could not understand what they were doing and they either could not hear him or would not answer him.

Not only did Tony appear to be tapping into psychic remnants or spirits of the ancestors of native peoples, but his inability to communicate at all is a typical experience when one's awareness is split between realities, and therefore, limited by this world. Tony also experienced these visions with the element of tremendous fear that he would somehow lose his son.

Tony's greatest fear at this point in his life was being alone. Tony had watched both friends and family members die of Alzheimer's and knew their predicaments very well. In his shamanic wandering, he created or attracted situations where he could not find his son.

The combination of projected fear and other shadow aspects with shamanic wandering can be absolutely terrifying for these people. This can exacerbate their conditions and the constant trauma may lead to soul-fragmentation. It is vital that loved ones, particularly the main caretaker, work to restore a sense of security.

If the individual is open-minded enough, we can discuss spirit guides with her. We can work with this person so that she may call upon a spirit guide, and possibly see the guide, whenever she feels threatened. This guide should be one that is non-threatening and makes her feel safe and protected.

You can also work to strengthen awareness of the cord binding you together. If she is aware of this, it is possible to deepen a memory of this cord, through frequent discussion and journey work. When she feels alone or lost, she may call up that memory and either find you or feel safe knowing that you are connected and that she will never be truly lost. Also, through deepening your own awareness, you are likely to be more aware when she is in need. You can then go to her on any level of being.

Alternatively, I have learned that these so-called delusions can be related to a prolonged breakdown of the body's energy systems. This leads to a premature release of stored memories and shadow aspects. This is what Don meant when he said that part of his aunt had already passed over. As is described in detail in chapter five, the death process begins with the breakdown of the lower energy centers.

As these systems dissolve and pass over, the dying person becomes aware of old memories and experiences that have been stored in these areas. In situations such as Alzheimer's disease, the awareness of these becomes a reliving of them. The individual's entire focus is on these experiences and to us it may appear to fluctuate randomly as each new memory is released.

It can be very difficult to reach these fragmented individuals. Trying to contact them through the physical body can result in a frustrating mass of confused fog. All assistance in these situations must take place through energy work and journeying. Shamans use varying methods to heal the energy bodies and dull physical pain. We work to balance their energy and ensure that all chakras are clear. I also recommend contacting the Monroe Institute for feedback from individuals who have used the Hemi-Sync tapes with Alzheimer's patients.

Even more important than this energy healing is the shamanic journeying. In order to reach these people and help them understand what is occurring, we must get beyond the limitations imposed by their condition or their medication. In order to do this, we focus on the being behind the fog. Through journeying, we go straight to the core of the person and allow that core being to lead us to him. This might be described as the higher self of the individual, although we also connect directly with the personality in transition. We enter the journey with the specific goal of contacting the core of the fragmented individual. This is beyond mere personality, we are going for the totality of who he really is.

My step-grandmother was hospitalized in Pennsylvania for some time with Alzheimer's disease. Whenever I visited her, I felt her energy scattered all over the place. She was unable to maintain her focus on any one place or time. Each time we saw her, this lack of conscious control seemed to be more serious. It was very difficult to get a fix on her in this reality.

Understanding that within the shamanic journey there is no time-space as we experience it in our physical Middleworld, I decided to find out exactly what was going on and see if I could assist her from our home in Connecticut. At that time, we had a small room that was used only for journeying, meditation, and ritual work. I let my husband know where I was off to and entered this room, closing the door behind me.

We had constructed a circle of stones within the small room. In reality, it was more of a walk-in closet, but the circle was large enough to contain the two of us and our altars. Since it was a room devoted to this type of work and had been used frequently, the energy was actually tangible upon entering. I was so conditioned to working in this room that I immediately slipped into light trance as I entered the circle.

I seated myself on the floor before my altar and lit a central white candle. I then lit some sage, angelica, and sweetgrass smudge. Using a feather fan we created from feathers we had been given, both by other humans and by the birds themselves, I smudged my entire energy field. As I smudged, I *felt* my energy be cleansed and I *saw* the energy of the room become more intense. My trance deepened as my own energy quickened.

I stood up and smudged the entire area, calling on the smoke of the sage, angelica and sweetgrass to purify this space. I asked that the Spirits of these sacred plants allow only the most beneficial energies to penetrate this space. I allowed this to continue to burn throughout the journey.

With my drum, I called upon the Spiritkeepers of the four directions: the Golden Eagle and Hawk of the East, the Serpent and Coyote of the South, the Bear and Great Stag of the West, and the Buffalo and Owl of the North. Each came through with their own resonance and rhythm on the drum. I watched and listened as they entered the room and filled it with their strength. I invited them to join me in this work and asked their guidance and protection in my work. I called upon them to bless me with their wisdom and energies.

In the same fashion, I called upon the energies of Father Sky, the Earth Mother, and the Great Spirit: the Creator that permeates all things. I received their blessings then gave them honor and thanks. Then I sat back down before my altar.

I lit our silver and gold candles, which for us symbolize the balanced energies of God and Goddess, male and female. As I did so, I invoked Their presences and asked for their blessings and assistance. They came easily through and joined with the others. Next, I called upon my personal guides and guardians, and all allies in all realms to join with me in this journey and offer any assistance I might require to be successful in reaching my step-grandmother, Kathleen. They filled me with their energy and I spoke each name as they joined with me.

Then, I lay down and began to drum once more. As my trance deepened, my physical body continued to drum. I was barely aware of this as my free soul began to

63

rise. A part of me watched as my body released the drum and my spirit departed the room. I called for Kathleen, asking to communicate with her true self. I felt myself pulled at incredible speeds through a mist. Suddenly, I was face to face with her. She was as I remembered her, but different. She appeared lighter and younger, yet now I felt a strength and wisdom I had not known in her before.

We were in no particular shamanic World, nor in any time-space that I knew. It was just the two of us, separate but together and able to communicate easily. I asked about her scattered energy in the physical realm and if I could do anything to help her. She said the disease and hospitalization had been difficult on her physical and emotional bodies. She had needed to separate and close down a few parts of her so that she could make the jump beyond the Veil with ease.

She smiled knowingly and told me that she was just waiting here until the other parts released her body. She also made it clear that she was already in close contact with her own spirit guides and needed no additional assistance. She told me they were all aware that, once the body died and the other parts were released, she would have no difficulty assimilating them and would return swiftly Home.

I hugged her one last time and returned to my body. Once more back in this reality, I sat up and thanked all those who had come to my aid for this work. I released all I had called, saying that they were always welcome and could stay or go as they chose. I doused the smudge and extinguished the candles. I put away my drum and went out to record this journey in my journal.

Through journeying some of us have found that other "versions" of ourselves are acting as personal guides. In *Ultimate Journeys*, Robert Monroe writes of discovering that the Being who began his instruction out-of-body and guided him in his continuing work was actually his future self.[32]

This is also interesting in light of the parallel worlds theories of quantum physics. According to Fred Alan Wolf, there are an unlimited number of parallel universes and information moves equally between past and present as a result of quantum waves.[33] This does appear to confirm Monroe's experience of being guided by a future self. This also leads me to believe that in some of these Other worlds, our counterparts are not only aware of us, but have developed the ability to communicate with us in various ways. Whether we are aware of it on a rational consciousness level, we may frequently guide and be guided by our Other selves.

Those who are experiencing spirit fragmentation in addition to mental fog will appear disjointed, incomplete, or lifeless when we encounter them through journeys and dreams. These individuals require soul-retrieval before any other work can be effectively done. We seek their fragmented parts, return them, and assist the individual in reintegrating them. As I said in the first chapter, it is a Saami belief that all people journey. Sometimes this journeying free soul will become lost, fragmented, or stuck somewhere, unable to fully return to the body.

Many shamanic cultures believed that this free soul could wander into the realm of the ancestors, who would then attempt to hold or steal the spirit. This would normally be done out of misguided love or jealousy of the individual's physical life. The shaman would then be called upon to journey in search of the soul, or soul fragments.

A form of soul-retrieval is practiced in Michael Harner's basic *Way of the Shaman* workshops. Several years ago, my husband and I decided to attend one of these workshops for ourselves, after hearing so much about them. We had a wonderful time and experienced some real insights, as well as learning more of how other people and other cultures work shamanically.

I had a wonderfully powerful experience of one type of soul-retrieval journey, the retrieval of a power animal, which is also taught in Harner's workshops. During the course of the weekend, we would switch partners and undertake the shamanic journey for each other, alternating journeys. At one point, we went in search of a power animal that had been lost by our partners and was needed by them at that time.

While I was waiting for my husband to return from his journey for me, I wondered what type of animal he might bring back with him. I managed to clear my mind so I did not influence his experience. Since we are so close and so attuned to each other, we often experience shared journeys and dreams, as well as finishing each other's sentences. Sometimes we joke that we just waste energy actually talking since we already know what the other is thinking anyway.

This is one reason why some people find it difficult to work shamanically or psychically for those they are emotionally very close to. These attachments can interfere, creating blocks out of fear and denial. They can also cause one to initially pick up on what is currently in the other person's consciousness. Some people will accept at face value what they first see without going any deeper or looking for verification. I always stress the development of accuracy and learning one's personal symbolism when dealing with inexperienced healers or shamanic practitioners. In order to work effectively, these two abilities are vital to the process.

When my husband returned, he held the energy of the power animal close to his chest as he sat up with eyes closed. He leaned over me and blew this energy into my heart chakra. I instantly felt a tremendous release and began to sob. I felt the presence of a huge buffalo surround me as I felt I had come Home. My heart chakra opened wide and blocks I had been holding onto since childhood were crushed under the power of this new presence. As they dissipated, I felt like a child who had lost a favorite stuffed animal or a security blanket and then had it suddenly returned out of the blue. As we wrote in our journals afterward, we compared notes and Buffalo is indeed what he brought back for me.

In many ways, this type of soul retrieval can be seen as returning a lost part of one's self that manifests as a specific power animal. We interpret the energies associated with these newfound parts of Self based on our current store of experience. They manifest to us as animals from our reality in order to ease their integration and accessibility to our conscious minds.

Whether you view these lost power animals as parts of one's own Self or interdimensional beings, they play an important role in bringing us the energies we need to continue and maintain the process of retrieving our own lost soul fragments. I find this technique to be particularly beneficial when working with someone who has an extreme fear of death.

In this way, the individual is more easily able to accept and integrate her own strength. The presence of a power animal not only offers a tangible example of the needed energies but it is a potent reminder that this person is not alone. There is no pressure to rely on her own strength or personal power. The acceptance of the power animal provides a forum for universal strength to flow though the individual.

Soul-retrieval is not always experienced as a return of power animals. There are individuals and situations that require other methods. The two most common alternate methods involve accessing past-lives, which is discussed in depth in chapter eight, and journeying to find our other selves, which can manifest as versions of ourselves, archetypal dramas and personalities, and missing memories.

Although soul-retrieval can be experienced spontaneously, often through dreams, when the individual is ready to reintegrate these parts, it most often requires the guidance of an experienced shaman. The shaman is able to prevent any further fragmentation, to persuade the missing parts to return to the main individual, and to keep the whole process flowing smoothly. In addition, the shaman can provide ongoing support and counseling to assist the reintegration of the individual.

Pain can be a powerful barrier to the soul in transition. Although severe and extreme pain has been known to spontaneously induce trance states and can kick the spirit out of body, this is also frequently accompanied by a fragmentation of the spirit, which will need to be handled with a soul-retrieval process. When the physical body is wracked with pain, it receives our full energy and attention, leaving nothing with which to open to the Other side or to enter altered states of consciousness. As stress and tension increases, one's ability to center and balance decreases.

Although in most cases I would not recommend foregoing them, most pain medications cause the mind to become foggy and often reduce our levels of control in altered states. Many of these medications do not really eliminate the pain. They just make it so we either sleep through it, or just don't care about the pain.

These situations can mimic the effects of psychosis, conditions such as Alzheimer's, and even comatose states. This is best handled as though the spirit were fragmented, which is often a result of the trauma of physical pain. We journey to connect with spirit guidance and communicate with the core being, beyond any physical pain or other limitations. We may journey to retrieve a necessary power animal for the individual in need, perhaps one that will provide them surcease from pain or the strength to handle things better.

As is true with the death transition itself, there are no quick fixes to handling pain. Shamans will often work in conjunction with medications. When the pain is less severe, medications are sometimes replaced with other therapies such as shamanic or energy-healing techniques, acupuncture, homeopathy, hypnosis, and herbs. The topic is far too involved to be covered in any real depth here, but there are a number of books out devoted specifically to this topic. I highly recommend the works of Barbara Brennan and the Silva Method courses for anyone interested in healing. I also recommend the Monroe Institute tapes. They produce two, which have had astounding results in decreasing and eliminating pain, "Energy Walk," and "Pain Control."[34]

Stroke is one of the leading causes of death in the elderly today. Head trauma, often leading to coma, is a leading cause of death and disability before old age. While these conditions can be devastating for both patient and family, they are interesting in that, although the physical body is generally significantly affected, the mind often functions quite well.

In the case of stroke, it is vital for us to remember that, although this individual may not be able to respond to us in this reality, it is very possible that she understands us perfectly. Unless there are mitigating medical conditions that would indicate a loss of mental capabilities, stroke victims frequently feel stranded within a body that no longer responds as it should. These individuals often respond very well to drumming and the Hemi-Sync technology of the Monroe Institute.[35]

Coma is another condition, which seems to be a mystery to many, including medical professionals. It has been described as extended unconsciousness; unconsciousness being the lack of reaction to a stimulus. No one can tell us for sure if the coma patient is aware of this reality or not. Sometimes people are encouraged to speak to the patient, just in case they are aware.

Studies have shown that a maintaining a positive attitude when in the presence of a coma patient may be beneficial to the recovery of the patient. This leads many people to believe that the coma patient is aware of what is taking place around them. Most psychics, and many of those who awaken from a coma, report a distinct to vague awareness of physical reality. Some coma survivors even remember things that were said to them while they lay in a coma.

For example, a young man named Andy shared his experience as a coma survivor. He described hearing someone say that he was in a coma and the confusion and fear that evoked within him. He was aware of activity around him, of waking up from time to time but being unable to move or respond in any way. He spoke of having a fragmented memory and difficulty staying awake. He said it felt as though he were drifting on an ocean. He kept trying to reach the shore, to go home and somehow make himself known to those around him, but the tides kept carrying him away.

Andy clearly experienced uncontrolled shamanic wanderings associated with an involuntary slipping of identities. As a result of his injury, he was unable to focus his attention on any one reality. Just as we all commonly travel about during sleep, when the physical body is in a period of hibernation, it appears that the coma patient is experiencing a prolonged and very deep sleep-state. During this time, they are so disconnected from physical reality, they are unable to establish a lasting connection.

I believe don Juan Matus would call this an inability to "assemble" any specific reality or world. As Victor Sanchez describes it, "(for the average person) . . . his or her assemblage point produces a singular alignment, which is perceived as the everyday world."[36] It is our ability to focus our attention on a specific range of energies that determines which reality we perceive at any given time. When we are unable to focus this attention as a result of injury or a physical or mental condition, we are also unable to align with any one world.

This can be experienced as a drifting or a feeling of being pulled around at random. These individuals are often frightened, helpless to control their realities. They feel increasingly more alone as they are unable to communicate or establish any physical connection with loved ones. This inability to focus can continue after physical death, as the departed carries the fear and loneliness with them.

Andy also spoke eloquently of wanting his loved ones to talk to him, to tell him something familiar. He wanted physical contact and some type of connection to familiar things. This is an important link for any individual experiencing a condition, injury, or illness that prevents proper functioning of the brain. In order for these people to gain control over where they go, they must be certain where they are. Since the brain is no longer able to perform its functions as map and stabilizing guidepost, it is up to loved ones to do what they can to fill that position.

In everyday reality, we sit with these individuals. We hold their hands and talk to them about the things we did together or their favorite things. We tell funny stories and let them know what is going on with the other people in their lives. We do our best to maintain a positive attitude when we are with them. It is vital that we hold this positive attitude in our hearts and minds as we spend time with these people.

The individual in transition to death, or during a serious illness, is vulnerable both physically and energetically. It is the hospital or caregiver's responsibility to prevent additional infections and injuries. It is our responsibility as loved ones and shamans to prevent any further damage to their energy field. They will pick up on our energy when we are with them.

Walking into the room of a coma patient, pretending to be cheery, but feeling certain that this person will die or be a vegetable is analogous to going in with a full-blown case of a contagious and deadly disease. It works on them slowly and subtly, but you can be sure this *will* infect their energy systems. This infection may manifest in many ways. It may lead to a longer recovery. It may induce fear that can carry over beyond the Veil. It may also cause them to experience increased shamanic wandering and potentially traumatic out-of-body experiences that can lead to further fragmentation.

Am I saying that you must avoid a loved one if you are afraid, depressed, or believe something awful is in store for them? Certainly not! I am, however, saying that we need to take an equal responsibility for our psychic influences and our physical influences. In everyday reality, I expect that family and friends will either stay home when they are sick, or avoid sneezing directly on my toddler. In a similar way, I would not consider walking into the room of a psychically vulnerable individual without first clearing my energy and, if possible, handling some of these issues I may be holding onto.

It is usually best to deal with these individuals from your own center, also known as your higher self. In this place, you are beyond the limitations of beliefs and fears. You are better able to be a clear conduit for healing energy. Below I have outlined three exercises that can be used to purify your own energy and assist you in finding your center or higher self.

Earth–Star Meditation
To Clear and Balance One's Personal Energy Field

....

Preparation to enter the energy space of an ill or otherwise vulnerable person.

Calm and center yourself. Count down from ten to one. It may help to visualize yourself going down one step with each descending number. Remember to take deep, diaphragmatic breaths and feel yourself going deeper.

See a ball of light at the center of the Earth. This is the embodiment of the Earth energy. See this energy flow up out of the Earth's core and into your body through the soles of your feet and the base of your spine. If you like, place your hands, palms down, on the ground and allow this energy to be drawn up into your hands and arms directly. Feel this energy fill your entire body. Feel it exude from the pores of your skin, your eyes, your hair, your navel. Feel it flow completely though you and out through the top of your head. Fully experience this flow.

See a star at the center of the universe. This is the embodiment of the universal or Sky energy. See this energy flow down from the center of the star and into your body through the top of your head. If you like, raise your hands, palms up, to the sky and allow this energy to be drawn down into your hands and arms directly. Feel this energy fill your entire body. Feel it exude from the pores of your skin, your eyes, your hair, your navel. Feel it flow completely though you and down into the Earth. Fully experience this flow.

Experience both of these flows together for as long as you like, until you really feel them. See and feel your total energy space cleansed and purified by this light.

Visualize yourself completely attuned to your higher self. See yourself acting as a clear channel for healing energy. You are revitalized by these energies flowing through your being.

You may now choose whether to count back up from one to ten or not. In any case, you are now ready to enter the space of a vulnerable individual.

One note of advice: maintain this energy flow while you are with this person. If you begin to feel drained or irritable, take a moment alone to call forth this flow. As long as this energy is flowing through you, you are protected from any draining or damaging energies.

Smudge Ceremony
For Purification of One's Personal Energy Field

This ceremony may also be used as a prelude to the above exercise.

You will need:

A source of purifying smoke. I recommend smudge sticks or loose herbs such as sagebrush (*Artemisia* spp.), sweetgrass, or incenses such as sandalwood and myrrh.

Matches or a lighter; a candle is recommended for a continuing flame, especially for smudge sticks, which may be difficult to maintain smoking.

A heat-resistant container or incense burner

Optional—a feather or fan

Take a moment to center yourself. It may help to count (to yourself) down from ten to one, remembering to breathe deeply and from the diaphragm.

Light your smudge with respect. Invite the smoke of the sacred herbs to purify your energy and this space.

Using your feather or fan to move the smoke, or carrying the smudge stick with you, offer the sacred smoke to the six directions: North, East, South, West, Earth, and Sky; and to the Great Spirit in the center, which permeates all things. Offer blessings of respect and gratitude to each of these.

Beginning at your navel, bathe yourself in the sacred and purifying smoke. Move the smoke up to your heart area, then over your head, along your back, down to your feet, and back up to your navel.

As the smoke moves along your body, feel yourself center deeply. Deeply breathe in the smoke. See your worries and tensions dissolve in the warmth as they are carried up and away by the smoke. Ask the smoke of the sacred herbs once again to purify your energy, to clear you of all limitations, and to help you become a clear and protected channel for healing energy.

Offer the smoke once more to each of the six directions and the Creator. Give thanks to them for their presence in your life. Thank the smoke of these sacred herbs for their assistance in purifying your energy and preparing you to meet with your loved one.

Some individuals and groups believe that once a smudge is burning, it should be left to burn itself out. The truth of this will depend on your beliefs and experience. In my experience, allowing something to burn for extended periods of time is not always possible or preferable. In my journeying and work with these sacred plants, I have been taught that whether I extinguish the flame or leave it to burn itself out is not important, provided my every action is made in respect and honor.

Drum Purification Ceremony
To Purify and Energize One's Personal Energy Field

Take several deep breaths and center yourself. Begin to beat the drum. In determining the tempo of the beat, go with what feels right to you at the time. It is generally recommended that this be faster than a heartbeat.

Continue to beat the drum until you feel yourself center deeply and enter the trance state.

Holding the drum up and out from your body, offer its sound to each of the four directions. Then offer it to the Sky and the Earth. Then to the center again, to offer it to the Creator.

Continue to drum at the pace that resonates best for you along your entire body, stopping at each chakra for a few moments. Allow the sound and energy of the drum to harmonize your energy systems and clear away unwanted vibrations. Hold at each chakra, or any area that feels the need, until you feel this area come into balance with the rest of your system.

Hold the drum out to center once more as an offering of thanks to the Creator. Beat four times more quickly and then end with one strong beat.

With the physical body out of commission and usually a minimum of pain, stroke and coma victims are often nudged out of body. The ability to remain open to the Other side and to function in Other realities is often enhanced during these situations, particularly in the case of stroke where a measure of nonphysical control often remains. A basic shamanic journey can be quite effective for these individuals, even though they often need to be led through it.

Although the basic shamanic journey can be found in most books on general shamanism, the following is an outline of a semi-guided Upperworld journey for the stroke or coma patient. This particular journey is designed to assist the patient in recovering control over the energy body and to facilitate her in establishing a conscious connection with guides.

As a guided experience, this is not a true shamanic journey. As I have said, the shamanic journey cannot be led. Therefore, any journey described and led in a book is really a guided meditation with shamanic elements. This distinction is unimportant in most cases. However, it is important for readers to know the difference. I have attempted to leave enough of the meditation guidelines open so that the shamanic guides and experience may flow through.

Semi-Guided Upperworld Journey
To Free the Energy Body and Connect with Spirit Guides

To be read while drumming or with a shamanic drumming tape in the background. If possible, smudge the area or burn incense.

If the individual has some control over the physical body, it is beneficial to have him use a specific sign when each step is completed or when he is ready to move on.

Say: "Find an opening to the sky that feels familiar to you, perhaps a chimney or the branches of a favorite tree." (*pause*) If you are unable to find an opening, find something that will carry you up to the sky, such as a hot-air balloon, the smoke from a fire or a bird." (*pause*)

Speed up your drumming. Say: "Feel yourself floating or flying up, higher and higher. You leave this earth far behind as you become lighter and freer. You will pass through at least one opening as you seek a place in which you can comfortably regain control of your energy body. When you feel the urge to stop, do so." (long pause)

Slow your drumming. "When you stop at this place, take a good look around. (pause) Notice if anyone or anything meets you. (pause) Go with whatever feels right to you." (Pause for at least a few minutes to give him time to experience whatever may occur.)

"Now prepare to leave this world. You may return here whenever you choose to. (pause) Feel yourself moving higher up to other worlds. Soon you find another world, which seems to draw you." (pause)

"When you stop at this world, you are met by your spirit guides and guardians. (pause) Greet them and thank them for their presence in your life. (pause) Ask their assistance in developing control in Other worlds and in moving on to whatever your next step may be. (Do not mention physical death during a guided journey or meditation, unless it is specifically designed around death) Ask them to help you with any lessons you still need to learn. (long pause) Ask them if they have any messages for you at this time. (long pause) Thank these beings for their continued support and guidance. (pause) Invite them to continue working with you through spontaneous journeys and dreams from now on. (pause) Now say goodbye and prepare to return to your body."

Pick up the tempo of your drumming. Give him some time to return, then say: "When the drum beats three times, then three times again, you will have returned to the here and now with full memory of this journey. You will be able to return to your guides and any world you choose. You will continue to work with your guides through dreaming. (Beat drum three times, then three times again, and stop.)

I would recommend repeating this journey several times along with several journeys to the Lowerworld. A semi-guided Lowerworld journey is outlined below. The basic idea is to assist the individual in establishing a solid connection with spiritual guidance and to reacquaint them with the ease of spirit travel.

Semi-Guided Lowerworld Journey
To Free the Energy Body and Connect with Power Animals

....

To be read while drumming or with a shamanic drumming tape in the background. If possible, smudge the area or burn incense. If the individual has some control over her physical body, it is beneficial to have her use a specific sign when each step is completed or when she is ready to move on.

Say: "Find an opening in the earth that feels familiar to you, perhaps a cave, a water drain, or a hole to the roots of a favorite tree. *(pause)* If you are unable to find an opening for yourself, find something that will carry you down deep into the earth, such as a burrowing animal, an elevator, or a subway." *(pause)*

Pick up the tempo of your drumming. Say: "Feel yourself sliding or riding down, deeper and deeper. *(pause)* You leave the earth's surface far behind as you slip deeper still. *(pause)* Soon you emerge in a place in which you can comfortably regain control of your energy body and meet with your power animals." *(long pause)*

Slow your drumming. Say: "When you emerge into this place, take a good look around. *(pause)* Be aware of who or what meets you. *(pause)* Go with whatever feels right to you." *(Pause for a few minutes to give her time to experience whatever may occur.)*

"If you are not met immediately, go exploring. Follow any trail or road that feels right for you. *(pause)* Be aware of your surroundings. Take a good look around. *(pause)* Allow yourself to follow your instincts in your exploration. *(pause)*

"Take notice of anything that presents itself to you three or more times. This may be an animal, a tree, a cloud, anything that you notice near you at least three times. *(pause)* When you see this for at least the third time, know that this is a spirit guide for you. This is something that holds power and learning for you. Do not judge this experience, allow it to flow freely, and be open to your guide. *(long pause)*

"Greet this guide or guides and thank them for their presence in your life. *(pause)* Ask their assistance in developing control on other worlds and in moving on to whatever your next step may be. *(Do not mention physical death during a guided journey or meditation, unless it is specifically designed around death.)* Ask them to help you with any lessons you still need to learn. *(long pause)* Ask them if they have any messages for you at this time. *(long pause)* Thank this guide or guides for their continued support and guidance. *(pause)* Invite them to continue working with you through spontaneous journeys and dreams from now on. *(pause)* Now say goodbye and prepare to return to your body."

Speed up your drumming. Give her some time to return, then say: "When the drum beats three times, then three times again, you will have returned to the here and now with full memory of this journey. You will be able to return to your guides and any world you choose. You will continue to work with your guides through dreaming." *(Beat drum three times, then three times again, and stop.)*

There are those individuals for whom the shamanic journey is inappropriate or may be offensive for religious or other personal reasons. However, guided meditations have become a generally acceptable part of modern society. Thanks largely to the New Age movement, guided meditations and visualizations are commonly used for anything from stopping smoking to losing weight to improving self-esteem. As a result, I would recommend using the following guided meditation in any situation where a shamanic-type journey is ill-advised.

Guided Meditation
Using the Energy Body and Connecting with Spirit Guides

It may be beneficial to have a metronome or a tape of soothing music playing in the background. It may also help to have the individual visualize walking up or down a stair with each number they count down.

If the individual has some control over the physical body, it is beneficial to have him use a specific sign when each step is completed or when he is ready to move on.

Count down from ten to one, stopping periodically to remind this person that he is getting deeper and more relaxed. Say: "At the count of one, you will be perfectly relaxed; you will be feeling better than ever before."

At the count of one, tell this person: "You are now perfectly relaxed. You are feeling better than ever before." Have him go to his favorite place of relaxation, a place where he always feels completely safe and comfortable. This place does not have to exist in this reality. He should feel free to go to a place he has created or one he always wanted to go to.

77

"While you are in this place, you are completely safe and comfortable. You feel strong and healthy and are able to come and go as you please."

Suggest that he do something physical, like run or swim or dance. If he has a favorite sport, encourage him to imagine he is playing it. Direct him to really get into it, to really feel it. Give him reminders, such as: "Feel the wind and water against your face," "Smell the grass," and "See the ball fly from your hand."

Count him up from one to ten. If you used stair imagery on the way down, use it on the way up as well. Stop periodically to say: "At the count of ten, you will be perfectly comfortable. You will feel extremely relaxed and refreshed." At the count of ten, say, "You are now perfectly comfortable. You feel extremely relaxed and refreshed."

After taking him through the above meditation a few times, add the following step before counting him back up to normal consciousness.

"Now return to your favorite place of relaxation. (*pause*) In your favorite place of relaxation, notice a door to your left. (*pause*) As you turn to look at this door, see it slowly open. Your personal spirit guides (or guardian angels, etc.) enter the room through this door. Greet them as they enter and ask for the names of any you do not know. Accept whatever is given. (*pause*) Thank these beings for their presence in your life. (*pause*) Ask them for their assistance in whatever your next step may be. Ask them to help you regain a feeling of freedom and control. (*pause*) Ask them if they have any messages for you at this time. (*Long pause to give him time to experience whatever may be offered.*) Thank them again and let them know you are open to their guidance and protection." Count up from one to ten as directed above.

After he has met with his spirit guides a few times, you will want to switch him from physical to nonphysical activities. Have him meet with his spirit guides again in his favorite place of relaxation. Prompt him to ask their guidance and protection in his spiritual journeys. Then have him imagine he is climbing out the top of his head. Tell him to see his body below as he floats up high. Let him know that he is always completely safe when doing this and that he can return to his body whenever he wants to. Remind him that his guides are with him always and will keep him safe. Prompt him to really experience this with reminders, like "Feel how light and free you are," "See the ground far beneath you and the clouds up close," and "Hear the noise of the earth fade to wonderful silence." Give him time to enjoy these experiences. Then direct him to return to his favorite place of relaxation and count from one to ten as directed above.

Any of these techniques are recommended for those with serious injuries, illnesses, or during the transitional period preceding physical death. If the individual is not experiencing significant physical limitations, or if he is comfortable with out-of-body travel, you might choose to use only those portions of this meditation designed to establish a connection with personal spirit guides.

Even if you believe this person is experienced enough in working with spirit guides and does not to need this type of assistance, it is recommended. The instinctual fear of death can cause even those we believe to be very spiritual to lose all touch with their chosen beliefs and spirit guides.

I became acquainted with a man several years ago as a result of several neo-pagan festivals we attended with mutual friends. He always appeared to be carefree, loving, and dedicated to his spiritual path. To most of us, he seemed to be very attuned to his helping spirits and had a particular connection to the Goddess that came through him even in the most difficult times. He was a joy to be around.

Then he was diagnosed with full-blown AIDS. He became sullen and hostile. As time went on and his disease progressed, he sank deeper into self-pity and resentment. He lost all touch with his spiritual path and blamed the world for what he was experiencing. He blocked all attempts by friends to help him in this reality and shut himself down psychically. He allowed his fear and anger to completely control him and prevent him from receiving any healing.

In this situation, many people are tempted to try to force the issue. They react from within their own ego-identities and their own beliefs. Often, these individuals who want to help will get angry themselves. They will confront the dying in an attempt to blast through the walls. While this may work in some situations, it most commonly causes the dying person to retreat even further into his protective shell.

I have known people to try and force the issue on a spiritual or magical level, as well. Believing they know exactly what this individual needs, they hammer away at him on a psychic level, trying to communicate or heal through the resistance. The love and concern that prompts such action is commendable, but the means do not justify the end. And the end is rarely what was intended.

79

This type of approach most frequently only serves to send the individual on the receiving end running for cover. Once again, the dying will very possibly retreat behind the walls they have erected to prevent further emotional pain. They close themselves off even more tightly, further reducing the possibility of healing and acceptance. These walls can continue after physical death, preventing the newly departed from establishing connections with spirit guides and moving on to the next step.

Although it may sound rather trivial and nonshamanic, often the best thing we can do for an individual who is experiencing this degree of emotional distress is to simply continue to be there unconditionally and be open and nonjudgmental when and if they do decide to open up to us. This can be one of the most difficult and most important tasks we can perform for a loved one.

To stand in the face of rejection and hostility from a loved one during their death transition and say, through word and example, "I am here for you no matter what," takes incredible strength and an enlightened lack of self-importance. Once again, we face our shadow sides and take our egos down a notch or two for the greatest benefit of all. Often this means taking a huge leap of faith in that universal flow from the Great Spirit. It means trusting that all things happen in their time and that we do not know everything that is involved in the processes and cycles of life.

It has been my experience that many of these individuals who feel the need to decide what is best and to force a confrontation, whether physical or psychic, are acting out dramas triggered by their own fears and beliefs. This is another reason why it is essential for anyone dealing with a dying individual on a spiritual, shamanic or magical level to engage in significant personal work toward self-knowledge. The most common trigger I see is fear. These people fear death on a deep, instinctual level. They may have convinced their rational consciousness that they have overcome this, but it remains deep within, waiting for a reason to reassert itself.

These individuals also tend to fear losing control, which, in my opinion, is related to the fear of death. They do not trust in our interconnections or the continuity of life. They are deluded into believing that they must rely on personal power and intellect. Quite often, these people are divorced from or limited in their own experience of universal flow.

They fear being weak or helpless or alone. They have not yet fully integrated that letting go and allowing ourselves to become one with All Life is the path to true strength and power. That creative force, which brought us into existence does not abandon us, we block our experience of it as we create ourselves as separate. It is all a function of our beliefs.

When all we can do on a physical level is be present, we can do a considerable amount through journeying without creating a withdrawal response in the dying person. One of the most important things we can do on a shamanic level is to continue to gently radiate love and appreciation for this individual. Appreciation is defined as value, gratitude, and awareness.

When we honestly and unconditionally appreciate another being, we allow them into our awareness with gratitude. We value them for who they are and what they have done in this life. Even if they have created hardship and suffering this time around, we appreciate the value this may have to their continuing soul growth.

Love and appreciation are radiations of pure supportive energy. They gently suffuse all things they contact. The individual in need feels safe and comfortable allowing their walls to slip a bit in this type of environment. If they choose to use this energy while they remain in a physical body, they may begin to respond in everyday reality as well. Even if they are not comfortable enough to lower their shields while in the body, they emerge from physical life into a cocoon of loving safety. They will very often use this energy after departing the body as a boost to move on.

Another significant way in which we can work to assist this individual is to enlist the aid of her personal spirit guides. We do this through journeying and dreaming. In our everyday reality, we may see no tangible evidence that we are accomplishing anything of value, but we can be certain that spirit guides are already working on the situation. These guides may choose to work through you, even in this reality.

The spirit guides of the individual in transition may use you to plant a seed that will be activated once the physical body is no longer available. You may be unaware of the ways in which they work through you. Often, we will hear ourselves saying things that later we wonder where they came from. Have you ever noticed how occasionally you will see or hear something that seems unimportant, but then days or even years later, something else happens that triggers that seemingly superfluous incident? Suddenly this silly thing makes sense and fits amazingly well in with the big picture.

The same thing can happen during that period after physical death. Without realizing it, we are occasionally used as a channel to say or do something that can be triggered later on by this person's spirit guides. After physical death, this being may experience something that feels familiar to them, something they heard before. They may remember that it was associated with a loved one and as such, feels safe to explore. These innocent seeds we plant may very well be the catalysts for an easy journey beyond the Veil and for further soul growth.

Therefore, it is important that we remain open to communication from spirit guidance, no matter what form that communication takes. Through our meditations and journeys, we inform spirit guides that we are open to their communication. We invite them to work through us, if necessary, to help the individual in need. We maintain a personal awareness, so that our own beliefs and fears do not block or color any incoming communication, and we work to keep our energies clear and filled with unconditional love.

There are no easy, cookbook answers for the multitude of questions on how to handle the death process. Each situation is truly unique and must be handled in ways specific to those involved. It's a little like raising a child; while the books may be good guides and references, you take it as it comes and it gets more familiar with practice. Both situations require creativity, flexibility, and respect for all people as spiritual beings. Those we are assisting cannot afford for us to get caught up in the need to do things right.

We have not failed if someone dies while we are assisting or healing him. We work to heal body, mind, and spirit. It is not a shaman's place to decide whether someone stays in the body or moves on in spirit. If this spirit you have been working with is able to make an easy transition through physical death with the help of your healing energy, this is a blessing. You have contributed to the creation of a free and potentially joyful passing for this individual. Far from being a failure, this is truly something to cherish and rejoice in.

Respect, honor, and trust are key elements in creating the healing and unconditional love necessary for an easy passing from this life. It is vital that we respect the fact that the choice of passing is theirs alone. Each dying person enters the process with a unique set of variables, making each transition different. If we are to help them, we must honor the type of transition they have chosen.

There are those people who have chosen a relatively easy life in this incarnation and there are those who will choose an easy death. Then again, there are those who will choose a difficult death. Neither choice is better or more correct. Each spirit comes in with a specific plan of lessons and experiences they need for their continued soul growth. It is not for us to say which experiences are more valuable. Not only do we not have the big picture, but we are not walking that soul's path of evolution. Most of us have chosen some pretty nasty lives and deaths on occasion, to fully understand the vast range of human experience.

For the greatest benefit of all, we must release our attachment to the type of death they experience. Just as a parent does her child a disservice in completely shielding that child from the world, we only hinder their growth and transition if we try to force a different end for their current incarnations. Clear out those belief systems, which propose we are better shamans or guides if those we assist pass over with ease. We are friends, loved ones, guides and shamans. We are not gods. For us to presume to know what is best for any spirit in our care creates more harm than good.

The transition out of physical life can be a great gift. Those who are not suddenly pulled from the body are being given the opportunity to clear up unfinished business, to receive healing while still in familiar territory (the body), and to say their final good-byes. With compassionate and respectful assistance, this time can be used for reflection and preparation. It is our responsibility as shamans and loved ones, to do everything possible to enable them to take full advantage of this time. Whether we work on a purely spiritual level, or also in this reality, we establish connections and channel unconditional healing to support these people in greeting death as best they can.

Endnotes

29 Robert A. Monroe, *Ultimate Journey*, p. 1.
30 Harry Palmer, *Living Deliberately*, p. 90.
31 Ibid.
32 Robert A. Monroe, *Ultimate Journey*, pp. 197–198.
33 Fred Alan Wolf, *Parallel Universes*, p. 296.
34 See Contacts section at the back of this book, particularly their feedback Web site.
35 Ibid.
36 Victor Sanchez, *The Teachings of Don Carlos*, p. 9.

Chapter 4

RITES OF PASSAGE

One of the most tangible ways in which a shaman can be of service is through creating and performing rites of passage. Although much of the actual work involved in deathwalking takes place behind the scenes during shamanic states of consciousness, rites of passage are important to both the living and the departed. Death rites of passage serve to bring closure and healing to both the living and departed. Well-constructed memorial services are designed to encourage the living to grieve openly and to provide a safe forum for them to do so.

Most death rites of passage involve praying over the body, commending the soul to the god(s), and remembering the life of the departed. These are important elements that will be discussed throughout this book. In some cultures, particularly the Far East, a type of map is read to the spirit of the departed during these rites of passage. This is to assist them in finding their way along the Road of the Dead.[37]

Many people today are becoming dissatisfied with traditional death rituals. For many, the traditions of ancestors just don't apply to our world experience. We follow them out of habit, or to please family and community, but often they no longer hold any real meaning for us. Modern people can find these traditional rituals to be hollow, more of a "going through the motions" than anything else.

Too often, in modern mainstream society, funerals and memorial services become a social showplace and a burden to the immediate family. People dress up and come to socialize while paying their respects. Their hearts are usually in the right place, but there is a palpable need to keep up appearances and network. The immediate family is responsible for ensuring that visitors are accommodated and feel welcome. Few, if any, of those closest to the departed feel comfortable showing any real emotion.

In this world where our mechanistic science has replaced a Great Spirit (or God), in many ways, people *need* to feel there is something more. They want hope that their loved ones live on in some way and they need healing for their own pain and fear. People frequently tell me that they want to feel that these rituals have real meaning. They need ceremonies that speak to their souls.

A large number of modern people are straying from tradition and designing their own rituals. This is an important step in reclaiming our own power to heal ourselves, rather than relying on a religious authority or an omnipotent deity to do it for us. In this way we can focus our energies on personal healing, while bringing meaning to an otherwise cookbook ceremony. In personalizing, or creating our own ceremonies, we open to spiritual guidance and our own intuitive energies. Once the way is open, we can more effectively channel and receive healing and love.

Some individuals choose to stay within the basic confines of tradition, but make small changes and add personal touches. Some will go to alternative spiritual practitioners for something very different and follow those rituals. Still others will design completely new rites on their own. However they alter tradition, these individuals are creating ceremonies that come from the heart and soul, not merely from custom.

Personally, I have nothing against tradition and custom. I find it serves an important role in maintaining our connections to our ancestors and in creating a sense of continuity and belonging. However, it is obvious that tradition just does not work for many modern individuals. This may be due to new beliefs and radically different life experiences from their parents and ancestors.

This also due to the fact that many of us have mixed heritages leaving us wondering where we fit into the scheme of things. Several people have expressed concerns about what path they "should" follow. I know several women who are of mixed Native American and Celtic or African-American heritages. They feel it would be dishonorable to reject some of their ancestry to follow the path of others. Unfortunately, some of them have experienced a lack of acceptance, even hostility, from Native communities when mixing Celtic or African practices with traditional Native American spirituality. This is a difficult situation that is experienced in many other ethnic communities.

When walking a traditional path, it is generally best to remain within the confines of that path for a number of reasons. However, if we find something is missing from this path for ancestral or personal reasons, it is our responsibility to our spiritual growth to find what is correct for us. Regarding rites of passage, the most important factor in determining what type of ceremony to use is not where it came from or how old it is, but whether it catalyzes growth and impacts one's total self.

Rites of passage are, by definition, a marking of life changes; a ritual acknowledgment of the death of one chapter of life and the birth of another. Today, rites of passage are often superficial excuses to buy cards and presents. In fact, many rites of passage are completely overlooked by the majority of society. The death ritual, in particular, has lost its focus as a rite of *passage*. It is viewed as a "final goodbye" due to our societal inability to persuade our rational minds that death is *not* the end of one's being. More and more new rituals are designed as an expression of the continuity of life and love.

The main point to keep in mind when creating any ritual is to follow your feelings. While many books detail certain elements that should be included, this is not necessarily true for all people. If we are to truly empower ourselves to create from our hearts and bring about healing for ourselves and others, we need to release those deeply ingrained feelings of "should." Open to yourself and your spirit guides. Go with whatever feels rights to you. If that works, excellent; if it doesn't, work with it a bit more. You will get it right for you.

In general, there are four major elements to any rite of passage. These are the invocation, experience/release, closure/grounding, and celebration. While many people view the celebration as being completely separate and following the ritual, it is an important element and is part of the ongoing ritual process.

For a death rite, we first set up the altar or area of the rite with symbolic or special items. The basic goal is to use sensory and symbolic input to bypass the analytical mind and create an atmosphere that is conducive to interdimensional communication and experience. These sensory and symbolic elements are vital in evoking the emotion of participants and encouraging that energy to release.

In shamanic rites, the use of sound is incorporated in most of these elements. Drums and rattles have been used throughout the centuries to evoke and release the emotions of loved ones, to guide the departed beyond this world, and to encourage them to return to this world for another lifetime. I have found that drumming, in particular, can be tremendously healing in its ability to help us release emotion, realign our energy systems, and ground us.

I generally smudge all present and the area before stating the purpose of the rite and going ahead with the invocation. Invocation, or calling in, of specific energies, deities, the spirit of the departed, spirit guides, etc., follows this stating of purpose. This should be done in whatever manner feels right to you or is in keeping with your spiritual tradition.

The experience/release element is essential to bring the death into reality. Without this portion, the rite is in danger of becoming a mental activity rather than a deep rite of passage. It is necessary for this to be done in a safe space because the emotional charge created will often release deep and repressed emotions. This element of the death rite catalyzes our own release of grief and permits us to fully experience the effects of this passage.

Many rites are designed with some type of ritual action to physically manifest this element. If possible, all of the senses should be activated by this ritual action and this can be as simple as a guided meditation or the reading of a poem. Again, we use sensory input to bypass the analytical mind. I have seen many wonderful ritual actions from a cutting of symbolic cords to a purification by fire of photos or pieces of paper with things to release written on them.

The action of this element makes it absolutely clear that we have the choice of remaining where we are, or passing through this symbolic action. We can remain stuck in old patterns or fully experience the rite to break us out of old stuff. This can be a powerful tool for internal change that will manifest as external change once the rite is concluded.

After this great release, we require closure and grounding of all this energy. This may be accomplished in many ways, from meditation to discussion to asking for support and guidance from spirit guides and deities. This is a wonderful time to lie down and connect one's chakras with the Earth and perform the Earth-Star meditation. Through this element, we accept the new phase and our new identities.

And finally comes celebration. Many people feel it is wrong or disrespectful to celebrate at a death rite. While most people do opt for a more subdued celebration rather than a wild party, the point is that we all need to uplift the energy. We honor ourselves by releasing our need for life to remain stagnant and unchanging. We honor the departed by recognizing that we will miss his or her physical presence, but by also rejoicing in the newfound freedom and the new adventure this individual is entering into. These are beings that have just completed one physical phase of life. In a sense, they have graduated. It is only our own limited perception of death that creates such morbid and depressing beliefs surrounding it.

When the ritual is a death rite of passage, the wishes of the departed are essential to the process. While it can be very productive for you to hold private rituals for personal healing, the main public ritual should, in most cases, be in keeping with the path of the departed. The main exceptions to this are those individuals who prefer a more mainstream or nondenominational public ceremony and a deeper, more personal private ceremony. If the departed has not already outlined her desires regarding her own rite of passage, it is up to the family to assume this responsibility. Maintain an open mind and allow yourself to receive intuitive ideas, many of which may be communications from the departed or from spirit guides.

There are many books available today detailing New Age or neo-pagan rituals, including death rituals. This is a clear indication of the need for alternatives to the usual ceremonies. Although the majority of these are excellent books, I normally recommend that people use these as guides or references. This is why I have chosen to keep the following rituals as nondenominational and basic as possible.

If a ritual feels perfect for you, just as it is written in a book, that is wonderful. However, if you feel the need for something more personal, or really want to work with your own creative energies, you might choose to use these rituals to spark your own ideas. Reach within for elements that truly resonate with your spirit. Feel free to alter these rituals if something feels wrong or missing. The idea is, again, not to conform to anyone else's beliefs about what is right, but to create an atmosphere of safety and healing.

Many organized religions today will permit a personalization of rituals to some extent, and this is something that should be discussed with the associated clergy. Depending on how spiritually open the clergy is, it is possible to combine the best of tradition with our modern needs. While it is true that the more rigidly structured religions only permit incidental variations, with some creativity these can be made to create the desired effects.

For example, a Catholic funeral mass often only leaves the choice of readings and flowers open to discussion. From both the Bible and a multitude of other sources, we can find literary pieces that strike the right chord within us. Flowers are extremely easy to personalize and with a little research, specific flowers or colors can be used to channel healing and comfort to the congregation.

Many people have some idea of the type of memorial or funeral they would like when they die. I would encourage everyone to think about this and write it down.

While many of us refuse to entertain the possibility of our own mortality, it can be a great comfort when confronted with that mortality, to know our memorials will be meaningful for us. It can also be a tremendous relief to the family to have even a basic idea of your wishes when faced with funeral planning.

If a ritual, or even an outline of ideas, was important enough for the departed to have written it down, it is our responsibility to honor that. This is one instance where the ability to set aside personal beliefs and the ego becomes absolutely essential to the process. This is often the last concrete thing we can do for these individuals and we need to be able to put their needs before our own, just as we would want others to honor our requests after death. Keep in mind that the departed may very well be there in spirit, looking for some type of release and closure before moving on.

Another significant factor in the need for new, more meaningful rituals is the fact that there are many today who do not follow the same religious traditions as the rest of their families. The huge growth of the neo-pagan movement has created a need for many to follow their spiritual beliefs in hiding from the rest of their families and communities out of fear of rejection, ridicule, or worse.

Often when one of these individuals dies, they receive the traditional ceremonies they rejected because no one knows they followed an alternative spiritual path. If the departed was part of a spiritual or religious community, that community will frequently honor the departed in keeping with their beliefs. Unfortunately, family and other friends are commonly unaware of these alternative communities.

These situations require creativity and flexibility on the part of those who do know the true spiritual path of the departed. If at all possible, I would recommend discussing these wishes before their death, or encouraging them to write it all down in private. This is important not only when it comes to their "final" rituals, but also when dealing with mainstream family and friends.

It can become essential for you to know how they wanted the schism between their family expectations and their new path handled. See if you can help pave the way to greater honesty and understanding between the dying and their families. Whether they are able to successfully "come out" prior to death or not, as friends and shamans we will most likely need to tread a fine line when it comes to the death ritual unless, of course, we are not included in the family services.

On one hand, we want to be able to offer this soul the comfort of his personal beliefs. The beliefs of this incarnation are normally carried over into the initial stages after physical death. A newly departed spirit is frequently in need of meaningful ceremonies within the context of the beliefs he assumed while in the physical. Without the support of these beliefs, he may feel lost and abandoned, even hostile. These feelings can prevent or postpone his successful jump to the next reality.

On the other hand, choosing one's death to "come out" with previously secret beliefs is not generally the most beneficial time. This is a time of grief, and often shock, for loved ones remaining in physical life. To add the shock of a hidden life and religion at this time will bring healing and closure to no one. In fact, it can create hostility related to feelings of abandonment and dishonesty, which may prolong the pain and prevent any possibility for closure. If it is necessary for this to be disclosed after death, it is better handled at a later date by one close to the departed, or though a letter from the departed.

So then, what does one do when faced with this situation? In several other chapters, I discuss the importance of putting aside our own beliefs in order to allow healing to flow through us. This is a time when friends and shamans must be able to successfully release the ego if we hope to create a truly healing experience for all concerned.

This shelving of our self-importance and our cultural or personal beliefs is essential in our discussions with loved ones, with the deathwalk itself, and during any input regarding rites of passage. When we focus on projecting a persona or a belief in the rightness of our own beliefs, we block our receptivity to the needs of those around us. We also block the vast majority of communications from our spirit guides and from the departed. We may be experts in creating beautiful or elaborate rituals, but they serve no real purpose if they are meaningless to the departed and the grieving.

I have often created separate and very different death services for the same individual. One service is normally intended for mainstream or traditional family and friends, while the other is based on the beliefs of the departed, or loved ones who follow alternative paths. We have worked with open-minded clergy and personalized traditional services as much as possible without threatening the beliefs of those attending. These services are designed specifically to bring closure to mainstream loved ones. Sometimes this is a memorial service, sometimes it is a funeral.

In 1994, we created public services for the passing of my grandfather. We found a Christian minister who enthusiastically listened as we talked about what was most important to my grandfather. My mother related stories about his thirty-two years as a state park ranger. She spoke of how his family and the natural world were of utmost importance to him. From that conversation, this minister composed a beautiful and personal sermon for the funeral. It was spiritual rather than religious, and that was very fitting for my grandfather.

However, it was performed by a Christian minister. This satisfied those friends and family who have adopted a religious Christian belief system. Although several family members were aware that there were other rituals going on, they were not forced to come face-to-face with those rituals. They received their assurances that my grandfather was committed to God by a "man of the cloth." They were able to say their final goodbyes in keeping with their beliefs and they gained a real sense of closure as a result.

As those closest to my grandfather, we could have decided to forego these mainstream ceremonies. We were in a position to do whatever we wanted. Had we been coming from a state of self-importance or ego, we might have chosen to tell these people to find their own religious solace elsewhere.

In doing this, we would have only created a situation of greater pain and hostility. It would have effectively used my grandfather's physical passing as a soapbox, from which to preach about "right" and "wrong" beliefs. Rather than celebrate his life and his transition to a new plane of existence, this would have torn apart the family that he loved so dearly, and whose differing beliefs had already created tension and separation.

In choosing to put aside beliefs, we were able to forge new ties with friends and family. Those tense and distant relationships that my grandfather tried to smooth over were able to begin to heal. Rather than becoming a soapbox, his passing became a healing catalyst for renewed tolerance among family members.

When personalizing traditional services, be clear on what specifically is open to change. Work with the associated clergy whenever possible in order to avoid future misunderstandings and disagreements. Be mindful of the feelings of other attendees when deciding upon your changes.

Flowers and stones are often the simplest and subtlest means of personalization available. As I said before, with a little research these can be used to bring in the desired energies. I would suggest looking into the therapeutic uses of color and aromatherapy, as well as the social and magical meanings of the various flowers or stones.

Incense can also be a rather subtle way of purifying the area and carrying prayers to the departed and the Great Spirit. Most religions use some form of incense or smudge in their rituals. Find out what scents the clergy intend to use and research their traditional uses.

Since memorial services tend to be less structured, you might choose to use a light incense in the rooms where these will be held. This can be very productive in purifying the room, bringing in desired energies, and facilitating the release of unwanted emotions. However, there is one admonition I would give concerning incense. Keep in mind that some people may be allergic or offended by strong scents. It is usually best to avoid highly allergenic scents. It is also helpful to prevent the incense from overpowering the room.

For both memorials and funerals, just about anything can be charged with energy and included at the service. Stones are certainly the obvious choice for this, but flowers, memorial cards, pens, chairs, and even entire rooms are equally good candidates. In this way, we can make the most effective use of the total atmosphere to create a healing and safe space for those in mourning.

If you choose to charge things already present in the area of the service, take some time before the other guests arrive to do this. It may help to tell the family or funeral director that you need some time alone with the body, or in the room, before the service. It is the rare individual that would deny such a request.

Charging Items with Energy Exercise

Note: Clear your own energy field using any of the purification ceremonies from chapter three before proceeding with this exercise.

Place your hands on or over the items you have selected for charging. If you have chosen an entire room, or something you are unable to place your hands over, hold out your hands, palms facing the item. Feel this energy you have cleared and merged with, flow through you and out the palms of your hands. See the item completely cleared of any previous energies. Say aloud or to yourself, "May this _____ be purified and cleared of all unwanted energies and beings."

Call upon your guides, God, or the Source of All Life, and ask that you be used as the channel to fill this object or room with pure healing energy. As you direct this energy, see those who will be attending the service feeling safe and comforted in this energy. Clearly visualize the healing and unconditional love that is filling this object or room.

When you feel ready, lower your hands. It may help to rub them together to speed the desensitization. Many healers can experience overly sensitized hands and feet, often resulting in extreme heat, tingling, or numbness.

Give thanks to those you invoked and to all who assisted you in this process before returning to ordinary reality.

Keep in mind that we are not interfering with anyone's free will or belief systems in doing this. We are creating the most beneficial and personal atmosphere possible to contribute to healing and closure. All energy we channel and all choices we make in flowers, stones, or readings are unconditionally loving. Whether the individuals attending choose to accept this energy is their decision.

There may be times when you choose to hold separate services for those, including the departed, who hold alternative belief systems. In doing this, we are providing the means for these individuals to receive the blessings and comfort of their own belief systems. If the individual followed a relatively organized path, such as Buddhism or Wicca, it is usually beneficial to discuss the ceremony with members of that clergy. However if you are an experienced follower of the same path, this is not always necessary. Below, I have outlined nondenominational memorial, burial, and scattering-of-ashes ceremonies. These may be used as a rough guideline or explicitly as written.

Memorial Ceremony

Prepare the area using incense or smudge. You may wish to use any of the three purification ceremonies from chapter three.

Decorate with white flowers and clear quartz crystals. Use evergreens or acorns to symbolize the cycles of life and rebirth as well as eternal life.

Set up a central altar on a table or a blanket on the floor. Place a picture of the departed in the center. Surround this with objects that were special to this person, perhaps special stones, photos, mementos, etc. Also on this altar have white candles, feathers, and a bowl of earth. We use the candles to symbolize the flame of love and light that burns within each of us and continues to burn within the departed, as well as for light and atmosphere. The feathers symbolize the newfound freedom of the departed and the hope that she will fly swiftly Home. The earth is representative of our Mother to whom her body is returning.

With your smudge or by drumming, clear those attending as they enter. The ceremony leader should explain the symbolism of the altar and other decorations to those attending. Allow everyone some time to familiarize themselves with the room and altar.

Sit or stand in a circle. If you are indoors, lower the lights and light the candles. The leader should then invite everyone to hold hands and center themselves for a moment. It may help to have everyone count down from ten to one.

The leader then states the purpose for this ritual and invites the spirit of the departed to join. Any other deities or spirits you choose to include should also be called upon at this time. I would recommend calling upon the ancestors and all departed loved ones to participate.

The leader then initiates a guided or an individual meditation. You might suggest people focus on death and rebirth, on the joyful transition from physical body to free energy, or on merging lovingly with the Great Spirit. If a guided meditation is preferred, the leader will need to have one prepared. At the end of this ceremony, I have detailed a meditation for use in this type of situation. The leader is responsible for bringing everyone back to this room after a suitable period of time.

In order to encourage and allow each other to openly experience your grief, go around the circle and share stories or feelings about the departed. Offer prayers or jokes, whatever you feel. Some people may need to use jokes to get the energy moving. Whatever feels right is fine. This must be a safe, nonjudgmental space. Go around the circle at least three times and continue until everyone feels some sense of release.

Some people may choose to plant a tree or make a donation in honor of the departed. If so, this is the time to charge the donation or bless the seed or sapling with a long and healthy life.

If this ceremony takes place before a burial, a crystal or other object can be charged with blessings of release, joy, and love now. Later, it can be placed in the grave with the body or ashes.

Conclude with a guided energy working. Although more generally meta-physical than shamanic, I suggest this because these workings are fairly common today, and can be very beneficial in providing a tangible means of releasing emotions and attachments. The leader instructs everyone to visualize and feel the energy flowing through the circle in the left hand and out the right. As the energy builds, it rises in a spiral to a point above the circle. Focus your prayers for the departed into this energy. It may help to chant her name as you all see her happy and healthy. When the leader feels the time is right, direct everyone to shout her name and send this energy out to her.

Follow this with some form of grounding to handle excess energy or grief. You may wish to simply guide those present in sending this deep into the Earth for purification. You may use the pot of earth from the altar as a focal point if you choose. Please remember to return this to the Earth afterwards for clearing. If you prefer something more structured, the Tree of Life meditation follows the Cycles of Life meditation after this ritual.

Finish with a dinner where you can all celebrate this incarnation of your loved one. Take heart in the fact that you were able to speak your prayers and do something to facilitate her transition into a new life.

Guided Meditation
Cycles of Life

For use at any time, particularly during Death Rituals and Memorials.

If you have not yet counted down from ten to one, do so now. It may help to have the participants visualize descending one step with each number. Say: "Take a deep breath and relax. See yourself at the opening of a large beautiful meadow. The sun is shining brightly overhead and the scent of wildflowers is carried by the light breeze. *(pause)* To your right, you see a small pool of clear water that empties into a rocky brook. *(pause)* Stop at this pool and allow all of your worries and tensions to fall into the clear water. *(pause)* Watch as they are carried away and cleansed by the running water of the brook." *(long pause)*

Continue: "Now look up from the water and see the huge old oak tree at the center of the meadow. Watch this tree as you walk toward it. *(pause)* Hear the breeze rustle in its branches. Feel the grass against your ankles. Take a deep breath and smell the wildflowers." *(pause)*

Say: "As you approach the tree, feel its strength and timelessness. Study the tree. Walk around it. *(pause)* Touch it and give it a big hug. *(pause)* Feel yourself merge with the energy of this tree. Feel its strength in your body; its silence; its timelessness. *(pause)* As you walk around the tree, you notice a door in its trunk."

Continue: "Open this door. You see steps leading down into the center of this tree. Take a deep breath and go down this staircase. *(pause)* At the bottom of the stairs, you enter a large room where you quickly move forward in time to your own old age. (*pause*) Look back on the joys and accomplishments of this life; at the lessons you have learned and how you have grown spiritually. (*long pause*) Then you feel yourself pass comfortably from this body. (*pause*) You float lightly up, higher and higher, into the light of the universe. (*pause*) Feel the presence of loved ones and spirit guides as you are drawn to a beautiful white star." (*long pause*)

Say: "You feel the most complete and unconditional love imaginable emanating from this star. (*pause*) Know that you have returned Home and allow yourself to flow freely into this star, merging with it fully." (*long pause*)

95

Continue: "Soon, you feel an urge to move on. (*pause*) You become aware of a new life that offers you wonderful opportunities for learning and love. (*pause*) You are drawn out from this star. You become smaller, more defined." (*pause*)

Say: "You are in a warm, dark place. You feel safe and happy here. You are surrounded by a loving and protective energy. (*pause*) Suddenly, you are jolted out of your warm comfort by pushing and constriction. (*pause*) You are pushed down until you emerge into a bright light. (*pause*) It is colder here, but someone wraps you in a warm, soft blanket. You are placed on a warm body and held by strong arms. (*pause*) You realize that this body is the source of that warm, protective energy that surrounded you in the darkness. Soft voices call a name you recognize as yours now. You feel the loving vibrations of mother and father as they hold and comfort you."

Continue: "Now you move out of this body and become one with All Life. (*pause*) Feel the season change. (*pause*) Watch the land appear to die as winter approaches and then blossom with new life in the spring. (*pause*) See the deep greens of summer turn to reds and yellows in autumn, before becoming brown and gray once more with winter. (*long pause*) Watch a beautiful sunset turn to night. (*pause*) See the sparkling beauty of the stars and the glory of the moon give way to another sunrise." (*pause*)

Say: "Now come back to yourself, standing at the base of the stairs deep within the oak tree. (*pause*) Thank the tree for allowing you to experience the wonder of these cycles of life and rebirth. (*pause*) Offer a prayer of honor for the wisdom and strength of the tree. *(pause)* Now go back up the stairs and out the door into the meadow." *(pause)*

Guided Meditation
Tree of Life
....

For use whenever grounding is desired.

Stand tall and strong. Take a deep breath.

Feel your feet firmly planted on the ground. Feel roots growing down, deep into the center of the Earth, from your feet.

Send any excess energy in your body down into the Earth through these roots. Give the Earth your grief and fear and worry. Let Her purify this and support you.

Feel the strength and timeless love of the Earth flow into you through these roots. It fills your body and comforts you.

Now, stretch out your arms to Father Sky. Feel your arms as they become branches, gathering in the blessings of the multiverse. You are energized and invigorated by these energies flowing into your branches.

Take a moment and feel the blessings of the Earth and Sky together. Feel cleansed and whole.

Burial Ceremony

Purify the burial area and all ritual items using any of the three purification ceremonies from chapter three.

Call upon the Spirits of the six directions (East, South, West, North, Sky, and Earth) and the Creator to join with you in this ceremony. Ask for their guidance and blessings throughout this ceremony.

Call upon the spirit of the departed to join with you. Let him know the reason for this ceremony and make it clear that you honor him through it.

Say: "Through this ceremony, we commend the body of our departed _____ to the Earth as we entrust his spirit to the Creator. We gather here to honor his memory and send him our blessings for a joyous reunion with All That Is."

Optional: The ceremonial leader may choose to lead the gathering in a special prayer or song at this point. I would only recommend that this focus on the continuity of life and love as well as celebrate life, freedom, and rebirth.

Have either the ceremonial leader or a selection of people give speeches or readings in honor of the departed. These may be as personal or as formal as you feel appropriate.

If anyone would like to include anything extra in the grave, such as a flower, photo, or charged crystal, they should be permitted to do so at this point.

Optional: Using a ritually purified, ceremonial shovel, allow each of those attending to place a shovelful of earth into the grave. While digging, each person thanks the Earth Mother for the use of Her soil and for accepting back into Her the body of this loved one. As the soil is placed in the grave, each person speaks a prayer for the departed into the Earth.

Say: "Although we grieve for the times we will no longer share in this world, we rejoice in the freedom of our beloved _____ . We are grateful for the sharing of our lives during your time here in this world. Your memories and gifts live on within each of us as we freely release you to your next world. We send you heartfelt blessings of peace, love, and joy. We say not goodbye, but farewell until we meet again."

Allow everyone time to experience the ceremony and their feelings. They may wish to sit in silence for a while or spend a few moments by the graveside. Arrange to meet at a predetermined location for a meal. This allows any energy or grief to be grounded more easily and provides a supportive atmosphere for all concerned.

Scattering of Ashes after Cremation Ceremony

Purify the area where the ashes will be scattered and all ritual items using any of the three purification ceremonies from chapter three.

Set up a central altar on a table or a blanket. Place the container of ashes in the center along with a picture of the departed. Surround this with objects that were special to this person, perhaps special stones, photos, or mementos.

With your smudge or by drumming, clear those attending as they enter. The ceremony leader should explain the symbolism of the altar and other decorations to those attending. Allow everyone some time to familiarize themselves with the room and altar.

Sit or stand in a circle. The leader should then invite everyone to hold hands and center for a moment. It may help to have everyone count down from ten to one.

Call upon the Spirits of the six directions and the Creator to join with you in this ceremony. Ask that they bless your work. Request guidance, that your every action may honor them.

Call upon the spirit of the departed to join with you. Let her know the reason for this ceremony and make it clear that you honor her through it.

Say: "Through this ceremony, we release the ashes of our departed _____ . We commend your body and spirit to the Creator. May you once again become One with All That Is, in body and spirit. We gather here to honor your memory and send you our blessings for a joyous journey."

The leader directs the gathering in a special prayer or song at this point. I would only recommend that this focus on the continuity of life and love as well as celebrate life, freedom, and rebirth.

Holding the ashes, stand in the center of this circle. Have everyone go around the circle and speak their prayers for the departed. See these prayers enter the ashes. If you are aware of the departed there at the time, see these prayers flying directly to her.

If you need to travel to the specific area for scattering, do so now. If possible, have everyone follow the leader to this place. As her ashes fall to the Earth and are carried away on the wind, have all attending release her to her next world. Visualize letting go of the cords binding her to each of you and send your unconditional love for her out with her ashes.

Say: "Your ashes have been released to the directions and to the Great Spirit. You are now free to move on to your next realm. Although we grieve for the times we will no longer share in this world, we rejoice in your freedom. We are grateful for the sharing of our lives during your time here in this world. Your memories and gifts live on within each of us as we freely release you to your next world. We send you heartfelt blessings of peace, love, and joy. We say not goodbye, but farewell until we meet again."

Allow everyone time to experience the ceremony and their feelings. They may wish to sit in silence for a while or spend a few moments alone. Arrange to meet at a predetermined location for a meal. This allows any energy or grief to be grounded more easily and provides a supportive atmosphere for all concerned.

Rites of passage can be equally important for the living after a death as they are for the departed. Often in performing these rites, we tend to forget that the departed is not the only one experiencing a passage into a new life. Very often, the death of a loved one can propel the living into new roles, new identities, and an entirely new life. The associated changes in our reality are generally overlooked.

The experience of rites of passage that mark and assist these changes within our reality can help these individuals accept their new roles and move on with their lives, rather than resisting and attempting to hold on to old identities. Many cultures celebrate the coming of adulthood with ceremonies, but few (with the exception of traditional indigenous and some neo-pagan cultures) today maintain those rites which mark the entry into elderhood or parenthood or any other life change.

This is why I have chosen to include the following section on rites of passage for the living after the death of a loved one. To ignore these changes is to prevent our own easy transitions and to dishonor the continuity of change in the life cycle. Since the number of changes that occur as a result of a death, particularly one in the family, are as many as there are people on this planet, it would be impossible to publish a separate ceremony for each. Therefore, I have chosen to outline three, which can easily be altered to fit one's specific situation. Again, I ask that you view these as simple guidelines through which your own creativity and healing may flow.

Rite of Passage

From Partner to Single Individual/Single Parent

This ritual is also designed for the transition to single parent; see letters in parentheses for addenda.

It is recommended that this ritual be performed alone followed by a dinner with friends and family.

Purify the ritual space and all items used in the ritual using any of the three purification ceremonies from chapter three. Set up a central altar with photos of both of you together, and one photo of each of you alone. If you are now a single parent, also include a family photo and one of you alone with the children.

Call upon the Spirits of the six directions and the Creator to join with you in this ceremony. Ask that they bless your work. Request guidance, that your every action may honor them.

Call upon the spirit of the departed to join with you. Let her know the reason for this ceremony and make it clear that you honor her through it.

Say: "Through this ceremony, I honor the life and passing of _____ , my lover/wife/ _____ . I enter sacred space this day/night to also honor my passage into a new life as a result of her transition from this world."

Pick the photo of you as a couple. Meditate on what this relationship meant to you; the love, lessons, and accomplishments you shared and those you created for yourself as a result of this relationship. "We came together in love and respect to create a new being: the being that was Us. We balanced each other and contributed to our common joy and growth. We were truly blessed in this gift."

(A) Pick up family photo. "As parents we gave our all to create a truly loving and supportive atmosphere for our children. We came together, all of us, to create One Family, and we were truly blessed."

Replace these photos. "But now the time for Us has ended. We have completed all we came together to do and it is right that we move on in our own ways. Who we were and what we created will never die. It lives on within each of us forever."

Pick of the photo of her alone. "I love you now and always. Because of that love which is beyond physical existence, I release you to your new worlds. I send you blessings of joy and love in all your journeys and creations. I thank you for all you brought to Us and for loving me as you do."

(B) "I honor your role as mother to our children. I vow to keep your memory and love alive for all of us. Our children will always know your love for them and the special place you still hold for them in your heart."

Pick up photo of you alone. "I honor myself for contributing to this beautiful partnership. I accept that this life of mine is becoming something new. I have not lost a partner, but instead have gained a life of wonderful memories and growth. I carry the blessings of our partnership into my new life." Replace this photo.

(C) Pick up photo of you alone with your children. "I accept my new role as single father in this family. I know that you will continue to be a part of our lives and care for our children from your Other world. I know too, that I am never alone and ask the support and guidance of Spirit in caring for our children." Replace this photo.

"I recognize that I am greater than this incarnation, this physical body. I trust in that Higher plan for my life, even though I may not be aware of where that plan may take me. I am strong in my Self and in my connections to All That Is. I am never alone, yet now I courageously embark on my own new adventure. I willingly place myself in the flow of multiversal energies as I am once again reborn.

"I ask that the Creator and all your manifestations, support and guide me along the way. While my steps may occasionally falter, I know that with Your help I will learn to walk again. May my path be one of strength and beauty. May I honor Spirit in my every action."

Thank all those spirits who joined you in this rite. Release them and let them know they are always welcome with you.

Take a few moments to allow any guidance from Spirit to come through. Meditate upon your new life and the adventures ahead of you. When you feel ready, join your friends and family for a celebratory meal; or if you prefer, celebrate with a solitary meal.

This next rite of passage may not appear of tremendous emotional significance, but there is a great deal involved in this period of life. Obviously, the adult child is now an elder, with all that may entail in the individual family. Even more, an adult who has lost both his parents experiences a multitude of emotions beyond the usual grief for the loss of a loved one.

What we often do not recognize is that, eventually, most people in this situation recognize themselves to be orphans. The child identity that lingers, even when a child cares for a parent, is suddenly gone. This individual is really an "adult" now. No one else will perceive her as "their little girl." Those beings who changed her diapers and taught her to ride a bike and punished her when she missed curfew are gone from this reality. That can dramatically impact one's sense of self.

In addition, there is usually a long-term and complex mix of issues involved with one's relationship to parents. These are issues that are frequently repressed for the sake of family harmony. They are often some of our most sensitive and deep-rooted shadow aspects. When a parent dies, these issues are thrown into chaos. Now we are stuck with them. We'll never get that apology we felt we deserved. We'll never be able to say those things we were afraid to. We may initially feel that these issues will never be resolved. This is not necessarily true, but it is important to fully experience the feelings that arise in the wake of a parent's death.

It is for these reasons that I include this rite. This can be a surprisingly powerful ritual. We do not normally consider adults to be orphans, or to obviously need their parents. Even those who have only recently lost their parents may not be fully aware of this aspect of their grief. It often shows up as a later stage of grief.

As a result, you may wish to postpone this rite until you feel you have cleared a good deal of the issues surrounding the death. You may also want to consider performing it again at a later date. Follow your intuition and your own gut feelings when deciding when to perform this rite.

Rite of Passage
From Adult Child to Family Elder

Purify the ritual space and all items used in the ritual using any of the three purification ceremonies from chapter three. Set up a central altar with photos of you together with your parents (both one from your youth and a current one), one of just your parents (either separate or together), and a current one of you individually.

Call upon the Spirits of the six directions and the Creator to join with you in this ceremony. Ask that they bless your work. Request guidance, that your every action may honor them.

Call upon the spirits of the departed to join with you. Also call upon all your ancestors. Let them know the reason for this ceremony and make it clear that you honor them through it.

Say: "Through this ceremony, I honor the life and passing of _____ , my parents. I enter sacred space this day/night to also honor my passage into a new life as a result of their transition from this world."

Pick up the photos of you as a family. Meditate on what this relationship meant to you; the love, lessons, and accomplishments you shared and those you created for yourself as a result of this relationship. Consider who you were as part of this family. Meditate on your personal growth throughout the course of this relationship and on all that your parents gave to you during their lives.

"I honor the sacrifices you made for me and the love you hold for me. Although our relationships changed over time, you remain my parents. We came together in love and respect to create a new being: the being that was Family. We balanced each other and contributed to our common joy and growth. We were truly blessed in this gift."

Replace these photos. "But now the time for that part of our family has ended. You have both finished your time here in this world. We have completed all we came together to do and it is right that we move on in our own ways. Who we were and what we created will never die. It lives on within each of us forever."

Pick of the photo(s) of your parents without you. "I love you now and always. Because of that love which is beyond physical existence, I release you to your new worlds. I send you blessings of joy and love in all your journeys and creations. I thank you for all you brought to our Family and for loving me as you do."

Pick up photo of you alone. "I honor myself for contributing to this beautiful family. I accept that this life of mine is becoming something new. I have not lost my parents, but instead have gained a lifetime of love and growth. I carry the lessons and blessings of our family into my new life.

"I recognize that I am greater than this incarnation, this physical body. I trust in that Higher plan for my life, even though I may not be aware of where that plan may take me. I am strong in my Self and in my connections to All That Is. I willingly place myself in the flow of multiversal energies as I accept the role of family elder. I vow to live this new role with integrity, honoring all my ancestors.

"I ask that the Creator and the ancestors support and guide me along the way. While my steps may occasionally falter, I know that with your help I will learn to walk again. May my path be one of strength and beauty. May I honor you in my every action."

Thank all those spirits who joined you in this rite. Release them and let them know they are always welcome with you.

Take a few moments to allow any guidance from Spirit to come through. Meditate upon your new life and the adventures ahead of you. When you feel ready, join your friends and family for a celebratory meal.

Rite of Passage
For the Child who has Lost Both Parents

Note: This ritual is designed with the minor child in mind, although it may be used for anyone who has lost both parents. Since the main focus is on the young child, I have included a role for an adult ritual guide. This role may be easily deleted from the ritual, if not necessary.

The child should be included in all ritual preparations and encouraged to add or alter whatever she feels the need to. Throughout the ritual, the adult guide should allow the child to assist or perform whatever is appropriate and all meanings should be explained. Feel free to alter the language to the age of the child.

If you know who the child's legal guardian will be, include the addenda, which are indicated by the letter in parentheses.

Purify the ritual space and all items used in the ritual using any of the three purification ceremonies from chapter three. Set up a central altar with photos of this child together with her parents, her parents without her (either separate or alone) and a current one of her individually.

(A) Also include a recent photo of the child's legal guardians, or a paper with their names written on it.

Call upon the Spirits of the six directions and the Creator to join with you in this ceremony. Ask that they bless your work. Request guidance, that your every action may honor them.

Call upon the spirits of the departed to join with you. Let them know the reason for this ceremony and make it clear that you honor them through it.

From here on, the child should either read these prayers or say them after the adult guide.

"Through this ceremony, I honor the life and passing of _____ , my parents. I enter sacred space this day/night to also honor my passage into a new life as a result of their passage from this world."

Have her pick up the photo of her with her parents. Help her to meditate on what this relationship meant to her; the love, lessons, and accomplishments they shared and those she created for herself as a result of this relationship.

"We came together in love and respect to create Our Family. We were there for each other through happy and sad times. Our Family was a gift to us all."

Have her replace these photos. "But now the time for that family has ended in this world. We did what we came together to do and now we move on in our own ways. Our love and our family will never die. It lives on within each of us forever."

Have her pick up the photo(s) of her parents alone. "Mommy and Daddy, I love you now and always. Because I love you so much, I let you go to your new worlds. I wish you joy and love wherever you may go. I thank you for our wonderful family and for loving me as I know you still do."

(B) "I thank you for picking people we all love and trust as my guardians. I know you believe that they are the best people to love me and raise me. I know that they will never try to take your places or make me love them more than you. I promise to try to love them as you would want me to."

Have her pick up the photo of her alone. "I know I was the best child I could be and even though we may have had fights, we loved each other always. I have not lost my parents because they live on inside me. I know that they will always be with me as long as I live."

(A) "I accept my new guardians as family. They will never replace my parents, but I accept them as my new family. I am lucky to have such wonderful people become part of my family. I am lucky to have two sets of parents, one in this world and one watching over me from the next world." Replace the photo.

"I know that I am much more than my body. I trust that the Great Spirit has a bigger plan for me. I am strong and know that I am never alone. I am part of All of Life. I know that I will always be taken care of and loved. I accept my new adventure in my new life."

"I ask that the Creator and my parents keep on helping me along the way. I pledge to make myself and my parents proud by living an honorable life."

Help her to thank all those spirits who joined you in this rite. Release them and let them know they are always welcome with both of you.

Take a few moments to allow any guidance from Spirit to come through either of you. Help her to meditate upon her new life and the adventures ahead of her.

When you both feel ready, join friends and family for a celebratory meal; or if she prefers, celebrate alone together.

I end this chapter with the following ceremony to create a special Medicine bundle or altar to the memory of the departed. This can be extremely beneficial in the acknowledgment of the time it may take for us to completely release our bonds to the departed and to heal from these wounds. It may also assist the departed by showing them that they are not forgotten. They continue to be honored and recognized as a continuing member of the family, just one that inhabits a different world from the physical family members.

This is a common process among indigenous peoples for the remembering and gradual easing of grief, although they may take the form of ancestor dolls or other items. Generally speaking, these altars or bundles are kept and honored for one year after the death of the loved one. At the end of that year, the honored items are ceremonially either burned or buried in recognition of the end of a mourning period and to fully release the loved one to the next world.

Memorial Altar or Medicine Bundle Ceremony

Select the items you wish to include in this altar or Medicine bundle. These may include a lock of hair, a photo, items that were special to the departed, and anything else that you feel is important, including any symbols relating to the spirit guides of the departed. If you have chosen to create a Medicine bundle, also select the bag or cloth to be used to contain the bundle items.

Put together and bind your Medicine bundle or set up the altar.

Purify the ritual space and all ritual items, using any of the three purification ceremonies from chapter three.

When purifying any leather or other animal parts to be used in the construction of the altar or bundle, be sure to release and honor the spirits of these animals. Thank them for the gifts of their bodies and make an offering to their spirits of some kind. This may be anything from a donation to a wildlife refuge, to a direct offering of food or water.

Call upon the Spirits of the six directions and the Creator to join with you in this ceremony. Ask that they bless your work. Request guidance, that your every action may honor them.

Call upon the spirit of the departed to join with you. Let her know the reason for this ceremony and make it clear that you honor her through it. Ask her assistance in creating this altar/bundle.

Holding your hands out over the items to be used, bless them with the memory of your departed loved one. "This altar/bundle will be honored as the symbolic representative of _____ . Through this altar/bundle, we maintain a physical connection to you and you continue to share a physical space within our home. This altar/bundle will be an instrument of love and healing for all of us and will be ceremonially released when we no longer need its energy.

"In creating this altar/bundle, we acknowledge that we have not yet released all ties to our departed _____ . We ask the blessings of the Creator and all our spirit guides in our time of grief and healing. Guide us that we may fully heal and rejoice in this glorious transition."

Thank all those spirits who joined with you in this work, particularly the departed, spirit guides, and the Great Spirit. Release them and let them know they are always welcome at your home.

At the end of the year, or whenever you feel the time is right, you will ceremonially bury or burn these items. The burial ritual given above may be easily altered for this purpose. This basic outline can also be used for a burning. Rather than commending the altar/bundle to the Earth, you will ask that the fire purify and cleanse your grief and anything still binding this spirit to our world. Request that the spirit of your loved one be released by the fire; and that the smoke carry him or her directly to the Creator.

Whether we choose to simplify our lives with a minimum of ritual and other trappings or become very involved in ceremony, rites of passage are a vital part of our Earth journey. Both psychologically and spiritually, these ceremonies provide us with a tangible means of recognizing death and rebirth. Whether these life cycles are experienced as the death of the physical body or the transition between life phases, they are valid markers of change and growth.

We honor ourselves and all our relations through these ceremonies. This is part of walking a sacred path of honor and respect for Life. Ceremony speaks directly to the heart and soul allowing us to interact on a sacred level with Spirit. A rite of passage related to the death of the physical body is one of the most sacred acts we can participate in. Through the ritual celebration of these passages, we strengthen our ties to All That Is and reaffirm our continuing place in the Web of Life.

Endnote

37 Eliade, *Shamanism: Archaic Techniques of Ecstasy*, pp. 438–442.

Chapter 5

MEETING DEATH

Throughout this book, it becomes clear that death is not what most of us have been taught to believe. No matter what our culture or education, life *does* continue after the death of the physical body. Furthermore, there are an unlimited number of Other worlds through which we may pass before returning once more to a physical body. I have discussed the effects of unfinished business, medical considerations, and fear on our experience of the Afterlife. But what about death itself? What happens at one's death? And how can we better meet our own deaths?

Our experience of death in this reality is very limited by our perception. We see the physical systems cease to function. Often, we see blood or the effects of pain and illness. Sometimes, a physical death can be very raw and even frightening. And then all of a sudden, there appears to be nothing. The body becomes pale, rigid, and cold. It almost seems to be a fake body. We are left cold, as well. This person we knew and loved is no longer. We cannot see him or hear him and his body is nothing more than a decaying hull. Within our three-dimensional perception, we are unaware of the new state of being in which our loved one now exists.

But this is only a very limited perception of death as a process. I have a friend who has worked intensely with death and dying for many years, who likens these physical symptoms of death to the birthing process.[38] It is as though the physical body is birthing the spirit into the next world. In many ways, the physical experience of death is similar to the birthing process. A spirit, a being of energy, is making the incredible transition from one world to the next. This is an amazing transformation of energy, one that can only be experienced when entering or departing a physical world.

110

In order to accommodate this incredible transition, the physical body must undergo a similar change. In one case, the mother has grown the physical body for the incoming spirit. She has assimilated the returning being into her own energy field and during the birth process, the stress on her physical body creates an altered state of consciousness, much like a vision quest or sweat lodge will. This is necessary for the two spirits and the two bodies to separate. Labor and delivery is both a spiritual and physical rite of passage, just as death is.

In the case of death, the physical strain is often necessary to induce altered states and release the spirit from the body. Frequently, the energy produced by the release and reintegration of body soul and free soul will cause stress to the physical body, much like the birth process does. This can be seen as a type of shamanic initiation complete with initiatory "illness." The image of the phoenix that burns to death so that a new phoenix can rise from the ashes is perfect here. As the kundalini rises and releases the body soul, it is in effect burning off the ties to the physical so that the spirit may be reborn into the next world.

In truth, death is a change in energy. As beings of energy (matter being a form of energy), death is experienced as a complete transformation; a release from denser energy and a return to freer, more expansive energy. We release the more dense form of energy, which is matter. Along with the physical body, we also release those energy blocks and walled-off soul fragments that are generally associated with our repressed shadow sides.

Throughout this book, I have discussed chakras, energy centers, and energy systems. While I expect that most readers have a basic understanding of these concepts, I feel this is a topic worth delving into here. In the hope that you, the reader, might gain a deeper understanding of what actually occurs at death, I will briefly describe the interrelationship between the energy systems and the physical body, as well as how they relate to the death process.

The physical body is a manifestation of an energy template. We each have several energy systems, which are also called energy levels or bodies. These energy bodies correspond with the various energy centers, or chakras. I use these terms, chakras and centers, interchangeably to denote those areas of the total energy system, which give rise to and function as doorways between our various energy bodies. These energy centers also relate to specific areas of the physical body. It has also been suggested that these major centers as well as the smaller chakras are related to the crossing of acupuncture meridians and their associated energy flows.

It is the flow through and between these energy systems that maintains the physical body. This flow, as mentioned earlier, is often called *prana* and it is carried by the breath. Decreased flow to any area of the body results in decreased maintenance energy and eventually to decreased health. Those parts of the physical body which continually experience blocked flow will become weaker and sickly. This process can eventually result in the death of the physical body. Similarly, when the need for this incarnation is over and the spirit decides to move on, the death of the physical body is accompanied by a tremendous release of energy.

As I have said, this release is comprised of our energy bodies and shadow aspects, which are usually stored in various areas of the physical body. This is significant, in that upon physical death we finally re-integrate our shadows with the total energy of our beings. As this happens, we often consciously re-experience stored memories and shadow aspects. "I saw my life flash before my eyes," is a common phrase. Have you ever wondered where that phrase originated? Through the process of release, our consciousness becomes aware of these aspects of self; in effect, watching them as they pass beyond the physical body. It is interesting to pay attention to common phrases within our societies. They frequently give us clues to deeper and often forgotten understandings of life.

Within a few hours before physical death, our lower energy centers begin to dissolve. It is these lower chakras that ground us into the Earth and a physical body. When we are infants, these are usually the last chakras to stabilize, as our energy moves into physical form from the top of our heads down into the body. The reverse occurs at death, when these lower energy centers separate from the physical body and the rest of the chakras. As they break down, they release all memories, feelings, and shadow aspects. These often include soul fragments that have been shut down and walled-off.

Then, our physical and spiritual energy rushes up and out through the top of our heads (the crown chakra), taking with it all these released images and experiences. This is often described as a tunnel in the reports of near-death experiences. This tunnel is the central axis of our physical energy systems through which everything leaves the body at death. The light many see at the end of the tunnel is the exit point, the crown chakra, of personal energy from the physical body as well as the entrance into Other worlds. We become aware of these memories and stored experiences as they pass through and out of the physical body along with the rest of our energy body.

From a purely shamanic perspective, the free or journeying soul reintegrates the body soul as it leaves the physical body. When this occurs, all of the experiences of both souls combine to create a whole being that is aware of its sum total of experience. Whatever aspects have not been cleared are carried by the spirit into the next lifetime. Those experiences, which were released with the previous body soul return to the next body as the spirit splits once more during the process of incarnation.

As the lower energy centers are dissolving, our upper chakras are opening wide to Other realities, becoming Gateways for increased perception. Persons in the hours before and at the moment of death become very expanded in their awareness of all worlds. Mainstream belief systems tend to label the ensuing experiences as hallucinations. However, these individuals are simply reintegrating their total selves as their awareness broadens greatly. They are frequently aware of spirit guides and departed loved ones around them. They are also often aware of their Afterlife destinations. These are not hallucinations. They are valid and common experiences of the death process.

There are those who may experience fear and frightening images before the actual moment of death. These are most often those individuals who have a significant amount of repressed emotions and shadow aspects. To face oneself at the moment of death can often be easier than doing so during an incarnation for many reasons. At that point we don't have responsibilities to worry about or concerns of how this will change our lives. The exceptions are those who have not lived an honorable life, have avoided and denied the totality of themselves, or who have not fully integrated expanded beliefs regarding death and the continuity of spirit. These people often experience deep fears of an Afterlife as a result.

The images these people experience are also not hallucinations, but neither are they direct perceptions of the Afterlife. As I indicate throughout this book, when shadow aspects are denied and repressed, they gain more power over us. They grow in size and energy, until they may become truly terrifying. It is interesting that, in attempting to hide these aspects and not give them any energy, we actually increase their control over our lives. After a lifetime of repression, these images may be frightening to the ego of the soul in transit.

In truth, it is really only the ego that dies along with the physical body. This is also where much of our fear comes from. The ego is the personality, or identity, of this incarnation. It is the ego that believes it is the Self and fears its dissolution. In a misguided attempt to protect itself, the ego creates and allows soul fragmentation. At death, these fragments are reintegrated and the ego dissolves into total aware-ness. And this is what death really is, our separateness dissolves into a greater unity. But rather than losing our Selves in the process, we transcend our previous identities without losing anything but our fears and limitations.

There is an alternate view of the spirit's departure from the physical body that I would like to discuss here. Many people believe that the spirit leaves the body with the last breath. This is an innate recognition of the role of the breath as the vehicle for prana, which is the vital link between spirit and body. When a person dies, the breath stops and the energy leaves. Although brain and heart functions may continue after the last breath, unless the breath is re-established these systems will eventually cease.

There are several techniques that allow sharing one's life force through the shar-ing of the breath. Similarly, when we really want to experience something, we breathe deeply of it. We fill ourselves with its essence through the breath. There are also very involved shamanic and yogic techniques for achieving a fully conscious death, or bypassing the death of the physical body. In part, these techniques use the conscious control of the breath. While these methods are extremely involved and take a lifetime to perfect, we can use the conscious control of the breath during both life and the death process.

In chapter two, I discussed the importance of diaphragmatic breathing and an awareness of the breath during everyday life. While it sounds simple, this may take some practice. The breath does not stop when we forget about it. It automatically kicks in and continues one's habitual breathing pattern. Life has a way of taking one's focus away from the breath. This is usually when the shallower chest breathing returns along with its associated tension and stress.

Developing an awareness of the breath and working with its control when an indi-vidual is nearing death may be beneficial in assisting the release of attachments and fears, as well as centering and opening to spirit guides. We use the breath in this way along with visualization, through the many guided journeys and meditations outlined in this book. It certainly helps in removing attention from physical ailments and emotional distress. However, it is far more effective if this awareness is developed early in life. I would strongly suggest guiding children in an awareness of how they are breathing, how it makes them feel, and how to change their breathing at will.

When I was in elementary school band, our teacher showed us a wonderfully sim-ple way to determine just where you are breathing from and how to be sure you have switched to diaphragmatic breathing. Lying on your back, place one hand (or light book) over the center of your chest and one on your abdomen. As you inhale, whichever hand rises indicates where your breath is entering your body. Deeper and slower inhalations bring more oxygen, more energy, and less stress. This type of breathing, called diaphragmatic breathing, invigorates the body.

Once we have developed an awareness of this, we can move on to slowing the breath. According to *Science of Breath,* it is considered average to breathe between sixteen and twenty breaths per minute.[39] While pranayama is an involved discipline that also takes years to master, I will make two suggestions for exercises to practice with anyone who is ill or nearing death. Both of these exercises are very simple and will encourage the experience of calm and balance. These are particularly recommended for anyone who is experiencing pain, fear, difficulty saying goodbye, or difficulty letting go of this lifetime. I would also suggest these techniques for anyone involved in the death of a loved one, before or after death.

Breathing Exercise 1

Place your full attention on your breathing. Do not attempt to alter it, just observe it for a few moments.

Where does your breathing seem to come from? How do you feel at this moment? If there is any tension in your body, where is it localized?

Now, slow your breathing. Count to three on each inhalation and again, on each exhalation. Breathe deeply, filling your lungs from the bottom first. Feel your diaphragm stretch and expand as your abdomen moves out. As you exhale, feel your abdomen contract as the breath leaves from the bottom of your lungs first.

Breathe into any areas of tension or stress. Feel your breath fill and relax these areas. With each breath, tension and pain melt away.

Once you feel comfortable with this exercise, increase the count for inhalations and exhalations. Practice this several times a day, particularly when you are feeling stressed, or are in pain.

Breathing Exercise 2

Beginning with Breathing Exercise 1, begin to alter the count of inhalations and exhalations. Starting slowly, work toward a 1:2 ratio between inhalations and exhalations. For example, if your inhalation lasts for four counts, your exhalation will last for eight counts.

Do not increase this ratio too quickly. If you are gasping for air and desperately sucking in the inhalation, you should return to Breathing Exercise 1.

This exercise is strongly recommended for any time you feel stressed, in pain, or feel the time to leave your body has come. You may choose to ask a loved one to guide you in this exercise during the process of death.

While it is beneficial to understand exactly what occurs on a spiritual level when we die, and why the release of shadow aspects is important, this knowledge does not bring us a concrete means to facilitate an easy passing. A truly conscious death is created through a number of practical considerations and personal shamanic work *before* death occurs. Most of these considerations are discussed throughout this book. There are also a number of meditations that can be valuable in helping the passing of a loved one.

Although self-knowledge and integration of shadow aspects are invaluable to an easy passing, the meditation technique, which is outlined below, can be a great benefit in producing a more consciously chosen death experience for the dying. This meditation is intended to be practiced before death and to be used by the dying whenever they feel their time has come to cross over.

Conscious Death Exercise

Although the dying are not normally in need of assistance in inducing trance states, it may be helpful, at least in practice, to use smudge, drumming, or music to facilitate altered states of consciousness.

"Feel your hold on your physical body loosen. See your lower chakras and the energy binding you to this plane begin to let go. Easily release all cords and attachments that hold you here.

"Watch as memories of your life, and possibly other lives, pass by you. Allow these images to flow unrestricted by any judgment or fear. They are merely memories and cannot harm you unless you permit them. Embrace these pieces lovingly and accept them back as part of you.

"See a tunnel open above you. At its end is a glorious white light. Follow this tunnel up into the light. As you pass by your upper chakras, notice that they are wide open. They act as windows allowing you your first glimpse into the Afterlife. You see loved ones from beyond the Veil and spirit guides waiting to assist you on the Other side.

"Permit the rest of your attachments to this realm to slip easily away. Feel the freedom as your spirit rises out of your body into the light. You feel complete and joyous. You are filled with this glorious white light as you fully integrate the totality of your being. Greet your loved ones and spirit guides and allow them to lead you to the next world."

At the completion of this exercise we do not count up to bring the individual back in any way. If she has not chosen to pass over during this meditation, we allow her and her spirit guides to return her to this reality in their own time and in their own ways.

To be present at the death of a loved one and to know that you have contributed to a beautiful and spiritual passing can be a great gift to all concerned. This is truly a sacred event and is analogous to witnessing a birth. I have a friend who works with a group devoted to creating this type of passing for anyone in need. They have maintained constant spiritual vigils at the bedsides of the dying. At one point, they kept up a sacred circle around a dying man. They chanted and drummed as he took his final leave from his body. This is an experience without compare in our reality and is one of the most sacred acts we could hope to participate in.

While guiding loved ones through these meditations and ceremonies can be of tremendous benefit, it is equally important for us to allow them some time alone. We sometimes make it difficult for them to go because of our constant presence at their sides. The dying often choose to pass over while they are alone. If this is their preference, they may hang on longer than necessary, waiting for loved ones to leave.

We generally remain at the side of a dying loved one for a number of reasons. Sometimes we feel we would not want to be alone at our own deaths, so we do not want to risk leaving a loved one alone. Often, we do not want to miss a loved one's final words, so we fear leaving her alone even for an instant. Occasionally, we do not want them to feel they were abandoned when they need us most.

It is essential to the healing process for us to release these feelings of guilt or frustration. If a loved one truly has words to impart or does not want to go alone, they won't. If the departed decides that there is still something left unsaid or undone, they will attempt to contact someone after death. This also tends to hold true for sudden and traumatic deaths due to violence or accidents.

If we truly want to help those loved ones who are dying, we must step outside ourselves and place their needs before our own. This includes providing them with the opportunity to pass over in solitude and peace. Most people who are aware of this potential need will schedule short periods of time, anywhere from ten minutes to an hour depending on the situation, to leave the loved one alone.

This is usually accomplished through careful planning. The dying individual is made comfortable and all her needs are taken care of before her caretakers depart the room. Goodbyes are said as the dying person is assured of love and told that if she needs to go while the caretakers are away, she should feel free to do so. Sometimes, a monitor will be turned on so caretakers can respond to calls for help or the sounds of pain, or a difficult death.

While they are out of the room, caretakers respond to their own needs. They go for walks, or take showers or baths. They eat or meditate or nap. In this way, the energy of the caretaker is diverted away from the dying individual allowing her to slip away unfettered by our needs. In addition, caretakers are able to care for themselves and as a result they are more effective and healthier caretakers for the dying.

I feel it is important to note that there are some individuals who do not want to be left alone at any time while they are dying. This is usually due to unreleased attachments and fear, but it is not our choice to tell them what is best for them at this time. If it is possible for someone to be with this dying individual constantly, that is also a tremendous gift to the dying. This is often particularly important to dying children. To have this support at the moment of death can be exceptionally comforting to some people and can greatly ease their passing.

However, this is where the importance of family and community come into play. We as a society need to give more support to both caregivers and the dying. Caregiving, especially for the dying, is one of those "rotten jobs" that no one wants to deal with. We avoid it, and although we sympathize with those who must do it, rarely do we jump in and lend any real assistance.

These caregivers are performing a selfless and sacred service. But they need to be able to take a nap or a shower or grab a cup of coffee without feeling guilty for leaving a dying loved one alone, or in the care of a competent but impersonal hired nurse. We need to put this situation in perspective and then take the leap and do something. Yes, we have our own lives and our own responsibilities. Perhaps we do not live nearby or feel we just can't face it. If we take a moment to consider what we would hope to receive from our family or community were we in either situation, we gain a very different perspective and a personal motivation for action. We do receive what we give out.

There are those dying individuals who are not part of an indigenous shamanic family or culture, and who are open to shamanic ceremonies. These individuals may be assisted through the death process with a ceremony of release. This ceremony is designed to help the loved one accept his place at the end of his life, while establishing contact with spirit guides, and providing a continuing safe space around him. This safe space encourages comfort and security before, during, and immediately after death. If a full ceremony is inappropriate (for example in a hospital), more obvious elements may be deleted, such as smudge or drumming.

Release Ceremony
For Any Person Nearing Death

Purify the room or even the complete home where the dying person is staying, using any of the three purification ceremonies from chapter three. Also purify the personal space of this person and any involved in this ceremony, or in his care.

Call upon the Spirits of the six directions and the Creator to join with you in this ceremony. Ask that they bless this ceremony and all involved in this death process. Ask them to watch over and protect this loved one throughout the death process. Request guidance, that your every action may honor them.

Call upon the spirit guides of all involved and ask that they contribute to a beautiful, easy death for this person. Let them know that this ceremony is a rite of release and ask for their blessings throughout the process.

Say: "We come together this day/night to honor _____ , our loved one who is departing this life. We offer prayers of gratitude that we were able to share in his life in this world."

Say to your loved one, even if he is not conscious or fully aware: "We are honored to have learned from you and grown with you. We honor you now in this ceremony. As we have loved you in this life and before, we will continue to love you when you depart from this body. Because our love for you is so great, we release all ties that may bind you to us. We know that our love will continue in all worlds and we will not hold you in this body."

Call upon the spirit guides of this person. If he is capable, this person may wish to do so for himself. Call them to his side and ask their assistance to ease his passing. Let them know he is open to their guidance and ask that they be there for him at the moment of his death. Give him time to experience their presence.

Say to him: "You are _____, in this body. You are and have been child, brother, lover, . . . But we all recognize that you are much more than these identities. You are a glorious being of spirit who is nearing the end of this Earth journey. As you embark upon your new journey, we offer to you prayers of blessing, love, peace, and release. Let go of your attachments to this world. We assure you that we will all be healed and we will pull together to heal each other. When you are finally called from this world and this body, go easily with our blessings for your joy."

Drum, rattle, or chant for a period of time. Do it at least long enough to experience an altered state of consciousness and to feel the energy shift in your circle. Allow yourself to remain open to any feelings or rhythms that may come through.

Thank all those spirits and the Creator who have joined you for their presence at this ceremony. Ask that they remain through the death process, continuing to bring their blessings and protection to this person and this place. Again, ask for their guidance, that your every action may honor them.

Be prepared for the possibility that this person may choose to go during the ceremony. If so, be comforted with the fact that you provided a safe space with spirit guidance present for this person to go in peace. This is not something you have caused through the ceremony and it is certainly nothing that should create guilt. On the contrary, you have contributed to a sacred process and have honored your loved one in the deepest way possible.

With the exception of the physical death of the body, true death only occurs on an emotional level. Each time we create a new block or allow a fragmentation of our spirits, we experience a little death. We separate even more from our Selves and the multiverse through these experiences. Every time we permit this to occur, we shut down more of our access to the totality of who we are and close the Gates to the richness and abundance of all our worlds.

In living this type of life, we also increase our potential for an incomplete transformation at death. When the soul has become excessively fragmented, a total release and reintegration does not occur at death. When all those memories, experiences, and blocks are released from the physical body, not all are re-experienced and acknowledged by the departing being. The spirit carries these attachments and fragments, along with strong belief systems, into the Afterlife.

These blocked experiences can result in a spirit becoming stuck between worlds and prevent a successful transition. They can also increase the amount of time needed in various waiting areas and belief system worlds before the spirit can move on. If the trauma of facing these blocks is too great for the departing spirit, these experiences will be further separated from the rest of the being and denied.

This trauma can lead to further fragmentation of the spirit and will often cause this spirit to remain close to the Earth plane in search of familiarity and comfort. They may even seek other bodies to attach themselves to for safety and a semblance of feeling alive. At this point, it can require an experienced deathwalker to retrieve the soul fragments, assist their reintegration, and guide the spirit to the next level. If this does not occur, these beings may reincarnate without the benefit of a life review or the assistance of spirit guides, carrying these blocks with them to a new body.

These repressed experiences are also the basis of karma. Until these experiences, attachments, and fragments are cleared and integrated into the total being, we must continue to return to the physical. Just as we took these with us from previous bodies, so too, do we carry them with us and store them in our new bodies. This process and its effects are discussed in detail in chapter eight.

This phenomenon of incomplete transformation is discussed elsewhere in this book. However it is important to consider here, in light of how a person chooses to meet his death. Even (or perhaps especially) those of us who are most afraid of death want to meet it on the best possible terms. We don't want any nasty surprises. We want it to be easy and peaceful.

While we may not be able to completely control the manner of our physical deaths, we each have the power right now to begin to work towards making death a time of beautiful transition and freedom. Living a conscious life leads to creating a conscious death. As we expand our awareness and self-acceptance during physical life, we become more conscious beings. Rather than living our lives as confused victims, we learn why we create what we do, and how to expand our creation of self.

With an awareness of death in our everyday lives, we can find the courage to live honestly and honorably. When measured against the potential of imminent death, we remember to enjoy the beauty of a sunset, even if we are late for an appointment. We can overcome our fears of rejection or embarrassment and show affection to those we love. Indulging ourselves in frequent worry or anger, or even fear is recognized as a waste of time.

There is tremendous power in living a conscious and courageous life. Rather than just getting by until death cuts us down, we make a life worth living. One does not need to be rich or well educated to create a glorious life. We just need to give it our best. In being honest with ourselves, we attract honesty and become a shining example for others.

In many circles today, character has become more of a cartoon than a reality. As a result, people crave ethical role models. Sure, you may get some ribbing when making those first steps to an honorable Self. Along the way, you may also experience the loss of those individuals who are not yet ready for honesty and respect. This is one reason why shamanism is most often a solitary path. And that is truly all right.

121

I had a discussion with a man who has answered the Call of the spirits and is pursuing a shamanic path. He has experienced several old friends who are unable and unwilling to expand their awareness to accept his new identity. Rather than dragging his feet and attempting to stay stuck in the same old roles with these people, he is continuing along his path and not hiding it from these friends. Fortunately, he has enough trust in the Great Spirit that it is all right if these people choose to leave the relationship with him.

I had to tell him that it is not really "finding out who your real friends are," but more of a discovering who is ready for this type of growth and who is not. Perhaps, they will be ready later on, perhaps not until another lifetime. But that is not your responsibility, nor can you do anything about it for them. You need to be concerned with your *own* evolution. In taking charge of your own life and choosing to lead rather than follow, you will meet your death consciously and honorably. Your transformation at the moment of death will be more complete than had you lived your life for someone else.

Often our friends surprise us. After all, we have incarnated together for some reason. Who is to say what that specific reason is, from within our ego-identity? Friends and family can be spurred to their own growth and development through your example. For example, I worked with a woman many years ago who was from a very tough, rather poor neighborhood in the northeastern United States. When others she grew up with were involved with gangs and drugs, she chose to drive over an hour into the suburbs to work with handicapped children.

At one point, my friend was injured in a gang-related argument. Her old friends felt she was selling out to the rich, turning her back on her neighborhood, and avoiding the gang to go take care of rich people's kids. They refused to believe that those kids were often far from rich and were of many ethnic backgrounds. In any event, my friend stood her ground and began to do similar work in her own area.

She passed through this test of courage and began to find other people in her neighborhood following her lead. When I last spoke with her, she had returned full-time to her area to be a leader in the community and continued to work with children. Some of her old antagonists had become her strongest supporters and had turned their lives around as a result of her example.

If one young woman can stand up to these kinds of odds and create a courageous, honorable life, how can those of us with relatively easier communities and lives continue to believe that we can't do it? From the outside looking in, it may appear as though she may not have the ideal life. But she is serving her community and living an honorable life while working toward that glorious transformation that accompanies death. She is well on her way to an easy transition, passing over with the knowledge that she made a difference in her own and in others lives, just through being strong enough to follow her heart.

One excellent method of focusing on the kind of life you are creating, and how it may differ from the life you want to create, is to write your own eulogy, or memorial. Take some time, in a quiet, safe space, and imagine coming back after death to watch your own memorial service.

Visualize the people you would want to speak at this service. What is it that you would want these people to say about you and your life? Write these things down in your journal. Take some time to really consider the kind of eulogy you would be happy and proud to hear. What is most important to you, at the end of this life?

Once you have completed your eulogy, put it away for a few days. Don't give it another conscious thought. Then, when you have some time to be in a quiet space for some time, review your eulogy. Take an honest look at how it compares with what might be said, were you to die this moment.

Make a written plan of action to align yourself and your life with this eulogy. Follow through by taking concrete actions to create the life and the person that you would respect. Be courageous and know that any progress you make is something to be proud of. Then, review both the eulogy and the plan periodically. Make any changes you feel are right and important for you. Honor yourself for the progress you have made and do not berate yourself for not moving as fast as you might hope to. You are doing the best you can at any given moment.

There are some more practical things to consider in meeting one's death with ease and satisfaction. These include death rituals, which are discussed in chapter four, and other physical preparations for one's death. This usually entails purchasing a burial site, deciding between cremation and burial, deciding whether or not to donate organs, and creating or finalizing wills, including living wills.

Part of living a conscious life is facing and handling what needs to be done instead of postponing and procrastinating. It can be a burden to the family, and even to the dying if they are aware, to have final preparations for the care and disposal of the body unplanned. What happens to the physical body can be very important to the dying individual and these needs are often carried over into the next world. This is particularly true in societies that place a great deal of value on material aspects of life and on the physical body.

The decision between burial and cremation is very personal. Most people I speak to just don't know which is best for them. While they don't like to think of their bodies taking up space or decaying, they are also unsure of the spiritual effects of cremation. Some people are equally concerned that their ashes will be mixed up with someone else's and not be returned to the correct family.

Some traditions believe that the body should be cremated as soon as possible after death to encourage the spirit to move on. Some believe that cremation is the proper way to dispose of a body but that this must wait for three days after physical death in order to allow the spirit to fully release the body. Others feel that we should follow a more natural process of burial and decomposition. In some cultures, it is not uncommon to take dead bodies up to a high point and dismantle them so that carrion birds may more easily feed on them.

The point is that, although the disposal of the body may initially be important to the departed spirit, once that being has moved on, the body is no longer of any value to them. It returns to being a purely material part of the Earth. It is like an old car we were once attached to but have outgrown. The effects of cremation or burial on the spirit are nonexistent once that spirit has fully passed over.

If there are concerns regarding the return of ashes, or any other practical worries, these should be discussed with the funeral professional. Most crematoriums allow for a witness to be present during cremation to ensure that the ashes received are from the correct body. I have heard that some states now require this.

This can be a very difficult role for a loved one. It all depends on one's perspective. I would only make two notes of advice here. Prepare yourself for the experience as much as possible in advance and do not succumb to pressure from anyone regarding the clothing or casket or any other material concerns. You have made your choices for the good of all and this body is no longer your loved one. Other people's opinions or desires (especially those outside the family) are not important.

There is no correct choice for all people. However, it is important to take the time to consider what feels right for you. This does not have to be carved in stone. In most cases, you can change your mind later, if you want to. But after your death if

123

your family does not know what your preferences were, they will be forced to make the choice for you.

The choice of whether or not to donate organs can be an even more difficult one to make. This also tends to be a choice that varies with different life phases and spiritual beliefs. The greatest hesitations seem to involve the appearance of the body for funeral services, a rejection of such advanced technology, and whether or not some of our spirit remains in the donated organs. Few people today fear that they will be an incomplete being in the Afterlife without the donated organs.

From a shamanic point of view, we can look to our animal relations and the Earth itself for guidance in this matter. Our animal relations are viewed as the physical manifestations of our power animals. They are killed, dismembered, and eaten by us as well as by other animals. Although there were specific parts of the bodies of sacred animals that traditionally were kept together to provide them a new body in the Afterlife, most organs were not included in these parts. We did not fear that we were doing a disservice in following these natural laws. Those same organs that fed and nourished us, when taken from our animal relations, can provide new life to another human when taken from us.

All of Nature follows these same natural cycles. The physical body is the means by which we continue life on this planet. We eat the plants and the animals. Unless we are locked in a steel and cement grave, when we die and decompose, we are eaten by worms and insects and become food for the plants, which continue to feed the rest of the food chain. Whether or not we donate our organs, we still decompose and return to these cycles.

It is true that some parts of the dead body of an animal have been used throughout time to impart some of the essence of that being to another. This is often accomplished through eating a body part, such as the heart or drinking the blood. More often today, it is through the use of feathers, fur, and bones on altars and in Medicine pouches and shields. It is also true that some organ recipients have developed similar appetites to the donor after receiving organs.

I personally view this as a similar phenomenon to psychometry. We do not worry if part of our spirit is lost each time we throw out a broken watch, outgrow our favorite jeans, or clean out a hairbrush. Nonetheless, a good psychic can pick up images and feelings related to us from holding these items. We are not bound to these items, but they do carry left over energetic imprints from us, just as the sand retains our footprints until the waves clear them from the beach. Likewise, we can use the various purifying ceremonies in this book to clear our energy from the body and its organs before donation.

This is a highly personal decision, which should not be made based upon anyone else's beliefs. If the time involved in completing the donation or the condition of the body afterward is a concern in making this decision, you should discuss the possibilities with a doctor or funeral professional. In addition, continue to work with your spirit guides and getting to know yourself better. Again, there are no right or wrong answers that work for everyone. Go with whatever feels right to you.

The legal will seems a final and somber issue. Many people refuse to discuss this because they prefer not to think about ever needing one. This is also one of the most important issues to finalize *before* ever needing one. Not only does it bring peace of mind to the dying, to know that her affairs are in order and will be executed according to her choice, but it prevents a potentially tremendous burden for those closest to the departed. The legal issues involved in a death without a will can break a family both financially and emotionally, particularly if there are financial assets to be distributed.

Although we had practically no financial assets, my husband and I chose to complete our wills, including living wills, when we were just thirty-one years old. We had discussed it ever since my grandfather passed over but had not gotten around to it. We had no reason to expect an early death, but our son had just been born. Rather than avoid discussing the possibility of leaving him an orphan and not knowing who would raise him if we both died, we chose instead to get the details of our wishes should that happen, down on paper legally.

We still have no money, but we do have the knowledge that our son will be taken care of by people we trust and respect. Unless we have another child, and change our wills, our son will have no difficulty accessing whatever assets we do have when we die. In the face of possible death, this is the greatest peace of mind a parent can have.

As I said, we also completed living wills at this time. I had been through enough death situations to know what kind of death I preferred. I encouraged my husband to think about this and within a few months of each other, we completed the necessary forms. Now we both are aware of each others' preferences for medical issues and death services. Not only that, but these wishes are legally binding.

There are a couple of ways today to complete a will and a living will, without the services of an attorney. There are software packages that allow you to customize your will to your particular region or state. These also provide access to changing legislation and experts who can answer your more complex questions. I have also seen generic packaged forms sold in stores for wills. They are usually in a display, along with rent agreements and promissory notes. These are legal in the states in which they are sold, although with both of these types of forms it is recommended that you have them notarized.

125

The best way for us to meet that powerful transition that is death is to be mindful of how we live our lives. Being courageous is possible for all of us, in our lives and in our deaths. Permitting the continual creation of self-importance and self-pity is nothing more than a waste of time. It does not bring happiness while we live, and it often precludes a complete and conscious departure for the spirit. When we walk our paths in this life with honor and respect for All Life, that is what we will receive and that is how we will meet our deaths.

Endnotes

38 Oz Anderson, personal discussion, April 1998.
39 Rama, Ballentine, Hymes, *Science of Breath*, p. 109.

Chapter 6

DEATHWALKING

As previously discussed, one of the most vital and traditional roles of the shaman is that of deathwalker, or psychopomp. Throughout time and across the globe, societies have called upon their shamans to assist the dead in their journeys to the next world. In the role as spiritual guide for the community, and because of a familiarity with Other realms, shamans are the few people who are truly capable of performing the deathwalk.

As modern deathwalkers, we find that the departed will seek us out when they need assistance. As a result of that continually open Gateway to the Other worlds, we are often aware of spirits everywhere. Many of these are departed humans and animals that are hanging around this reality for one reason or another. Although we do not make it a habit to try to escort every spirit we meet to another reality, we do develop a feeling for which beings are in need, and which have a real purpose where they are. Those spirits that are in need will let us know this in various ways. Through dreaming or as a result of our shamanic awareness, they often will directly request our assistance. In the next chapter I will describe the ways in which psychics and shamans see and hear spirits, and receive other communications from other realities.

127

Sometimes these spirits will attach themselves to us energetically. Many traditional shamanic healers believe that some illnesses are caused by the presence of a disembodied spirit within the energy field of a living person. These are rarely malicious spirits. They are more like lost puppies that are frightened and unable to fend for themselves, or they refuse to accept the death of their own bodies. So, they latch onto whatever they think may be able to support them.

However the spirits make contact, the point is that they have a way of knowing instinctively who can hear them. While they may first attempt to contact those they were closest to in physical life, they are frequently unable to reach these people. When their initial attempts at communication fail, they eventually come to a shaman or psychic or a sensitive member of their family, often a child.

My mother and I have often jokingly referred to our homes as Grand Central Station. Thousands of travelers and commuters pass through this huge New York City transportation station each day on their way to work or other places. When loved ones pass over, they inevitably come to our homes on their way to Other places. In many families, the confirming telephone call usually comes soon after their arrival.

A connection seems to be made with a shaman or psychic that allows these spirits to know who can understand them. I have friends who find it very difficult to spend time in large cities due to their constant awareness of both spirits and those thoughtforms resulting from emotional disturbances and violent crimes. Sometimes we feel as though we have neon signs over our heads, "I can hear you! This Way!" One must keep one's humor, but this is no laughing matter to those in need.

In her role as deathwalker, a shaman often serves as a bridge, transmitting messages between the world of the dead and that of the living. The deathwalker is called upon, both by the departed and by their loved ones remaining in physical life, to facilitate and conduct communications through the Veil. Although this topic is discussed in detail in other chapters, it is worth touching on here as well because it is an essential element in the shaman's role as deathwalker and as healer.

The main reason the recently departed do not immediately pass on to the next world is their enduring attachments to those remaining in this reality, or to this reality itself. For some of these departed spirits, this may be due to a fear of being without a spouse or parent; for others it is a feeling of responsibility to their family. Still other spirits need to comfort their loved ones who remain in physical reality with the knowledge that they are happy and still alive. There are as many reasons as there are spirits but the result is the same for all: they are tied to our plane of existence.

One of the ways a deathwalker can be of service to these spirits is to assist the communication between them and those they are bound to. Obviously, this will not always be possible. There are those on our side of the Veil who want no part of this type of communication. They rarely believe that this communication is even possible. Nonetheless, there is a growing number of metaphysically minded people today who are willing to accept the possibility.

Often the mere knowledge that our loved ones continue after death is enough for us to release them. When a deathwalker is able to effectively communicate this to the grieving, we contribute to their ability to let go of the bonds keeping a departed loved one tied to this world. We may be able to do this through direct messages from the departed, a discussion of the dreams of loved ones, or even through describing the deathwalk of the departed. Some people get tremendous relief in knowing that their loved ones successfully passed into the next world and were met by spirit guides on the Other side.

129

Frequently, once a departed spirit has been able to say goodbye, he feels enough closure that he is able to move on. He has finally been able to reach his loved ones and let them know he is still alive. He can now turn his focus to his own journey. This is particularly true once the departed realizes that he can return at any time to check up on his loved ones in this reality.

As I said, hearing the details of the deathwalk of a departed loved one can be extremely comforting to loved ones who remain in this reality. If these individuals are at all metaphysically minded, they generally will feel a sense of closure as well as relief and solace in knowing that their departed loved one was not alone and has made an easy leap to the next world. Many people also find hope and comfort for themselves in knowing that death is not the end and that there are spirit guides and shamans who are there to assist us when we die. The personal fears of these people can be alleviated, paving the way for greater confidence and, eventually, an easier passing.

Often, the individuals who gain the most from learning of the deathwalks of loved ones want to do something concrete to assist the process. They feel that deathwalking is such an important role that they want to be a part of it. Many times they feel the need to give something back to others because their loved ones have been helped by someone else. These are honorable motivations and I respect any who are loving and brave enough to want to assist the dying and the departed.

However, the actual shamanic deathwalk is not for everyone. We each have strengths in our own specific areas. I recommend that people focus on their special gifts and assist the dying or the departed in these ways. This is particularly important in cases where the deathwalk would be attempted mainly for a perceived excitement or glory. It can take many years to reach the point where you are comfortable enough in the shamanic journey and past enough of your own shadows that you are ready to guide another being to another world.

Although I recommend that anyone considering attempting a deathwalk first obtain some training and gain a good amount of control and familiarity with Other worlds, I do recognize that there are those individuals who will take that step whether they are prepared for it or not. Whatever the motivation for taking on the deathwalk, without proper control and personal work, it is frequently a misjudgment and often does not turn out how the guiding individual hoped.

On occasion, an inexperienced individual will convince herself that the death-walk has gone exactly as planned. This is generally easy to determine through additional journeying and remaining open to spirit guidance. This is commonly the case when someone honestly wants to do the right thing but forces the images or performs a mental exercise rather than a true shamanic journey.

This can be healing for the inexperienced journeyer in creating images that help her to believe her loved one has successfully passed over. However, if it was a mental exercise, the potential need for a deathwalk still needs to be addressed. If it was a true journey but was forced, a complete deathwalk may still be necessary.

As a result, I would like to stress some points of advice for any that may consider making the leap to deathwalker. First and foremost, obtain the assistance of your guides and guardians before embarking on any journey, especially one to the Lands of the Dead. This is absolutely essential, especially if you do not have a considerable amount of experience in this area. If at any time you feel frightened, lost, or out of control, call upon your spirit guides to take you back to your body safely.

Another important point to keep in mind is that we do not go looking for a death-walk. Again, this is particularly applicable to those with little journeying experience, but we perform the psychopompic journey only in two situations: if and when someone in need approaches us; and if it is absolutely necessary to protect another person. No one who is inexperienced or is not prepared for any potential consequence should attempt to Walk a bothersome or dangerous spirit to the Other side.

A third recommendation is to enlist the assistance of another person who will not be journeying. This person should be fully informed about what you intend to do and will be given explicit instructions on how to handle an emergency. You should choose to set aside a specific time limit for the journey. If you are not back and fully conscious by that time, this individual has permission to do whatever is necessary to bring you back. If this person is shamanically or magically inclined, they may also act as a guardian, maintaining energy shields around your body until you return to it.

Finally, I strongly suggest a period of soul-searching prior to any such significant journey. Determine your motives for undertaking this working. In the case of a deathwalk, be totally honest with yourself concerning your views regarding death and any feelings you may have about remaining in this life yourself. If you tend toward depression or suicide, or are going through a particularly difficult period in your life, I recommend that you wait or request that someone else perform the deathwalk. You will be of no service to those in need if you are confronted by your own shadows or find yourself unable to release your attachments to these beings.

I do not bring this up to frighten anyone away from learning to assist the dead through the transition beyond the Veil. It is a sacred responsibility that humbles those of us who perform it. Far from being a glorious power trip, we are constantly reminded of our interconnections and the equality between all beings. Those who would become deathwalkers embark upon a vital and honorable path of brutal honesty and clarity of Self.

However, the truth is that the deathwalk can be an exceptionally difficult and occasionally traumatic journey for anyone to take on. This difficulty becomes even more intense the closer our relationship to the departed. We may find at the end that we are not ready to release them, or we want to go with them. Issues of abandonment and loneliness can show up during a deathwalk.

There are also many people that are looking for attention or an escape from this physical reality. To use the deathwalk, or any journey, for attention and social status is to invite trouble. The spirits do not deal easily with those who would lie about sacred matters. Furthermore, we truly do receive what we send out. If we are creating a persona made up of dishonesty and ego, that is what we will attract into our own lives.

These individuals may also be enticed into not returning to their bodies by what they find on the Other side. They have not done enough work to understand that they will return to a physical body carrying the same issues that drove them out of this life in the first place. In addition, they may experience difficulty fully moving over as a result of their attempts to escape. This is not the same as a conscious death by those whose time is nearing. This is cowardice. The only real protection is training, experience, and self-knowledge.

As I said earlier, unresolved shadow aspects can and will show up during shamanic journeys. A journey to the realm of the dead, when another soul is counting on us for assistance, is not the time to come face-to-face with disturbing shadow aspects of our own. The inexperienced journeyer may be unable to recognize where these images and experiences arise from and become terrified or caught in the dramas. It is mainly the fears of our own identities that arise and hold us back, but these can be paralyzing. The manifestation of fears and other shadow aspects also has the power to fragment our spirits, if permitted to get out of control.

With all this in mind, I have outlined a simple meditation that will provide a basic forum for assisting the departed to the next world. It is not a true journey. As I said, those can rarely be planned. However, this type of meditation-visualization is familiar to most people. It is also beneficial in maintaining an objectivity and detachment for the meditator that works quite well, both in protecting the meditator and in assisting the departed.

Deathwalk Meditation

Enter the shamanic state of consciousness using a drumming tape, or count down slowly, to yourself, from ten to one. If you feel you need additional deepening, count down once more from ten to one, stopping occasionally to take a deep breath and go deeper. It may help to visualize each number as you count down.

Visualize yourself standing at the base of a beautiful spiral staircase. This staircase is filled with clear, white light. Take a good look at it. Take another deep breath and go deeper.

Perform the Earth–Star Meditation (see page 70).

Now call upon your personal spirit guides and guardians. When they arrive, greet them and ask their assistance and protection in this deathwalk you are about to enter into.

Call the spirit for whom this assistance is offered. See this being clearly before you. Tell him that you are here to help him move into the Light. Let him know that once he is free of this realm, he will be enveloped in the most wonderful love and light imaginable.

Now take his hand, or in some way lead him up onto the staircase. Notice any cords or chains binding him down. Some people experience this as heavy weights that are tied to a being; other see it as many layers of clothing. Trust what comes up for you as your own personal symbolism.

Encourage him to release these encumbrances. If he will allow it, you may physically assist him in removing them. As each one is released, clearly visualize him becoming lighter and freer. As you reach the top of the staircase, see and feel his joy and freedom. He is becoming filled with light.

When you reach the top of the staircase, all of those things that bound him to our world are gone. See his personal guides meet the two of you at the top of the stairs. If they do not appear right away, call them for him. When he does come in contact with them, he may immediately move off with them. If he appears unsure or apprehensive, take charge. Introduce him to these beings and assure him that these are his own guides who have been with him unseen throughout his life. Let him know they love him and are here to help him find his way. Once he has accepted their guidance, your job is done.

You may choose to watch from the top of the staircase for a short while, but then come immediately back down the stairs. If you feel the need of any comfort or assistance call on your spirit guides. Remember that they have been with you through the entire journey, whether you were consciously aware of them or not. They are always there for you when you need them.

Once you reach the bottom of the stairs, take a few moments to center yourself. You may wish to recall that Earth energy to help you ground your own energy. Again, feel free to ask your spirit guides for any help integrating this experience.

Keeping a journal or diary may also be greatly helpful in integrating your experiences.

The shamanic journey for the newly departed, the deathwalk, is usually performed after rites of passage in order to guide the spirit to the next world. This can occur anywhere from immediately after the funeral to forty days later or more. Again, this is largely a cultural difference. This journey is not always required and some modern shamans will wait to see if their assistance is needed before taking any action.

Shamans are also called upon to assist earthbound spirits who are either unable or unwilling to move on to the next step. These are most often spirits who either deny the fact that they are dead, or are bound to our plane of existence by fear and attachments. While it may seem fascinating to us that a particular house, hotel, or hill is haunted, this is not so entertaining to the spirit that is stranded, uncertain of how to take the first step toward moving on. The spirits that a shaman is most commonly called upon by the living to Walk to the Other side are those that are either projecting a strong sense of pain and sadness, or who are bothersome to the living.

Although there are a number of explanations for the poltergeist phenomenon, there are instances where the experience is brought on by the presence of one or more disembodied spirits that have attached themselves to a specific person or area. Most of the time, these spirits are looking for attention.

They crave recognition from the living, in any way they can get it. They act much like an ignored child does when she misbehaves to get some attention from her parents. There are others, though, who are so filled with anger and fear that they become bullies, lashing out at others in a vain attempt to make themselves feel better. They often feel weak and helpless to control their situations. As a result, they do whatever it takes to regain a semblance of strength.

Shamans help those who do not accept that they are physically dead face the truth. This is often the case with those who have died suddenly and unexpectedly. Frequently all it takes is some focused attention and strong discussion to convince these beings that their bodies are gone. Sometimes, stronger measures are required. It may become necessary to show the spirit his grave or physical body. A little show-and-tell, demonstrating how he is no longer able interact effectively with this reality while now having the ability to move about at will within this reality and Others, can go a long way to bringing the point home.

Once the reality of physical death has been accepted, each of these spirits is guided, with compassion, through whatever additional bonds may be preventing their entrance into the next world. The spirit guides of these individuals are always called upon for assistance and it is made clear to the spirit that these beings have always been ready to help. They were just unable to break through the walls erected by pain and fear.

Those spirits who exude sadness are usually the easiest to guide through to the next world. These beings often recognize that their bodies have died. Even if they have not completely integrated the full meaning of this, they are generally accepting of death as an explanation why their loved ones no longer seem to be aware of them.

In cases of sudden and traumatic death, the bonds tying them to this plane may be difficult to release and the trauma may have resulted in fragmentation of the spirit. We handle these issues just as we would with any departed spirit, according to the methods outlined throughout this book. However, when many years have passed since the death, departed spirits tend to welcome the surcease of the light and the Afterworld.

The bothersome spirit can be a challenge to handle. It can be difficult, at face value, to determine the actual cause of certain physical or emotional manifestations.

There are plenty of people in this reality who assume that the cause is a disincarnate spirit, when there are very different issues at work. Since this is not something I recommend that anyone attempt to take on without significant training and experience, I will not go into this situation in depth. If you know of a shaman or psychic who has experience with this type of situation, I strongly recommend that you ask him or her to handle the situation.

Suffice it to say that for the inexperienced shaman, the best course of action is to call upon your spirit guides for protection and guidance, while offering no resistance to the annoying spirit. This does not mean we sit back and accept abuse. What this means is that when we react with strong emotions, particularly negative emotions, we feed the spirit, providing it with even more energy to continue plaguing us. If we are unable to gain control over our emotions, we become a constant source of energy. Once the spirit no longer has an energy supply, they will move on.

I have found that the need for a deathwalk varies according to the individual, as does the timing. Some people are ready to go as soon as the body dies. They immediately connect with spirit guides and need no assistance from a shaman. Others do need assistance but have no need to linger in our reality before asking for guidance. These spirits will go in search of assistance as soon as they are able. Then there are those who have unfinished business that they need to tie up before they can move on. This unfinished business may be anything from just needing to say goodbye to healing troubled relationships. It can be difficult to tell when the deathwalk is needed without a considerable amount of experience.

When an individual is in real need of assistance, they will often show up in dreams. Unfortunately, most modern people discount dreams as unreal and, in effect turn their backs on loved ones who need them. While it is important to be watchful of emotional and psychological issues that may indicate a need for some form of therapy, some of the signs that are used to judge whether the grieving are mentally stable are frequently misunderstood communications from beyond the Veil.

Dreams are only one of the ways in which the departed may attempt to contact us. Dreaming is usually the easiest way for interdimensional beings to reach us, because it allows them to bypass our rational minds. Our rational minds are notorious for analyzing away anything in physical reality that does not fit with accepted belief systems. Because dreams are so commonly filtered out of everyday awareness, it can become necessary for the departed to find other means to contact us.

Many people have reported hearing a departed loved one's voice when there was no one physically present. Some people believe that they see a departed friend out of the corner of an eye, only to find upon rational investigation that it was just a shadow, or their imagination. In addition, many spouses who have lost a mate experience a feeling of arms around them or kisses and comfort as they retire for the night. I have been very aware of the presence of a friend's departed husband around her, years after his physical body died. He pops in every now and then to be sure she is all right and to let her know he still loves her.

More often than not, these experiences are chalked up to grief or habit. We are told that we expect to see this person because we are used to seeing her, so our minds conjure up her image out of habit. Grief is the number one excuse to blame these hallucinations on. We hear hours of psycho-babble regarding the projection of our grief onto the external world producing momentary delusions. While this is certainly a possibility in some situations, the mechanistic belief structure of our society has eliminated any possibility of communications from Other worlds by labeling them delusions and indoctrinating an automatic repression of them.

However, it has been the experience of countless shamans and psychics that Otherworldly encounters are real. Frequently, these experiences are our perceptions of loved ones who have managed to reach us from beyond the Veil. For a deathwalker, these experiences will take on new significance when it becomes obvious that a spirit is not merely popping in to say "hello," but is in serious need of assistance.

My grandfather refused assistance immediately after his death. He was not ready to completely move on and wanted to stick around for a while. He indicated that he was fine but had things to do first. He wanted to say some goodbyes and visit the State Park that he helped to reforest and had cared for during his thirty-two years as a ranger. He also had a job or two to do. He shepherded two other family members beyond the Veil within a week of his death.

Two days after his death, my grandfather went to his sister, who passed peacefully in her sleep that night. Both her son and grandson were aware of my grandfather's presence in her room that night, and they were comforted by the fact that he was with her when she passed over. A few days later at my great-aunt's memorial, my mother found her father and aunt outside watching all the goings-on through a window. They appeared to be enjoying themselves immensely and were not in need of anything from my mother. Having no further contact from either of them, I put it out of my mind.

About one month later, my grandfather appeared to me in a dream, after having been seen several times by my parents. It was one of those dreams that are obviously not mere dreams. I was fully lucid and aware of our presence in an alternate reality. As often happens among my family, my trance state deepened to the point that my physical body was paralyzed.

In this dream, my husband was driving us past the cemetery where my grandparents are buried, when I saw a man standing by the side of the road. The man looked just like my grandfather had many years ago and he was dressed in the same state park uniform that my grandfather had worn. This man appeared to be asleep or even dead, as he stood absolutely still and silent.

When I realized that this was my grandfather, he suddenly became animated. It was as though my awareness of him had given him the energy and motivation to move about. I had the distinct feeling that he had just given up after having been unable to effectively reach my parents. His clothes turned blue and he was very excited to see me. He ran after the car waving at us, but I was unable to tell my husband to stop the car. I began to hyperventilate and my husband shook me back into ordinary reality.

As I re-emerged into everyday awareness, it became clear that this dream was a desperate cry for help. I knew with certainty that my grandfather had taken too much time or had in some way gotten himself stuck between worlds. I determined to take care of it the very next evening.

I was acutely aware of the presence of my grandfather as I prepared to assist him on his way the following night. His pressing need for assistance was physically tangible as soon as he arrived. I let my husband know where I was off to and shut the door to our altar room. I easily entered the journey without drumming. Since I had been working with one specific Monroe Institute Hemi-Sync tape for several weeks, I chose to use this tape instead of drumming to facilitate my trance state.

As I greeted my grandfather, I noticed that we stood at the base of a long spiral flight of stairs. He looked dull and listless, but I did not feel this was due to spirit fragmentation so we continued. He again asked for my help and we began to climb the stairs. He had a number of attachments that were binding him to this world. They appeared to me like cords tied around his waist, weighing him down. Some were small and fell easily away. Each time a cord released, we moved up a step.

As we neared the top of the stairs, he became brighter and less focused in physical form. His eyes, which had always been blue, were the only recognizable part remaining to him and they were an astonishingly brilliant blue. I told him that the remaining ties were his to release on his own. He released all but one. This one was a thick, heavy rope tying him to the Earth plane. He needed my assistance in struggling out of this tie. Once he was free of this final bond, he was amazingly light and happy. He appeared to me to be an amorphous mass of pure white energy, with bright blue eyes. He thanked me and told me to let everyone know he loved us.

When we finally reached the top step, his spirit guides met him there, along with many of his loved ones. His sister who passed over two days after him was there to greet him as well. They all welcomed him and took him into their midst. Then they entered a kind of waiting room, where they shed their forms and personalities, as we would shed an overcoat.

They passed through two huge doors and entered what appeared to be a star. I watched as they all merged with the star, losing individual identities and becoming the star itself. The huge double doors shut behind them. I stood alone at the top of the stairs, feeling almost jealous. I said one last prayer for them all and returned to this reality.

138

This deathwalk illustrates not only how the recently departed are often met by their spirit guides in preparation for their jump to a new reality, but also how one might be tempted to try to follow the departed into such a beautiful place. I certainly felt a little jealous of their freedom and effortless merging with each other and that star. It is for this reason that a period of soul-searching is strongly recommended before entering into the psychopompic journey. Individuals who choose to remain outside of our reality before their time has come will often find themselves stuck between worlds, if they are able to avoid being pulled back into their physical bodies. This is particularly true if the physical body is permitted to die.

In any event, this is a good example of how our guides will spontaneously meet us when we are ready. Often, our denial, fear, and attachments to this world can block their ability to connect with us right after death. In these cases, a shaman may need to assist the release of emotions and denial. As is later described in my experience with a cousin, a deathwalker may only need to call the spirit guides for the departed and then leave the situation in the capable hands of these guides.

I have also found that many families have a clan guardian who will sometimes show up to assist the death transition. In totemistic societies, it was a common belief that each family or clan had one specific animal spirit guardian that was inherited through one or both parents. It has become very obvious that our son has inherited some of the major spirit guides and guardians that walk with my husband and me.

Among some Saami, it was believed that this clan spirit was handed down from parents to their children. Many Native American clan guardians are indicated as part of the family or clan society name. It was often taboo for members of these groups to kill or eat any of the guardian species.

This belief is interesting in light of the fact that many of us have experienced a continuation of major spirit guides throughout several lifetimes. I have said that it is also a Saami belief that we tend to reincarnate along family lines. This is one explanation for the common spirit guide. It would appear that the clan guardian becomes not only the guide and guardian for the physical clan, but also becomes a recurring guide for the individual spirit that is reborn to the same family.

These clan spirits appear to be present more often during a time of illness preceding death. For example, in late 1996, I worked with a woman who came to me for assistance in handling the transition of her terminally ill mother. Through the process of discussions and shamanic journeys, we discovered that a family guardian spirit had been with her mother since the onset of her illness.

139

This guardian spirit had been introduced to the woman who came to me, when she was a child, although initially she had no conscious memory of this. When she was about eight years old, her grandmother had taken her into the garden at twilight. Her grandmother had taken her out to the garden to visit the nature spirits many times, but this evening was different. Her grandmother was very serious as she stood over her and called to the spirit. She was presented to this spirit as a child of the clan. Her grandmother considered this spirit to be a family guardian.

While the clan guardian was in constant attendance during her mother's illness, her personal spirit guides replaced this spirit when she finally left her body for the last time. It did not appear that the clan spirit called her personal guides, nor did it merge with or become these personal guides upon her physical death. I felt that once this woman's personal guides were in attendance, the clan spirit was then able to release the woman from her body.

Once this was accomplished and her spirit was safely within the care of her personal guides, the clan spirit relinquished its hold on her and returned its focus to the physical family. In this case, the clan guardian was with her, protecting her spirit until her personal spirit guides were able to take over her care. It is my belief that the clan guardian accepts responsibility for the physical clan, up to the point of transformation out of the physical realm.

Many physicists describe the quantum universe as consisting of an infinite number of conscious, although nonthinking, entities. In a way, it is these entities which create and run the universe. Of course, most of these entities are photons which, during quantum mechanical experiments, appear to instantly know what other photons are doing, even at incredible distances.

Taken to one logical conclusion, this could indicate the possible eventual scientific proof of the existence of these spirit guides. Although to be honest, no one who has direct experience of our spirit guides needs any scientific proof. We know they exist and work with us, even when we are not consciously aware of them.

As my experience with my grandfather clearly illustrates, we cannot deny that there are disincarnate spirits whose attachments to this world are so strong that they are held here, unable to move on to their next realities. These spirits seem to be so focused on their attachments to this world that they block any attempts by their spirit guides to reach them. Very often, they do not even recognize the presence of guidance when it is there.

It will often take a shaman, or gifted psychic, to reach these individuals, since they are so chained to our realm. They frequently refuse to believe that they are dead, and are traumatized by the fact that loved ones do not acknowledge them. The deathwalker is necessary to convince these spirits that their physical bodies are dead and assist them in moving forward to the next world.

Sometimes, deathwalkers need to have a talk with these spirits and convince them we are to be trusted. Occasionally, we will take them to see their loved ones who grieve for them. As I said earlier, it is sometimes necessary to show the spirit their dead physical body. While this is often extreme, it makes it very easy to prove they are indeed, dead. Once they have accepted this, the deathwalker does what is necessary to connect them with spirit guides and lead these souls into the next world.

Unknown to most people, there are deathwalkers who recognize the presence of large numbers of Earthbound dead in urban areas and in any area where a mass tragedy has occurred. I have heard stories of deathwalks in Nazi concentration camp areas, airplane crash sites, and in various locations where Native Americans were slaughtered by the United States military. Native peoples are very aware of this situation and are taking measures to free their ancestors from traumatic attachments.

The following are accounts of two very different deathwalks. Not only do they show the differing ways in which modern deathwalkers work and experience the journey, but they also indicate just how common this phenomenon is. These are by no means two isolated incidents. Modern shamans are aware of those in need on all levels of existence, and are working to effect healing for all concerned.

The first account is related by my good friend, Wolf Carnahan. It is a beautiful example of the role of the shaman and of the personal experience of the deathwalk. It begins with Wolf's description of how he knew the deathwalk was needed.

My daughter-in-law, Maria, and I were returning to her house after a day of healing work in Ashland and Medford, Oregon. We were driving by Table Rock, a prominent mesa that rises out of the earth near Medford, when a voice within me just said, "Come." Knowing I had heard a spirit-voice, I determined to go the next day.

The next morning before sunrise, Maria, Sean (my son), and I were climbing the rain-laden trail to the summit of Table Rock. There was a little stream of water running in the trail that wet our feet, and the pre-dawn morning was still and crisp. At the change of foliage where oak became madrone, I felt an energy shift, as if there were people watching us. Putting a piece of sage in my mouth, I continued to the top, where Sean separated from us and went to do his own work, leaving us to do ours.

Maria and I lost no time in making a stone circle, whereupon I smudged it and offered tobacco and prayers. After smudging ourselves, we entered the circle and I began calling in the spirits of the four directions. At that moment, time stood still. We stepped out of time and space into a different dimension where the Sun seemed to rise in the south, West became East and North wasn't anywhere specific. I found that I didn't have to call the spirits. They were already there; after all, they had called me.

The spirits of the directions were immediately joined by about three hundred Native American spirits who gathered around the circle and just stared solemnly at us, not saying a word. There were mothers with children, and women and men who seemed no older than about fifty. They didn't say anything to us, and we received no guidance from the spirits or from anywhere else, so we closed the circle and sat down to discuss the matter.

Soon, Sean returned and after listening to our story, he asked us to follow him across the top of the mesa. As we walked, we passed by a mound of earth that seemed out of place on that rocky top and as I approached it, I felt a deep sorrow coming from it. Stepping on it gently, I knelt down on it and got an incredible rush of pain and grief, and images of people being slaughtered and throwing themselves off the top of the rock to their deaths. I asked Sean if there had been a massacre here and he replied that he wasn't sure, but that he thought there was. I vowed to find out.

I returned to Eugene a few days later and told the story to a Karuk Elder who is the Native American Student Union counselor at Lane Community College. He put me in touch with a Rogue River Native in charge of archeological sites in Oregon. After telling him the story, he said he would get in touch with the appropriate people.

After doing some research and preparatory work, Wolf returned to Table Rock as part of the deathwalking group on March 1, 1997. His presence was requested by the Native deathwalker, the Spiritkeeper.

The Spiritkeeper contacted me Tuesday night. She will be coming to Table Rock to take care of matters and desires my help. The ceremony will last two days, from dawn until dusk. I will be there.

There were five of us: a Wintu medicine woman, a man from the Rogue Indian Council, Maria, Sean, and I. We met Friday night to connect with each other in the spirit world; to get accustomed to being together there. We only spent a short time there, but it was enough to find that we flowed together like water in a stream.

Saturday, we awoke in an altered state. Few words were spoken as the five of us packed wood, food, water, and sacred necessities into our packs for the journey. We decided the night before, that Saturday would be a "prep" day and we would do the major work on Sunday. So, after finding the place where we were to work, we settled in for a little "light" journey work. *Ha!* As soon as we entered the deep place, a spirit approached, a tall woman dressed in fringed white leather.

She was a messenger sent by the others to see if we were the ones and to prepare the way for the rest. She became confused by our brightness and wanted to enter Maria's body. Fortunately she wasn't real insistent and we were able to point her to the gateway. She was gone instantly.

After we came out of the deep, we talked for a while, shared food and water around the fire, left a plate of food for the spirits, and went home for the night. We arrived well after dark, too tired to cook, and not caring anyway.

When Sunday arrived, we again awoke in an altered state, deeper than before. Quietly and quickly, we packed what needed to be packed, grabbed our drums, and were off. From two miles away, I could sense the spirits' anticipation as they waited for our arrival. We started drumming just a short way up the trail, going deeper (into trance) as we walked. Spirits came to follow us from all around—old ones, young ones, children, and some that came to heckle us and try to stop what we were doing. The hecklers sang songs to us—old songs of the People that pulled at our emotions. They burned roots that the old ones used to confuse our senses. They danced. We walked. We drummed.

More and more came as we crossed the flat top of Table Rock. They seemed to come from everywhere, and from out of the ground. The heckler succeeded in getting into Maria for a moment, before we drove him out, but he would not give up. We made our circle and made offerings of tobacco and crushed angelica. But when we tried to light it to smudge the circle, it wouldn't light. The matches would burn all the way down without success. Finally, Sean called the Fire spirit, lit the fire, and put the angelica directly in it. It still would not burn. The 'Nay-Sayer,' as Albert named him, was exerting his force as much as he could to prevent the root from burning. After some prayers, it finally ignited and we were able to complete the circle. We all either felt or saw the spirit leave.

After blessing and banishing the circle, we cleansed ourselves and went into the depths. The wind picked up and swirled around us, first one way and then another when Albert and I started calling the spirits into the circle with our drums. With great force they came—many, many, many and from all sides.

They rushed into the circle and into the waiting open door the way a moth rushes a candle. Nothing was going to stop them. The door was right above the fire, their way Home. As they went, they turned transparent and thin, like paper. They flew up into the door and were gone.

The volcanic rock that the fire was built upon began exploding as the fire and stone accepted the energy of what was going on. After a long time, the rock gave one great explosion, scattering the firewood into a shape that looked like a lightning bolt and the wind stopped.

We took a short break then, connecting with each other in this world, discussing what we had seen and felt. We rebuilt the fire, smudged ourselves again, and went back down. The winds came again, swirling as before but different. It was more peaceful and there seemed to be a quiet joy instead of a desperate need.

The spirits came from all around again, more than before and for a longer time. The doorway blazed brightly. A light on the other side, almost blinding, shone through as if to call the lost children home.

Finally, there came a young mother and her daughter, who stopped in the door and looked at it, then at me, then back again. I could sense the fear in her: fear that she and her daughter would be separated. Time and time again, I pointed her to the door and told her that it was all right for her to go. I even moved the door directly in front of her, and she still would not go. I finally called the Creator to help, I could do no more.

The doorway opened wider and the light that was on the other side came to where we were, enveloping us in a light and love so pure that no human words begin to come close. It enveloped her and her daughter. She turned toward it went into it. As she started to diffuse, she turned around and looked at me—and was gone. The doorway closed. The wind stopped. We were done.

We cried for a long time. Some of us from grief, some from the recognition of the awesomeness of the love that was in the light—the power and beauty of that pure love in which we knew that there was nothing ever for it to forgive. It was unconditional.

The work is not done, it never is. What we did on Table Rock was felt by many. There are other Table Rocks and other kinds of journeys to be taken—other kinds of work to be done. I know too, that my life has been changed forever.

Wolf is absolutely correct in his poignant summation of this experience. Not only is the work never done, but each working forever affects those involved. Once the jump to deathwalker is made, we are never the same. We are empowered, expanded, and very humbled, all at the same time.

In the summer of 1997, I performed a deathwalk in an urban building that had seen a fair amount of crime, including violent crime, several years before. Two psychically sensitive girls came to me, with some of their friends, for help when these girls began having nightmares and hearing things soon after moving into the building.

After investigating to be sure this was not the result of active young minds that had seen too many movies, I determined that there was a real issue here that needed to be resolved. This deathwalk was interesting to me because I ended up being the catalyst, rather than the one actually leading the dead.

I informed my husband what I planned to do and where I would be. Using sagebrush, cedar, angelica, and sweetgrass, I smudged myself as well as the area I would be working in. I smudged my drum and purified the area with the sound of the drum. Then, I drummed in the Spirits of the six directions for guidance and protection. The energy of the area crackled and intensified as they arrived. They filled the entire area with their energy, bringing me the necessary protection and benefits of their individual energies.

Next, I called upon my personal spirit guides, the Great Spirit, and all the nature spirits who help me and generally accompany me everywhere. Again, they filled the area around me with their palpable energies. They all waited as I made offerings of angelica and corn. I began to drum, quickly at first, then more slowly as my trance state deepened. I lay down as usual so as not to drop the drum (or my body) when I enter a truly deep trance.

I set out for the Lowerworld, but had difficulty getting there. The tunnels were tight and I often plateaued out onto flat surfaces. While this was unusual, I plugged away at it until I reached the usual lake at the bottom of my tunnel. Rather than landing on the bank, I kept right on going. I saw a hole in the bottom of the lake and thought perhaps this was a *saivo* lake, so I decided to follow this hole down deeper.[40] I ended up going nowhere except stuck in the mud.

I climbed out of the lake and was met by a tribe of small dark men. They appeared to be made of this mud. Realizing that I was covered with mud and I looked like a large version of them, I danced with them for a short time before deciding to move on. I told them this was not where I needed to be right now and was swiftly sent (shot through a spear actually) to an all-white, rather sterile Upperworld.

A person in a white suit met me and shook my hand. I was unable to determine any gender in this being. I asked if this was where I needed to be to clear this building. The person said "yes" and led me to a dark, wooden door with a small window covered by bars. This was the door that opened onto the tunnel from that building to the next realm. The person turned a switch and we watched through the window as spirits, including a dog, were sucked up from the building. It was like a huge vacuum cleaner.

I could see above us where most of these people entered a park-like place. Most of them emerged onto a beautiful green lawn surrounded by big oak and maple trees. There was a clear lake in the distance and the sun glinted off the still waters. They were each met by a guide or loved one and moved on quickly from there. I do not know what happened to the dog.

A huge white-gold Angel took a place at the door in front of us. He appeared to be some type of guard. I asked the being in the white suit if this was all I needed to do and was told that this was not my Walk to do. I was then escorted to a room where I met and spoke with the spirit guardians of the children who had come to me for help.

I asked their help in protecting these children and making them feel safe once again. I watched through the eyes of each individual guardian as we cleared the bedrooms and apartments of each child. I felt the flow of white and golden light as it passed through us into the homes of these children. In the home of the two boys who lived across the street from the building that had been cleansed, extra care was taken in the room of their brother who had brain damage.

On my way back to the entrance of this world, we passed the door to the Gateway. Apparently, there was a time limit on the switch for this Gateway. I was told that, if it was left on too long, it could encourage any living beings that wanted to leave their bodies before their correct time. There was one angry young man holding onto the gate as it shut. I had the impression that he was the one following my young friends around. The Angel turned the switch back on just long enough for this man to pass through and then he shut it all down. I was escorted to the entrance where I was thanked for my part in the process.

These children were greatly comforted by the fact that something had been done to take care of them. They were particularly grateful to learn of their spirit guardians, one of whom turned out to be a boy's grandfather who had passed over a few years earlier. Interestingly, the brother with brain damage, in whose room extra care had been taken, has not experienced his usual nightmares and pains at night since the deathwalk took place.

This worked out extremely well. These children gained the best possible effects from this experience and I was honored to be able to assist them. However, I would give one word of caution whenever working with children: make absolutely certain that their parents are aware of what is going on and have given their approval for their children to be exposed to this. I strongly recommend that the parents be present for any teachings, discussions, or workings with their minor children.

This is not only to protect you from legal action by disapproving parents, but it is out of respect for their rights and responsibilities as parents. Just as we would not want our children exposed to, or indoctrinated with, any beliefs that we might consider dangerous or offensive, it is our responsibility to honor that same right for other parents. We may feel our beliefs are not dangerous, and may even be preferable to some. However, it is not our place to decide for other people or other parents' children. I encourage children whose parents are against this type of learning to explore the beliefs of their families first. There was a reason they chose to incarnate among this particular family. If they still feel drawn to a different path when they are adults, then it is their decision to go down that path.

There is another significant reason we are very careful when working with children: they are much more open and vulnerable to a variety of energies than most adults. The chakra and other energy systems are not yet fully developed in children. In my opinion, it is extremely irresponsible and unethical to expose children (or anyone for that matter) to potentially damaging energies before they are sufficiently prepared to handle them. I strongly suggest developing a structured training process, even for children within your own family, or for those whose parents want them to learn whatever you can teach them.

I have been asked to what World do we go after physical death? What happens after the deathwalk, when the departed has finally made it past the Veil? The actual location of the Lands of the Dead varies according to cultural beliefs. The Saami believe the dead return to an underworld Jabmeaimo where they receive a new body and continue a type of parallel life. In the Celtic worldview, Annwn is where the spirits of the dead reside while they await rebirth.[41] The Hopi people of the southwestern United States believe that the soul, or breath body, returns to the Underworld via the sipapu (hole) through which the Hopi believe their ancestors first came through to the earth's surface. Still others believe in an Upperworld resting place; and some cultures and religions believe in several different locations for the Lands of the Dead.

Disincarnate beings tend to retain their personal and cultural beliefs through the death transition for a period of time after death. As in physical life, these beliefs continue to affect their experience of reality. Earlier, I discussed the fact that our experience of spirit guides is our own limited interpretation of the totality of these interdimensional beings. This type of perception continues for a time after the death of the physical body. As a result, departed spirits often experience the next world based on their prior beliefs regarding an Afterlife. Therefore, the road to, and the location of, the individual Lands of the Dead can be very subjective.

It is for this reason that the modern deathwalker does not generally enter the psychopompic journey with any preconceived notions, particularly when assisting those not raised in a traditional shamanic culture. To bring in one's own beliefs or expectations of what will, or should, occur during any deathwalk is to potentially interfere with the easy passage of the soul in transition. Again, this is working from within the identity of the ego and is counterproductive to true shamanic work.

The following experience should give you a good example of the need to put aside your own beliefs in order to better assist the departed. A member of my extended family showed up at "Grand Central Station" about thirty minutes before we received the confirming telephone call. We all recognized that someone non-corporeal was there as we sat at my parents' dining room table. My mother said her usual, "Someone ought to take care of this," looking pointedly at me. I smiled, rolled my eyes, and went into another room where I entered shamanic states of consciousness without drumming or any other external facilitation.

This "guest" was a cousin we knew very well. She had died very suddenly and unexpectedly of a heart attack after leaving her doctor's office for a routine check-up. She could not understand what had happened or how she got to my parents' house.

I spent some time calming her down and explaining the situation. I put my arm around her and created a feeling of comfort and peace within my energy field. Often when interacting on a purely energetic level with another being, your energy field can have a significant impact on hers, particularly if she is emotionally uncontrolled or in unfamiliar surroundings, as is often the case immediately after physical death. This is particularly true in situations of sudden or violent death.

Our cousin had difficulty believing she was dead, since she had just been with her daughter at her doctor's office and could remember nothing else before her arrival at my parents' house. Fortunately she trusted me, so convincing her was rather simple. Her's was the third family death in one week and she was well aware of our family's tendency toward leaving in groups. There is rarely just one death in our family.

Once she was calm and accepting of the fact that her body was dead, I called on her spirit guides. A man and woman, dressed in Victorian-era clothing, appeared and immediately began to comfort her. Our cousin seemed to innately trust these beings, although she had no conscious recognition of them at all. Having not yet encountered angelic beings myself at that time, I was quite surprised to see the most incredible white wings unfold from their backs as they flew our cousin off into a bright light.

In this situation, our cousin was devoutly Christian and expected to have angels guide her into the light of Heaven when she died. That is exactly what she experienced. It was vital that I allowed this belief system to flow through me, without judgment, in order to assist this woman in an easy transition.

Had I attempted to force my own beliefs regarding guides or an Afterlife, I could have prevented her contact with her own spirit guides. In trying to create the reality

I would expect to follow this life for me, I might also have frightened her to the point that she could remain stuck here in this world looking for some measure of comfort and familiarity. The experience of a foreign Afterlife can threaten one's total belief systems. This shatters trust and faith, often fragmenting the soul, and creates or intensifies fear.

Many deathwalkers have reported the existence of an initial stage immediately following physical death. This appears to be some sort of intermediate stopping place where the newly departed spirit can rest, adjust to their newfound status, and meet with spirit guides before moving on to the next world. These departed spirits usually experience this place as a familiar and comfortable spot where they feel safe and calm.

148

Robert Monroe experienced a waiting area that he termed The Park. He believed this was an "artificial synthesis created by human minds, a way station designed to ease the trauma and shock of transition out of physical reality."[42] He also experienced that the departed would rest here and were often met by personal spirit guides.

Several modern deathwalkers have encountered this waiting area as a type of healing place for those who have died violently or after a difficult and prolonged death process. This appears to be a safe space where the departed seem to be mainly sleeping and only marginally aware of their situation. Some deathwalkers have seen this as a healing cocoon of light, while others have experienced a healing garden where the departed is held in loving arms by an ancestor or spirit guide. Again, it would appear that the experience of this place depends upon the individual and what is most healing or comfortable to him.

Mr. Monroe goes on to write that The Park manifests as various earth environments in order to be acceptable to everyone. In other words, each departed person experienced this "way station" according to his own beliefs and expectations, in a way that would be easiest for his consciousness to handle.

For example, a person from Switzerland may experience it as a spectacular mountain forest, while someone from the American Great Plains region may enter an expansive meadow. Similarly, Mr. Monroe found individuals that strongly identified with their occupations in the life that just ended, could experience The Park accordingly. He found that several doctors ended up in office or hospital settings, both at The Park and in the Belief System Territories, which are described later on in this chapter.

I have encountered The Park, as well. As I described in the mass urban deathwalk I performed, it often appears as a verdant green park with trees and benches; sometimes there is even a clear blue pond present. I generally find the newly departed waiting on a bench or strolling through the lawns. They are infrequently aware of other disincarnate spirits present, although when their personal spirit guides approach them, they often greet as old friends. This area does vary according to the departed individual, and I have found it to reflect the individual idea of paradise.

However, it has not been my experience that everyone passes through this waiting area, unless we can consider the energy field of the deathwalker a type of transfer point. This is certainly a possibility, in that the deathwalker functions as a safe haven and a connection to spirit guides for those who are unable to make this jump on their own. I do find that those who possess no strong attachments to any particular individual or belief system will quickly release all ties to physical reality and return to what I call the Great Spirit or Source.

This return to God or the Great Spirit has been referred to as becoming one with the universe and with the Source of All Life. Harry Palmer, author of the Avatar materials, describes Source as "awareness without definition."[43] Distinguished physicist John Wheeler calls it the "life-giving factor (that) lies at the center of the whole machinery and design of the world."[44] In returning to this Source, we merge with the energy of the multiverse, essentially becoming the Web of Life.

Those with extremely strong belief systems will sometimes pass immediately to what Mr. Monroe termed the Belief System Territories.[45] These Belief System Territories are realms adjacent to the Earth realm, or shamanic Middleworld. They manifest as particular beliefs about what happens after death. Some individuals go to a Christian Heaven (or Hell). Others go to a place just like Earth where inhabitants do not believe in an Afterlife and nothing intangible is real. There are as many territories as there are beliefs about an Afterlife.

If someone has formed a strong belief during this lifetime, they will follow that belief to the corresponding territory where there are others of the same belief waiting to help them. There are individuals at the entry point of most of these territories, standing ready to assist the acceptance and integration of the newly departed spirit. These greeters pave the way, assuring each newcomer that all is well and that they are in the correct place.

Individuals just disappear from these territories, or worlds, when they no longer need the associated beliefs. After a time, the spirit is able to release these beliefs and feels the pull to search for more. Once that point is reached, they no longer belong in these worlds, and they move on to other realms. The spirits remaining in these belief worlds have varying opinions as to what happens to those who have disappeared. In some worlds, they believe that something awful has befallen those who disappeared. In other worlds, it is believed that they have been chosen and taken by the resident deity. And in still other worlds, they do not even recognize the disappearance.

The life review stage is generally experienced after leaving a belief world and before deciding upon a new incarnation. This commonly takes place at the still-point, what I describe in chapter eight as the Center of The Wheel of Life. I have experienced this place as an open-air type of learning campus. This is where we meet with spirit guides, receive new spirit guides, and often attend various "classes." We do visit this place during physical life, usually during dreams or intense shamanic journeys.

During the life review stage, the departed will meet with personal spirit guides alone, either out-of-doors or in one the many open-air buildings. The preceding incarnation will be examined and compared to the growth and lessons that were originally intended for that life. Once that is complete, the next step is discussed. Sometimes, a period of time at the Center is agreed to be the most beneficial step for a particular being. If another incarnation is decided upon, the culture, birthdate, family, gender, and all other factors involved in that life are discussed to provide that spirit with the best set of circumstances to attain the desired level of soul growth and equilibrium with other beings.

Many people, including Robert Monroe and my mother, who is one of the greatest natural shamans I know, have experienced the presence of the departed in rings surrounding our world.[46] These rings appear to be holographic and are psychically similar to the rings of Saturn. They completely surround our world on many energy planes. The Belief System Territories occupy some of these rings. Other rings are home to various Other worlds, some of which are home to beings of similar soul growth who have chosen not to reincarnate yet. Other rings are mainly made up of emotional energy or mental psychic noise. This is interesting in that the Celtic worldview, particularly that of the druids, sees life and creation as a series of concentric circles as well.

According to the Welsh druidic tradition, the Circles of Creation begin in the Cauldron of Annwn.[47] Life begins here and advances outward through the Circles of Abred. Within these circles, we are learning and growing toward Gwynvyd, the White Life. A soul is believed to be beyond the cycle of rebirth once they attain Gwynvyd. Beyond this, exists Ceugant, which corresponds with what I call the Great Spirit, or Source.

People are often surprised to discover that modern physics is beginning to allow for the possibility of a multiverse of many interrelated worlds, as opposed to a single universe. As physicists gain experiential evidence that reality is not as we perceive it, several interesting new theories are emerging. According to the Many Worlds

Interpretation of Quantum Mechanics, there are an unlimited number of realities existing independently of each other.

These theories certainly have the potential to explain the existence of countless shamanic Other worlds. Some of these worlds are very similar to our own reality. Some of the cultural Lands of the Dead, in particular, are nearly identical to ours. Then there are others that are so different from our physical reality that our rational minds cannot possibly interpret them for communication within this reality. To get any deeper into the implications and possibilities of these theories would take another book, and someone considerably more knowledgeable about physics than I am. However, it does appear that science is learning to explain our shamanic experiences in physical and mathematical terms.

As shamans, the deathwalker's role extends beyond the Otherworldly journeys taken to guide and communicate with the departed. Many people fail to appreciate that the shaman's role is as an integral member of the community. The ways in which they serve the community are far-reaching and do not end when all the "shamanic stuff" is over. To the shaman, life on all levels is "shamanic stuff" and the path of shamanism involves every aspect of life. As I discuss throughout this book, shamans are called to work with the dying in their roles as healers of body, mind, and spirit. They are also called upon to aid the living through the grieving process and to facilitate the deathwalk through encouraging the release of attachments between the departed and loved ones.

Whether we hold a traditional or an eclectic worldview, none of us dies alone. That old saying about coming in alone and leaving alone just does not stand up to the evidence. Although we may block our recognition of them, we all have spirit guides. They often walk with us unseen, but are always there when we need them, particularly when this incarnation ends.

There are also a surprising number of modern shamans who answer the call to assist any in need. While this assistance is frequently offered in subtle and non-threatening ways, shamans serve their communities to the best of their abilities. They are your neighbors, your grocery clerks, and your nurses. True shamans work without interfering with personal or cultural belief systems, but with an expanded focus of the best interests of the individual and the society.

When this life is finished, we do not merely cease to exist. Loved ones, guides, and others who share our beliefs greet us on the Other side. We are taken lovingly to familiar and expected places. And when we no longer need those beliefs, we merge with the loving energy of the multiverse, becoming One with All That Is.

Endnotes

40 *Saivo* is a Saami term for spirit allies and the world of spirit. A saivo lake is believed to be two lakes on top of each other separated by a hole; or a lake with two bottoms.

41 Conway, *By Oak, Ash, & Thorn*, p. 87.

42 Monroe, *Ultimate Journey*, p. 249.

43 Palmer, *Living Deliberately*, p. 105.

44 Ross, *Design and the Anthropic Principle*, Wheeler quote. Original reference: Wheeler, John A. "Foreword," in *The Anthropic Cosmological Principle* by John D. Barrow and Frank J. Tipler. (Oxford, UK: Clarendon Press, 1986), p. vii.

45 Monroe, *Ultimate Journey*, p. 272.

46 Monroe, *Far Journeys*, pp. 238–246.

47 Per Philip Carr-Gomm, Chief of the Order of Bards, Ovates, and Druids.

Chapter 7

THE GRIEVING

The role the shaman fills with those remaining in physical life after a loved one passes over is an interesting one, particularly in that the shaman often grieves for this person too. The shaman is not only called upon to offer healing and guidance for others, but must be able to heal herself in the process. While this can be a period of tremendous growth for all involved, a shaman must maintain a constant awareness of her own Self. If her feelings become repressed or begin to dictate her actions, the best thing she can do for everyone is to step back and deal with it before attempting to help anyone else.

When I was a teenager, I worked several summers as a lifeguard. During our training, we were instructed not to enter into any situation for which we were unprepared and might endanger our own lives. True heroes are those who assess the situation first, then act accordingly. To jump into a dangerous situation for which we had no training and were unsure of our abilities would be foolish. To react and allow our emotions to take control, rather than acting with wisdom, would most likely get everyone killed, including us. Although most of us pushed the envelope of personal safety at least once, this is sound advice even from a shamanic point of view.

153

"The blind leading the blind" is not generally a productive situation. We can be blinded by personal emotional feelings, making us more of a hindrance than a help to other people. Refusing to experience and eliminate our own *stuff*, while attempting to heal others will only succeed in drowning us all in an emotional quagmire. We cannot be of valuable service until we are functioning with a clear mind and spirit. The ability to recognize our own needs and to take steps to heal ourselves first should be acknowledged as the strength it is.

154

In our pre-dominantly Judeo-Christian culture, we glorify those individuals that are totally selfless while deriding people who show signs of selfishness. Depending on the situation and the issues of those involved, one can be labeled as selfish for merely recognizing the need to take care of the Self. While truly selfless service is honorable, it is rare. People can donate time and money to selfless pursuits for any number of reasons, many of them selfish. In order to be honestly selfless, we must be Self-ish first. Only in recognizing our wounds and healing ourselves can we heal others—again, we find the image of the Wounded Healer.

Sometimes we need to step back and allow a new reality to settle and integrate within us before setting out to heal the world. In fact, I have observed some healers and seers who have not given themselves sufficient time for their own healing. Frequently, they felt pressured to be selfless and put the wounds of others above their own. Many of them did so, not recognizing that their attempts to heal others and their insistence in focusing outward, was a classic avoidance tactic.

Rather than committing to a period of going *within* for personal healing and integration, these individuals were projecting their feelings and needs onto those around them. While they often attracted and healed others who mirrored their own needs, many times they were unsuccessful in their healing efforts. There was also a tendency in these cases for the healer to assume the wounds and symptoms of the patient. Rarely did the healers recognize their own reflections within their patients. Their own denial created blocks in their abilities to channel healing energy and to receive necessary messages from their guides.

Shamans are obviously human. All of us incarnating in this reality are working through our own issues of growth and karma. While those walking a shamanic path have cleared much of this stuff and are often more aware of their own inner workings, they are not immune to the effects of grief. The death of a loved one can bring up shadow aspects that have not yet been examined and can impact one's life in significant ways.

Experiencing the death of a loved one can throw our entire reality into chaos. Not only do we feel the loss of that energy cord binding us to them, but we also experience a personal death of our own. The personality we were, with that departed individual, no longer exists. We are not exactly the same with anyone else in our world. This can create a confusion deep within as to who we really are. Our ego-identities go scrambling to try to determine how the loss of this part of us affects the whole.

When there are blocks interfering with the free flow of energy through these ties, it can be difficult for either being to fully move on. This is true even when both parties remain in physical life. How often have we all experienced a lost friendship or a broken romantic relationship? Many times, we feel as though a part of us has been lost as well. We are often unable to truly let it go. This can be equally true for those on the Other side of the Veil. Just because someone has shed the physical body does not mean these feelings disappear. This is partly because these feelings are also related to an energetic injury.

Our loved ones often plug right in to our heart chakras. People say, "He died of a broken heart," or "I feel as though my heart was ripped out." Again, we find clues to deeper meanings through listening to societal clichés. In this case, the individual has experienced a part of his "heart" ripped from him. When we lose a loved one, whether to death or something else, that cord that was so deeply entwined in our heart chakras (or other chakra) has been torn out, often against our wills.

This can actually produce a physical pain in the area where the bond was established. The removal of these bonds often causes an injury to the energy field of this area, which affects one's total being. We feel vulnerable as the resulting holes open up our auric fields. Our ego-identity is threatened and who we believe ourselves to be is thrown into confusion as that particular role ends. The identity we had with that person is gone.

This experience can feel very similar to soul fragmentation and, if particularly traumatic, can actually lead to a fragmentation of the spirit. Who I am in this specific incarnation is not an easy answer. I am made up of many identities and roles. I am a writer, a mother, a wife, a daughter, a lover, a friend, a teacher, and so on. Within each of these major identities, there are even more defined roles that I can identify with: customer, neighbor, voter, etc. Furthermore, I am not the same "daughter" with my mother as I am with my father.

When one of these identities that we have existed as for a long period of time or one we have strong ties to is gone, it opens one or more holes in one's energy field. Suddenly the conglomerate "I" is unstable. "We" are not the same and our remaining identities often struggle for balance. On an energetic level, this can be seen as a hole, often from the heart chakra, where a strong binding cord once was. This hole can be felt physically as pain, grief, fear, and anger.

Even those on a shamanic path, or anyone who has done a considerable amount of personal work, can be hit hard by this loss. While many of us are on the path to self-knowledge, this situation takes us to the core of *who we are*. And few of us are absolutely and wholly certain just who that is yet. With every death of a loved one, we each necessarily become a new person. A large portion of our grief response is mourning that part within each of us that has died, in addition to mourning the loss of the departed loved one.

Shamanically speaking, our most common function with regard to loved ones is facilitating the experience and release of grief. Grief is defined by most dictionaries as emotional suffering. This is true, but grief is much more than that.

The process of grieving allows us to fully experience the reality of a death. This does not mean that we must spend days sobbing in order to accept a death, but denial of the reality of this situation closes off our feelings. Often, we do not grieve because we allow ourselves to feel nothing. We go about our lives as though nothing has happened, subconsciously pretending that the death is not real.

In *Living Deliberately,* Harry Palmer writes, "To make something real we must believe in it."[48] Denial is usually defined as a refusal to admit the truth of something. In other words, when we are in denial regarding the physical death of a loved one, we refuse to believe in the reality of that death. Therefore, it is not "real" to us. We resist, rather than experience and accept the death.

The emotional outbursts that are often experienced as a function of grief are vital to the process for those individuals. They are reactions through which a person may release resisted and denied energy. In allowing ourselves these displays of emotion, we permit ourselves to experience our grief. We can face grief and move through it once we are able to experience it. Once we let go of our resistance, healing can fill the place of that blocked energy within us.

Part of accepting grief is acknowledging the reality that we will never again see that person or animal (or plant, or place) again in this lifetime. Even the knowledge that our loved ones live on without a physical body does not change the fact that our time with that incarnation of theirs is finished in this reality. As I said previously, this loss opens a hole in the personal energy field and often throws one's identities into chaos. This experience needs to be recognized and allowed to run its course. We grieve for ourselves at least as much as we grieve for the departed.

There is no right way to grieve. Some people need a huge emotional outburst; others let go in quieter or more private ways. As shamans and loved ones, we allow and encourage each individual to grieve in their own ways, while compassionately discouraging any attachments to these wounds. Again, we allow our ego-identities to step aside so that we may allow the most beneficial and healing atmosphere possible.

As we do with the dying, often the best thing we can do is to listen when and if loved ones choose to talk about their feelings. While we do not force the issue, the grieving generally need to share as much as they need their privacy. It is said that "misery loves company." Although this may sound depressingly negative, the principle is a sound one.

When we share these feelings with others in the same situation, it becomes acceptable to feel and express them. Through discussion and sharing, it becomes easier for us to get a fix on exactly how we feel, and these feelings become more real to us. Often those who have lost someone close to them are in shock, unsure what they feel.

Shock is generally defined as the physical, mental, and emotional effects of a trauma or blow. Even when a death has been expected for some time, the reality of it can jar one's entire self. Our minds and spirits have been thrown out of equilibrium and in many cases, are only functioning on automatic. You get through the day, but you are unable to even begin to fathom that huge hole in the center of your being.

Sometimes we are feeling so many things we cannot pin down any specific emotions. We feel like a swirling mass of confusion and emotion. To attempt to sort it all out just leads to frustration and more confusion. Those experiencing this type of response commonly have a more difficult time just getting through the day than those in shock, who have kicked into automatic. These individuals can be prone to mini-breakdowns and overt irritability.

Although there are a number of ways in which the shaman guides and heals her community, encouraging the release and sharing of these responses is most often the first step. We cannot truly release our emotions until we know what they are. Through commiseration, we are drawn out of ourselves. As observers to the responses of others, we are frequently able to view ourselves from a less vulnerable perspective. When these feelings are shared and directed outward, we see them for what they are. Finally, we can release them and avoid the depression that results from extended internalization.

Shamanic cultures make many uses of artistic expression. Through accepting the flow of creative energy, we honor our spirit guides, create sacred and ritual tools, and bring the spiritual into physical manifestation. This can become an outlet for our varied emotions as well as a means to explore and decipher those feelings.

Creativity can take many forms. As a result, I would recommend that anyone who might choose to use art as a therapeutic technique, be open to the personal expression of creativity. We obviously create through the traditional art forms, including music. However, we also express this energy in our creation of self, home, and work. While I may choose to sculpt a big hunk of alabaster, you may prefer to redecorate your office. My friend may rearrange the furniture in her home while your brother may experiment with a new personal look.

I would certainly encourage people to overcome personal resistance and experiment with more classical forms of creative expression. However, it is vital that we support this energy in whatever way it comes through. The main point is to get the energy moving and to find a concrete outlet for emotion. This combination can contribute to the release of grief and other feelings. It is also a powerful means of reintegrating one's Self.

Art, in its ideal therapeutic form, is one of those sensory experiences that bypasses the rational mind. When we experience it as an observer, or when we participate in its creation, we are touched deeply and we feel. No longer are we able to block our emotions or deny that we are vulnerable. And we must feel grief in order to move through it.

One of my best friends, whom I will call Becca, lost her mother soon after we graduated from college. Her family is Catholic and there was a full mass for her funeral. All of our closest friends attended the service along with other friends and family. My husband and I took charge of the after-funeral gathering at Becca's house, along with a Hindu couple. None of us had any religious issues about leaving the mass early. We were able to make all the preparations and keep the gathering going as long as people stayed.

While this is another role, which may seem simple and non-"shamanic," it was the best thing we could do for our friend at the time. As I have indicated, a shaman is many things to many people. In order to heal our communities, we must be able to fill whatever role is most beneficial at the time. In this situation, Becca was free to bask in the solace of her faith and then return and allow her time with friends and family to lighten up her mood for a while. She did not have the added stress of playing hostess or dealing with the details of the gathering.

After all the guests had left, and many beers were drained, Becca and I went outside alone to talk. We have always had a special connection and, at that point, she needed to share her feelings with someone who understood her. She needed to be able to be herself, without any concerns about appearances or identities. We sat out back and I listened appreciatively and compassionately as she talked about her mother.

It would not have brought my friend any comfort to try to discuss this in anything other than a Catholic worldview. It was not an intellectual or philosophical debate; it was a sharing of heartfelt emotions between friends. I encouraged her to talk about

158

their relationship, the love they shared, the fun they had, and her close connections with her siblings. We discussed the wonderful things her mother did while she lived and how her memory lives on in her children and everyone who knew her.

Like all religions, Catholicism is based on a belief in a higher spirit and an afterlife. That night, Becca and I discussed the continuity of the soul and the possibility that her mother could still hear her in some way, just as God and the angels do during prayer. In not attempting to bring in a new belief system, I was able to help my friend focus on the joy her mother would find in the Afterlife and find some surcease, even a bit of joy for herself in that knowledge.

159

Being able to spend some time alone talking about this brought Becca a great deal of relief and allowed her to release her emotions in a safe space. She knew without question that she could say anything and would be totally supported. She knew that I loved her and would always be there for her unconditionally. She did not need to worry about saving face or how she would be seen afterward. This safety is vital during times of stress.

When faced with the loss of someone we love, there is a great need for an unconditionally loving and supportive, safe space. Not only does this allow us to freely release our feelings without any risk of ridicule or misunderstanding, but the energy in this type of space is also innately healing. It is a gentle radiation that coaxes us to let go while we allow healing and love to flow into us. In many ways, the role of the shaman, with regard to those loved ones remaining in physical life, is very similar to that of the ideal friend.

Effective rites of passage are equally beneficial catalysts for the release of bottled-up emotions. If constructed properly, these ceremonies can focus solace and closure to those in need. The purpose of ritual is to use symbolism that speaks to our souls. It connects with us at a spiritual level and gradually conditions us to enter light trance states upon the experience of the various stimuli present in the ritual.

Prayer has been used for millennia to achieve communication with Spirit and to gain healing or other blessings. The use of prayer crosses all cultural and religious borders as we attempt to communicate with a higher being or the Source of All Life. The belief in the results of prayer is such an innate leap of faith that several medical professionals and other researchers have recently begun to study the healing effects of prayer.

Researchers have found, in many cases, that prayer not only has observable, concrete results, but it also induces a change in brain-wave frequencies. True prayer can bring about the alpha brain-wave frequency, as can meditation, ritual, and shamanic journeying. It is at these slower, yet more expansive brain-wave frequencies that we are able to connect with All That Is and impact the collective energy of our multiverse. Prayer can be used for distant healing, telepathic communication, and gaining the guidance of Spirit.

Although millions use prayer daily outside of ritual, it remains one of those ritual elements that we have become conditioned to as a society. The alpha brain-wave frequency is the beginning of a light trance state. The shaman also uses prayer. However, some of the more obvious shamanic elements for trance induction are drumming, dancing, and the use of incense or smudge.

For example, I have been working with sagebrush (*Artemisia* spp.) intensely for many years. As a result, I have been conditioned to enter trance when using sagebrush. Now, all I need to do is smell it and my brain-wave frequencies automatically slow down, bringing about more expansive levels of consciousness. This is one reason many cultures use incense along with prayer. Direct sensory input bypasses the rational mind.

The symbolism we use in ritual is taken from our personal or collective unconscious. It is often a cultural interpretation of a direct experience of the Great Spirit, of other realities, and of interdimensional beings. Whether taken from mythology, fairy tales, or personal feeling, the composition of ritual serves to focus our rational minds on images that innately evoke altered states and bypass analytical consciousness.

When we remain open to spiritual guidance, we can facilitate the creation of truly healing rituals for the departed. Through meditation, shamanic journeying and dreaming, we can maintain open channels for guidance from beyond this reality. Often, we may receive ideas from the departed and their spirit guides. We may also be open to communication from the spirit guides of loved ones who remain in physical life. Trusting in our visions and intuition is the first, best way to bringing these communications into our reality.

It is important to keep in mind the belief systems of those involved when creating or planning death rituals. As I noted in the chapter on rites of passage, many people will hold more than one type of service for the departed. This is not always necessary, nor is it the preferred way to go in all situations. While it is a shaman's role to create ritual and to facilitate healing, it is counterproductive to pander to each individual's smallest whim. A large part of the role of healer is to encourage growth and change.

We are appreciative of other's beliefs and we maintain an awareness of this during preparation for the death rituals. We do what is necessary to create a comfortable and healing atmosphere but we do not enable intolerance or hostility from other adults. We honor and respect them by expecting that they will act as adults and treating them accordingly. How they choose to behave is not our responsibility. That is entirely the decision of the individual and reflects only upon that person.

As is true with the rest of life (and death), dealing with a variety of loved ones regarding death rituals requires flexibility, creativity, and an ability to move beyond the ego. A perfect example occurred when my grandfather passed from this life. Our family has, over the years, divided itself between those who have adopted a strict Christian worldview and those of us who remain followers of a nonreligious, spiritual path. Then there are the multitude of other reasons why we just "have nothing in common."

Even before my grandfather passed over, there were a wide variety of issues plaguing both sides of the family. When it came time for the death services and burial preparations, the "other" side of the family was insulted by the presence of a photo of my grandfather's second wife on his coffin. It made no difference that this was a woman with whom my grandfather had found happiness and adventure for many years; she was not our "real" mother, or grandmother. This began a series of defensive moves and hurt feelings on both sides of the family.

161

We could have responded through the filter of our own beliefs and allowed our egos to assert themselves through anger and retaliation. This probably would have been seen as a psychologically normal reaction to a lifetime of misunderstandings and emotional distances. However, this would not have contributed to a healing atmosphere. Furthermore, it would have been disrespectful to all of us, including my grandfather.

By allowing ourselves to remain open to spiritual guidance, maintaining compassion, and being mindful of others' beliefs, we were able to create a more beneficial situation. Although the other members of the family knew there would be "pagan" rituals performed as a result of my grandfather's death, we kept that aspect of it completely out of any communication with them. To actually have to face these rituals would bring about even more distress for these individuals; they deeply believe that without a proper Christian burial, a soul is unable to return to God.

All ceremonies they experienced were simple, yet mainstream. There was one evening memorial service that was open to the public. Each family member was encouraged to take time alone in the room with my grandfather before the other guests arrived. We made it a point to be absent from the room during these times. In this way, they were able to say their goodbyes in private with others of their religious faith present. They were afforded this comfort without the added stress of facing those who were different, or whom they may have viewed as opposing.

This is possibility the easiest way to provide comfort to loved ones of differing beliefs, particularly when those beliefs are of a spiritual-religious nature. When alone, or surrounded by others of like-mind, these people can call upon their faith and receive healing directly from the source of that faith. Their egos are not on the defensive, blocking any communications from beyond this reality, because they are in what they believe to be a safe space.

As described earlier, my mother and I worked with an open-minded clergyman for the public funeral service. While both the sermon and the blessing were performed by a Christian minister, it was not an overtly religious format. He stressed the joys of my grandfather's life. He commended his body to the earth and his spirit to the Creator. This satisfied everyone. No one's beliefs were offended and everyone was able to put aside their differences for a short time. No matter what path we followed, we all shared this grief.

Unless the ritual planning is already complete, perhaps by the departed, or is rigidly structured by a religion, it can be beneficial to enlist the assistance of loved ones. Listen to what holds meaning for them and make suggestions as necessary. If possible, use this time of planning to focus everyone's energies on similarities and togetherness. This can be a period of renewing family ties as well as for personal healing.

Even those people who appear to be far from intuitive will often manage to bring in poignant elements from the heart that work well within the focus of a death ritual. I have known some individuals who, on the surface, seem to be much more mind than heart. These people have been able to draw on their minds to provide symbols that activate their hearts. I also have known those who have created wonderfully cathartic rituals for themselves, especially those who have lost children.

The loss of a child strikes a heartbreaking, protective chord in most of us. The mere idea of a suffering child can send the media and society into a frenzy of anger and righteous indignation. For a parent, the loss of a child can be devastating. Most parents have a deeply ingrained resistance even to the possibility of losing a child.

One Wiccan woman, whom I encountered online, held an entire ritual for herself after the loss of her child. She used a perfect, unopened rose and a crystal egg to symbolize her child's innate beauty and unrealized potential. She called upon the Mother Goddesses to aid her in her grief and help her to find ways to go on living. At the conclusion of her Circle, she buried the rose and the crystal deep within the Earth. In doing this, she commended the body and spirit of her child to the Great Mother. She prayed to the Mother of All, asking that She carry her child's spirit to the next world with the enveloping love of a mother for her own child. As a mother myself, this beautifully simple ritual brings tears to my eyes.

Years ago, it was customary for children to be excluded from the death process. For their own "protection," they were frequently not informed when someone close to them was terminally ill. Many children were even told that their loved ones had gone away or gone to sleep in a misguided effort to protect them from the reality of death.

Fortunately times have changed, but many people still attempt to shield children from this horrible fact: sooner or later, we all die.

Children, particularly those who have been told that a loved one has gone away, sometimes feel they are responsible for the death. Far too often, they believe their loved one went away because they were bad, or somehow unworthy. Occasionally, they wished this person would go away and they fear that those thoughts caused the death. This latter feeling is especially common among children who have lost a sibling. Only through encouraging the release of these fears, and through explaining the truth of the matter do we have any hope of clearing up these misconceptions. Once the facts are discussed, we can begin to work on healing feelings of guilt and the damaged self-esteem that so often is the result.

163

Even the best of intentions can go astray when the truth is eventually discovered. Children who have been "protected" from the reality of death often feel that adults are not trustworthy. The adults that our young children look up to as superior beings, in whom they can safely place all their trust, suddenly become the bad guys. These children are hurt and find themselves adrift in a world that was not what they believed.

Trust is a tricky thing. It is the basis for all faith and makes us feel safe and secure. Once trust has been broken, it creates a wound that does not readily heal. A child's trust in family, especially parents, is usually instinctive. Once broken, this trust must be earned the hard way. Few children go willingly into trusting relationships with anyone after having been hurt so deeply by family. If left alone, without any attempt at healing, this wound can prevent a child from ever developing healthy relationships, let alone a healthy respect for death.

When we give children the respect they deserve and tell them the truth about death, they often surprise us with their resiliency and acceptance. Certainly we are responsible for discussing the subject in a manner appropriate to the age of the child. But, in dealing with death in an honest way while stressing that life and love continue in the next world, we allow our children to learn to accept death as a natural part of life rather than a horror to be feared and hidden.

This is another instance where supporting and encouraging a child's belief in visits from the departed, as well as in his own spirit guides, can be vital in his handling of the reality of death. Some children may fear that they will die and be torn from their families, stranding them all alone. Unfortunately, this reaction is normal. But, it is much more common among children who have been raised in a modern, mainstream environment.

Children who grow up in families that experience spirit guides and encourage discussions of the continuity of life after death accept with certainty that they will not be alone when they die. These children understand that they are more than this incarnation and they can always come visit their families, if they choose to. Often these children have direct experience of spirit guides and past-life regressions that have given them a personal reference point for understanding the life-cycle process.

Another relatively common reaction among children in our society is the fear that their parents will die and leave them. When cultures were more like those in Hillary Rodham Clinton's book, *It Takes A Village: And Other Lessons Children Teach Us*, a child had no fear of being homeless, alone, or bounced around in foster care if something happened to her parents. She knew without question that, while she would grieve for the loss of her parents, she would be taken care of and loved. This is not necessarily the case in our current society.

Again, we must be honest with our children. We cannot promise them that we will never die. I have heard parents assure their children that they will never leave them and that the child should not worry. Rarely are these parents referring to the fact that they will always be there in spirit for their children. I often wonder if they consider how this broken promise will affect their children when they do die, particularly if they die young.

What we can honestly do is promise our children that we will always love them and will be connected to them spiritually for as long as they live. We can explain the energy umbilical cord and tell them we will watch over them from Spirit. In addition, we can be brave enough to take responsibility for choosing legal guardians to care for our children should we die before they grow up. We can put this into a legal will and discuss it with our children. If we become terminally ill, we can also be brave enough to create time together so that our children can grow to know and possibly love those guardians before we die.

In guiding children through the process of death and grief, we must be careful not to tell them how to feel or how to act. There is no "right" way to grieve, and children, like all of us, must find their own way. Here again, the shaman or parent, becomes a guide and counselor, encouraging the child to talk about it, helping him to sort out his feelings, and allowing him privacy when he needs it.

Children are naturals at make-believe and imaginative creation. Art as a therapeutic technique can be powerfully healing to children. Engaging them in mask-making, painting, stories, or sculpture is often the ideal way to move them through their fear and pain, into an expression of their emotions that will pave the way to healing. The use of everyday items in multimedia sculpture has been particularly effective for us.

Take your children on a Junk Walk. Take along a bag or box and encourage them to pick up anything that strikes their fancy. Play along, and pick up stuff that catches your eye as well. It is not necessary to go out keeping the death or other issue in mind. What needs to come through at the time will flow into the sculpture. Pick up small items, such as feathers, pieces of paper or metal, wood chips, etc. Also, keep an eye out for larger items that may serve as a base for your sculpture. Bring it all home from your Junk Walk.

Have things like glue, tape, string, clay, and wire ready at home. When you return from your walk, dump everything out onto a big table, or the floor. Then allow yourselves to create. Experiment and play. Feel free to rip something apart if it doesn't work and start over.

With time and practice, you will all be able to create sculpture that comes from the heart. It will be a concrete means of getting those emotions and images out; a manifestation that separates you from them, allowing a more expanded perspective for clearing. It is a reminder that these issues are not who we are, although we experience them.

I used this technique after my grandfather's death. I did not have him in mind when I went out on the Junk Walk with my mother. I tried a few things and nothing seemed right. I was working on other issues at the time, but nothing seemed to flow with them in mind. Then, I found an old piece of metal. I don't know what it was, but it resembled a ladder. Suddenly, the deathwalk flowed through. I attached this ladder to piece of cement with gray clay. On the base, I fixed some wood and rocks. In the lower sections, I bound puncture vines (a thorny vine native to the southwestern USA) and deadly nightshade fruits to the ladder with leather and wire. Moving up, I looped a long, wide wood shaving that reminds me of straw, and glued a feather beside it. In the other top corner, is a piece of discarded metallic paper, in brilliant blue. All of this is symbolic (to me) of death, rebirth, and my grandfather's deathwalk.

Because of their natural creative openness, children can obtain even more comfort and closure from rituals than do adults. Rites of passage, in particular, speak to them from the depths of their hearts and imaginations. Including children in the planning of these ceremonies provides them with the opportunity to do something concrete for the departed loved one and for themselves. This allows children a vital feeling of inclusion, which is often lacking for them at times like this.

Due to their relative lack of energy filters and their readiness to trust, children are generally very open to interdimensional energies, including communications from spirit guidance. Trusting in their intuitive suggestions for rituals can result in a simple, yet truly profound ceremony. They often have a way of innately *knowing* at a heart level, what is needed by those around them.

Permitting children to participate in the commiseration associated with funeral and memorial services not only encourages them to share and release their emotions,

165

but it also lets them know that they are not alone in having these feelings. Our society can tend to make one feel weak, childish, or ashamed when expressing emotions, particularly any form of sadness.

As a result, many children grow up believing that they are the only ones that feel this way. This is particularly true for boys. "Big boys don't cry" and "Don't be such a baby" are still common admonitions to indoctrinate our young people to suppress any emotions other than triumph and victorious celebration.

Our children need to know—from experience, not merely through being told— that it is healthy and "good" to feel and to express those feelings. This can be a growth challenge for the adults in their lives, especially the men. Real men and women *do* cry, and they are strong enough to admit it.

To actually experience an adult, particularly a parent, expressing emotion in an honest and healthy manner goes a long way to establishing trust and instilling self-confidence in a child. We learn though example and experience. There is no better way to learn to effectively handle our own emotions than to have the example of a strong role model leading the way.

Another issue to bear in mind when facilitating the grieving process is that grief does not just disappear when the ceremonies are over and the three-day (if we are lucky) "death-in-the-family" leave from work is over. It may take quite some time before the emotional pain fades, especially if all issues have not been resolved. Everyone attains solace and closure in their own time.

Some people easily release their sadness and attachments soon after the death. Other people convince themselves they have done this, and are frequently praised by society for "handling it well." Still others may take months or even years to get over the loss of a loved one.

As shamans and friends, we need to maintain an awareness of how each person *feels* to us. We do this by being open and aware of the state of their energy systems whenever we are with them. If we are continuing our own work, we will intuitively *know* who is struggling, who is repressing, and who is easily on their way to healing. It is also possible to check on people's progress through the shamanic journey.

We need to counsel those who have not fully released their attachments and let them know that this is normal. We provide them with a healthy forum for the expression and release of these feelings without allowing a codependency situation to develop. We take care not to foster the continuous creation of these feelings. We respond with compassion, gently guiding the individual past this wound into healing, rather than sympathetically becoming enmeshed in an ongoing emotional drama.

I knew a woman named Charlene in college. Charlene had experienced a terrible earthquake many years earlier, in which her family lost everything. Her mother died in the quake. Unable to release her attachments and her feelings regarding this situation, Charlene continued to create fear, sadness, and feelings of guilt and abandonment well into adulthood. She had frequent nightmares during which she would relive the earthquake.

Charlene gathered friends and acquaintances about her, never feeling that she had enough. Popularity was very important to her and she continually worked on her public image, afraid to look at what was going on inside herself. She clung to her few good friends and her boyfriend desperately, as if she expected to lose them at any moment. Since Charlene always seemed happy and well adjusted in public, very few people suspected the deep pain and fear she carried with her.

Charlene was one of those people that subconsciously needed to continually create the wound. She had not been able to achieve any personal healing for her pain and fear, but had finally devised a way to make it work for her, at least on the outside. Rather than face the earthquake and all it meant to her life and her sense of security and *self*, Charlene came to feed on the emotional roller coaster.

There are many people who are so unable to find their own centers that they have become emotional vampires. They have become addicted to emotional extremes much like an adrenaline addict needs to continue daring or dangerous stunts. These individuals will be attracted to, or will create, situations of strong emotions. You will often find them in groups where there is a great deal of fighting or constant stress. They plug into the energy of the group and gain an energy boost from these extremes. Often, these extremes are a reflection of the inner emotional state of the individual and as such, this energy resonates with their own. These people will become so addicted to this energy roller coaster, that they will become unable to connect with their own centers or the flow of balanced universal energy.

In Charlene's situation, her nightmares attested to the fact that she was reliving the earthquake in her subconscious. She acted out her loss of security and the loss of her mother in every relationship she had, not only through collecting acquaintances (as if to have a "back-up," just in case) but also through desperately clinging to those she considered to be close friends.

Charlene had become so used to a lack of emotional control and personal feelings of security that these things eventually made her uneasy. She was afraid to feel anything real, particularly any form of safety or security. They were unknown to her. Her fears and her resultant protective bubble of superficiality had become a known quantity. As such, she felt relatively comfortable within them.

167

We frequently encounter people who react to death in this way. Most of us have heard about children whose behaviors change as a result of their "acting out" after a death, especially that of a parent. This reaction is fairly common and is certainly not limited to children.

Often, we feel so hurt by the death that it triggers issues deep within us that have remained dormant, possibly even for lifetimes. Our egos take over to prevent us from being hurt anymore, or to retaliate for the pain. One of the most common issues the death of a loved one triggers is the fact of our own mortality.

There are individuals who sometimes become reckless, even dangerous in their actions, when forced to face the truth of mortality. Often, they turn to drugs or alcohol in a mixed attempt to shut off the pain and to bring about their own deaths. Somehow they feel a little better knowing that death is not just out there, waiting for them. They are back in control, even if it means killing themselves in the process.

These types of reactions can be the most difficult to deal with. These are also some of the main situations in which we must maintain our objectivity and not get caught up in the dramas. I perceive a big difference between compassion and sympathy. When we sympathize, we feel sorry for; we pity. We lend energy to the continuous creation of the wound.

On the other hand, when we are compassionate, we empathize; we have an experiential understanding, yet we do not give it more energy. We acknowledge the need for healing and the pain the individual presently feels, without giving that pain any reason to stick around. Instead, we channel energy that is supportive and buoyant. We appreciate the current situation and focus on the individual's eventual healing. We do not allow everyone to continue to drown in uncontrolled emotional pain.

The maintenance of these wounded feelings also serves another role for the grieving individual. It creates an effective block, not only for healing but also for any communications from beyond the Veil. As has been discussed throughout this book, it can be stressful and even traumatic for some people to experience Otherworldly communications. Emotional blocks prevent this contact while protecting us from getting too close to anyone else.

This is nothing more than an emotional self-defense reaction and in some cases, this is a necessary initial response. However, if allowed to continue, it can prevent us from developing healthy relationships in the future. Furthermore, we become blinded by our own feelings, making it virtually impossible for our loved ones who have passed over to reach us. As a result, they will frequently go to whomever is most accessible.

In the absence of a shaman or psychic, the departed will commonly visit the children of the family. Children, particularly those under seven years of age, have not yet built up the filters and blocks we adults have. Their energy systems are still developing and they are relatively open to the Other side. Depending on the age and the child, they may experience this during waking consciousness or in vivid dreams.

Unfortunately, this type of communication is generally discounted as mere imagination or wishful thinking. Sometimes, it is greeted as hurtful lies with an angry response. These reactions are normally quite effective in shutting down a child's psychic or shamanic abilities and in teaching them not to trust their intuition. Children who receive this type of response will usually stop remembering their dreams, experience lowered self-esteem, and often exhibit heart chakra wounding and blockages.

Very rarely does a child report these types of occurrences, especially in a mainstream home, if they are merely wishful thinking. It is far more common for these children to have honest experiences with departed loved ones that are so real and comforting that the children feel compelled to try to help their remaining loved ones with the truth. What better way to demonstrate the continuity of life and love than to be open to their descriptions of life beyond the Veil?

Passing on messages is an important facet of the role of shaman after the death of a loved one. Although those closest to the departed are usually visited first, the shaman is often the only one to recognize the visit. As a result, the shaman is frequently called upon to speak for the departed.

A rather humorous situation developed soon after the death of my grandfather. While he lived, it had been important to him that my grandmother's grave be well maintained. The year after she died, he planted a flowering tree beside the gravestone. The morning of his funeral, my mother and I decided to buy some flowers for the grave area, in addition to the funeral flowers we had already ordered. Since Grandpa always placed geraniums at the family graves, this is what my mother wanted to buy. Although I meant geranium, I could not stop saying begonia in every conversation regarding the flowers. It became slightly annoying to everyone around me, once the initial humor had worn off. They just wanted me to get it straight or shut up.

Just before leaving to get the flowers, my mother felt a strong urge to prune the tree my grandfather had planted. She knew he would be there and would want it to look nice for the funeral. As she got the pruning tools together, I asked what kind of tree it was. We all burst out laughing when she said it was a begonia tree. Okay, Grandpa! I finally got it.

Messages are often simple requests just like this. Even if they are not hugely dramatic statements of love from beyond the grave, they are important to the departed. The personal identity does not immediately just diffuse after physical death, at least not in most cases. These are beings that were frequently able to speak for themselves

169

and even do for themselves just a few days ago. Now, they find they are invisible and generally unable to affect our reality. What was important to them a few days ago is usually still important, but they are helpless to do anything about it unless someone hears them and honors their requests.

Many people have asked me how I receive these messages or how I know when we have noncorporeal guests. This is another area which often instills fear and uneasiness because it is commonly an Unknown. Once it is known, it is just another natural part of life, a slightly different means of communication and awareness.

The translation of any direct experience into language that another can understand is not easy, particularly when the other person has no frame of reference for the experience. To borrow an analogy from Harry Palmer, it is the difference between tasting an apple and studying what an apple tastes like, without actually biting into one.[49]

We use words as symbols to evoke an understanding of common experiences. To describe something does not truly create the experience for another. It can approximate or guide using the mind and even the emotions. However, nothing but direct personal perception can bring about true understanding, and this may vary from the experience of another. Having said that, I can describe how we receive Otherworldly communications.

This experience does vary for everyone. It can also vary depending on who is contacting us. In general, those people who tend to be visually oriented in this reality will receive mental images and see spirits. Other people lean more toward the auditory or sensory. These individuals will hear voices or feel the touch of the departed. For a great many, it is more of a *knowing,* an unexplainable awareness of a presence. This is similar to how we know someone in a room is staring at us without needing to actually see them doing it. Most of us tend to be a combination of any of these, with greater emphasis in one or two areas.

Often contact with departed loved ones is similar to the above story concerning my grandfather's begonia tree. Those we are close to in this life can have the ability to bypass the conscious mind. You may notice this while they live as the ability to finish each other's sentences or frequently having the same ideas simultaneously. These people are in your head before you realize it. They may be communicating with you from beyond the Veil, often without your conscious recognition, much as our spirit guides do.

The best way to develop the ability to recognize this is to maintain an open awareness. Watch for things that you might not normally say or think of, like the begonia tree. In order to be clear, I have said to whomever might be listening that I am open to the communications of the departed and our guides. I continue by acknowledging that a specific thought or feeling has come to me and I would like clarification whether it is correct or it is a communication from the departed. I ask for it to be somehow repeated or strengthened three times. This can result in anything from a stronger urge to actually seeing it on a billboard while driving.

The vast majority of people will receive visits and messages from other realities through dreams. While we are dreaming, our rational minds are shut down. Dreaming helps release limiting beliefs and fears, allowing us to expand our awareness, receive Otherworldly communications, and freely journey out-of-body. This is the easiest time for departed loved ones to reach us without the possibility of being analyzed out of our consciousness.

I highly recommend paying attention to dreams all the time, but this is especially productive during the time before and after the physical death of a loved one. We are often warned of the illness or death during dreaming. My mother and I knew my grandfather was having circulatory problems (that would eventually kill him) long before he had the first stroke, as a result of similar dreams. We were also able to look back at these dreams and see how we were warned about the septic infection that was the final cause of death. I would suggest the dreaming exercises in this situation as well. They may be varied to develop the ability to remember significant dreams or to meet with your loved one to exchange messages.

The most common messages we receive are to let those on our side of the Veil know that the departed still live, that they are well, and they will always love us. As I described earlier, it was very important to my grandmother that my mother relay her message that she was all right. Unfortunately, not everyone is ready to accept the implications of this type of message.

As shamans, we must weigh both sides of the situation before deciding how to proceed. It may be important to the departed to be able to let her loved ones know that life continues after physical death. On the other hand, the intent behind her desire to communicate this will not be realized if the individual receiving the communication is traumatized by it.

A shaman must maintain control of the situation. Just because we can understand these communications, does not mean we are servants of the spirits. While they do remain part of our "community of responsibility" until they make that final leap to their next step, we also have a responsibility to the welfare of the whole community. Here again, the importance of communicating within the worldview of others is to be stressed. "When we perceive that the only difference between us is our beliefs and that beliefs can be created or 'dis-created' with ease, the right and wrong game will wind down, a co-create game will unfold and world peace will ensue."[50] Working

171

shamanically, we move beyond the beliefs that limit this reality. We travel beyond consciousness itself.

From that space, we recognize that there are no right or wrong beliefs, there are just beliefs that serve or do not serve the personal growth of those who have adopted them. The belief that God will always honor her and take care of her lovingly may serve Sheila quite well. However in this incarnation, Sue may have chosen to experience a vengeful and harsh God who blames women for the world's suffering. Whatever our reasons, we chose various beliefs and experiences for our personal evolution.

When working with grieving loved ones, this is a vital point to keep in mind. As I have indicated before, it will not bring healing to a follower of a rigidly structured religion to tell her that her pro-golfer husband is now teeing off in a version of Robert Monroe's The Park, with other disembodied spirits. Not only that, but chances are she will probably never speak to you again. We structure our communications and responses within an acceptable framework to minimize additional trauma, to heal, and to support unconditionally.

For example, say your aunt has passed over after a long illness. Everyone on her side of the family is a devout Catholic, believing that she has passed into the Light of Heaven. This aunt contacts you in a vivid and lucid dream and asks you to let her husband and children know she is happy, well, and that she still loves them very much. She is not in a Christian Heaven, but is instead in a kind of outdoor learning center with her guides reviewing this past incarnation. You know her family will be very upset with you for telling them such a story. Do you contribute to their distress and tell them the "truth, the whole truth, and nothing but the truth?" Well, obviously you need to do what you feel is best and right for you, but I would suggest another route.

First of all, you can honestly tell her family that she told you she loves them dearly. When she told you this is unimportant and they do not need to know, the point is that she loved them enough to actually say this to someone else. The fact that she spoke of this love to you can bring them great comfort during this difficult time of grief.

Second, you can focus their attention on the fact that she is now free of suffering and is in a happy, safe place. This will not conflict with their beliefs and is the truth, as you have experienced it. You can use your dream about her to help in this diversion of focus. It can be beneficial to describe the simple, healing parts of your dream, such as the fact that she was happy and healthy, or that she again spoke of her love for them.

Although we each have differing views on what dreams are and where they come from, dreams tend to cross cultural barriers as opportunities for hope. To all but those who have adopted a purely mechanistic viewpoint, dreams remain as possibilities of communication from a higher source. We may not actually believe dreams are real, but the fact is we just don't know.

Therefore, your aunt's husband and children may receive your dream story as the possibility of a blessing from God. They may see it as a comforting dream resulting from your own hopes for your aunt. However they perceive it, chances are it will serve as some type of comfort to them, even if it just refocuses them on the possibilities of Heaven.

You may choose to tell them the whole dream, including your belief that your aunt is not in Heaven. This is a choice that will, hopefully, be made wisely and with compassion. If you do choose to relate the entire tale, consider your motives for doing so. If they are amused or disbelieving and you choose to push your belief in the truth of what you experienced, I would recommend that you first reassess your intent and goals in doing so.

Keep in mind that healing is not effected through force and tearing down reality constructs when another person is vulnerable. It is channeled unconditionally through supportive, loving, and gentle energy. And to be quite honest, our interpretation of any such experience is often filtered through our own belief systems. We can't really say for sure what your aunt experienced, or that another individual may not experience her as being in Heaven.

In many cases, it is a great comfort for loved ones to know when the departed has successfully moved on. Some people get tremendous peace in knowing the details of the deathwalk of a loved one. They often find hope for themselves when hearing how the guides of the departed came to help or that they passed into a beautiful light. The communication of messages from the departed can often be a healing in and of itself.

My husband's grandmother passed on after a long and difficult time of strokes and illness. She stopped by to visit us soon after she passed from her body. Although she had no need of assistance in moving on, she wanted to see my husband one last time and pass on some messages. I allowed her to share my body and hug him. He knew instantly that it wasn't "just me." She wanted to tell him how much she loved him and how proud she was of what he had done with his life and who he was. She said she felt healthy and free now. He not only received emotional healing for his feelings of loss, he was also reassured once again that death is just another journey and is nothing to fear.

Although my husband holds a worldview similar to my own, we must always bear in mind the viewpoint and beliefs of those with whom we are communicating a deathwalk or other message from the departed. In this case, my husband *knew* and few words were necessary between us to comprehend and accept the occurrence. This is not often the case and we do need to be aware of how we communicate these experiences.

In a similar way, the shaman can perform his role, during the transitional period before a physical death, as an emotional and spiritual healer for those with differing belief systems. As I have said throughout this book, this all takes creativity, flexibility, and an enlightened lack of self-importance; the ability to move beyond ego. In many cases, it may also require learning a bit about the differing belief systems you may encounter.

We work from within the beliefs of others if possible, to create a change in their energy. In learning about differing beliefs, we expand our own awareness along with our abilities to heal and assist our communities. While we may expose these individuals to new ideas and even encourage them to explore varying viewpoints, we do not attempt to change the beliefs of others. We respect their decisions and the identities they have chosen for this incarnation, as the creation of their higher selves.

A shaman's role during the death process is to guide these individuals through the grieving process. We help release denial and resistance. We encourage and guide the grieving and the departed through the completion of unfinished business and we pave the way for an acceptance of death as a natural, unavoidable part of life.

When I was in college, a good friend was seriously injured during a football game. Although he did eventually recover, we were unsure whether he would live or die for more than a month. His fellow football players and other friends were traumatized. A few friends felt guilty, many were angry, and all felt helpless. We were all from differing spiritual and cultural paths. By keeping religion out of it for the most part, we were able to pull together and support each other through what could have been a disastrous situation. Initially, some people reacted with accusations and blame. Our friend was a small man and many felt he should not have been playing football. Some felt we should all pray together for our friend, and others just wanted to get drunk and rowdy.

This is the type of situation that has the potential to rip apart any group. Through careful and, often subtle, redirecting of the group energy, we were able to pull together and channel unified healing to our friend. Although very few members of the group were aware of the shamanic or spiritual effects of what had occurred, we all became a closer group as a result.

Since this is such an important issue, I will give you a hypothetical situation to further illustrate this point. Suppose your brother has suffered a severe heart attack and stroke. He remains in the hospital for care but is getting sicker each day. There are four siblings in your family: you, your brother in the hospital, and another sister and brother. Both of your parents have passed away.

Your brother in the hospital is not religious at all but does believe in some form of a higher Spirit, a Creator. He holds no structured spiritual beliefs. You walk a non-religious shamanic path; you adhere to no organized religious dogma and work shamanically for the benefit of yourself and your loved ones. Your sister has recently declared herself to be an atheist and your other brother is a born-again Christian. There is no real understanding between any of you. You see each other mostly on secular holidays and even then, communication is limited and often strained.

Obviously, all of you are grieving for the current suffering and the eventual loss of your brother. However, each of you experiences this grief in a different way, from differing viewpoints. As one on the shamanic path, your role includes many things, including peacekeeper. You attempt to bring everyone together beyond beliefs for the common good.

This is not to say that we coddle each and every individual, catering to their specific beliefs. We do not. Keep in mind that, as with the spirits, we serve but we are not servants. We also work toward the expansion and growth of our communities. However, during the grieving process, we usually invest a bit more compassion in other people's need for the security of their beliefs.

This type of situation, as described above, can go many ways. The three most common possibilities are as follows. The family can completely shatter as a result of asserted egos and clashing beliefs. I have seen this result and it is not pretty. Often, each individual carries around the wound of this for the rest of their lives. In many cases, family members will reincarnate together again, in an attempt to restore balance and harmony in the relationships.

This type of situation can also go nowhere as a result of emotional distance, fear, and lack of communication. This is a fairly standard reaction that concludes with a continuation of the status quo. These families continue their superficial communication, unless someone is drunk or otherwise reckless. Most individuals are unsatisfied with the relationship but it is safe and known, so no one dares disturb the barriers.

The third most common conclusion is the creation of stronger family bonds. This is also the least frequent of these outcomes. Families who are somehow able to move beyond ego-identities and beliefs catalyze deeper understanding, tolerance, love, and personal growth for all involved. While no shaman can force a situation to create growth, we can work toward that potential.

In this example situation, you can speak with each of your siblings individually, from a space of understanding and respect for their chosen beliefs. When relating to them, do not allow yourself to get caught up in the *stuff*. Each person is not merely their words or their identity in this life; he or she is a much more expansive, wiser,

175

more connected being at the core. And within the context of this life, each individual is learning about life and working toward the same basic goals as we are.

Keep in mind that all religions are based on a belief in a higher Spirit and an Afterlife. This is a common thread that can be used when assisting these individuals through any process. Even most of those who do not follow any specific religion tend to retain some basic beliefs from the family or culture they were raised in. Those who have chosen not to believe in anything nonphysical may appear at first glance to be tough cases. This is often far from the truth.

You might choose to read up on your physics or general science before attempting any in-depth communications with your sister. Discuss the law of conservation of mass-energy with her, as discussed earlier in this book. If you do not feel comfortable with a scientific discussion, focus your communications on your brother's immortality as a result of the things he did and the lives he touched. You can discuss, either in private or as a group, the need to put aside personal differences in the best interests of your brother. Remind everyone that your arguments and tensions will only add to his stress. Think back on the times you were all a team; a family who stuck together despite your differences. Find ways to rekindle those feelings and those memories.

It is usually best to direct conversations away from religious or spiritual belief systems, whether subtly or overtly. Redirect all attention towards a sharing of the facts and preparations, as well as a sharing of the emotional well-being of your brother. Since the brother in transition was not very religious, a nondenominational, personalized memorial service should be acceptable to everyone, provided they can put his wishes before their own. It is strongly recommended that the brother in transition be included in as many of the discussions and preparations as possible.

If your religious brother is adamant about church services or the presence of a minister, this should be discussed with the brother in transition. He may be amenable to the presence of a minister, provided the service is meaningful to him and not overly religious. If he prefers not to have any interference in his services, it may be helpful for you to offer to attend a separate service at your other brother's church with him. At no point should the uncompromising insistence on one belief system be permitted to override the wishes of the dying or the departed.

This is another situation in which our work in this reality may be best served if supported by a considerable amount of work on a shamanic level. We can more easily plant the seeds of understanding and tolerance beyond the filters and barriers of the rational mind. This is not mind control or brainwashing in any form. We are planting a seed, and like any other seed it contains the potential for growth. It is not guaranteed to develop into anything.

All seeds require proper nourishment and an acceptable environment. When we plant these seeds, we are making energy imprints available to the individual when and if, they choose to take that path. When they reach the point where their internal environment is conducive to the possibility of such seeds, these imprints will become accessible to the individual. The individual may then choose what to do with them.

On a shamanic level, we journey for the healing of each individual as well as for the group as a whole, if possible. We remain open to the possibility that, for whatever reason, these wounds may not be fully healed within this incarnation. Enlist the assistance of everyone's spirit guides and work toward your own increased understanding. We do our most effective work when we are a living example of what we teach. Let these guides know that you are open to their communication. Ask their help in releasing your brother from his body, and in healing family rifts out of this difficult situation.

Just as it is often easiest for the departed to contact us while we sleep, it is similarly effective for us to reach others in our reality while they sleep. One way to do this is to work with variations on the dreaming exercise described in chapter two. Another method is to journey specifically for this purpose, as outlined below.

Middleworld Journey
To Establish a Shamanic Contact with Others in Our Reality

Enter the journey as you would to contact a fragmented individual. Do not journey to any specific Other world, but focus on who the person is at her core, beyond the beliefs of the conscious mind.

Call upon both your spirit guides and her spirit guides for assistance in reaching her and in communicating effectively with her. As your trance state deepens, call to this person and allow yourself to be pulled to her.

When you are aware of this person before you; when you can see her or feel that she can hear you, tell her what you have wanted to say in everyday consciousness. Discuss the possibility of improved understanding and communication between you in this reality.

Accept whatever comes up and follow up in this reality, if possible.

The following is a simple visualization to make contact and improve understanding between you and others in this reality.

Visualization Exercise
To Establish a Psychic Contact with Others in Our Reality

Just before falling asleep, count down, to yourself, from ten to one, as though you were going to meditate. Stop periodically to take deep breaths and remind yourself to go deeper and deeper. It may help for you to visualize descending a staircase, one step with each number.

At the count of one, go to your favorite place of relaxation. This should be any place, real or imaginary, where you feel perfectly safe and comfortable. Call upon your spirit guides for their assistance in contacting this person and in improving relations in everyday reality with him.

With your guides at your sides, enter a doorway to your left. You enter the next room and find the person you wished to contact sitting comfortably on a chair. Greet this person warmly and sit down near him.

See the guides of this person standing behind him. Greet them and tell them you honor their presence.

See the person you wish to speak with as being open to hearing what you have to say. Tell him what you cannot effectively say in this reality. When you are finished, remain open and silent for a moment to allow this person to respond to you, if they choose.

Say to this person and his spirit guides that this communication will reach him at his most receptive point during the night. Then release the communication and allow yourself to fall asleep.

I have had a tremendous amount of success with both of these methods. In one situation, not related to a physical death, I was involved with a group of people who had been very close friends at one time. Although superficially, they were still friendly to each other, there was a significant amount of hurt feelings, hostility, and backstabbing going on. Remaining neutral as I normally attempt to, I had no desire to either choose sides or become enmeshed in the chaos.

While I listened compassionately when someone needed to vent, I discouraged people from consistently whining to me without making an attempt to change their situations. Although I was able to handle much of this in everyday awareness, I felt a shamanic supplement was required to help this community get on with their lives.

Using both of the methods outlined above, I contacted each of these individuals. I let them know that I would be there for them if they needed help or healing. If they chose to move beyond the pettiness, I would be more than willing to assist them. I also described my point of view on the situation, including the fact that no one was totally at fault, nor was anyone totally to blame. I viewed it as a co-creation in which everyone needed to release the past in order to continue to grow.

I received some very interesting responses to this combined approach. People, who had always preferred to complain and talk about others without recognizing the similarities within themselves, suddenly began to make productive, concrete plans for their futures. Many of the individuals involved forgot about the situation and began to focus on their own dreams. Some even came to me and thanked me for my part in refocusing the energy. Of course not everyone was able to be friendly or even honestly civil to each other, and I certainly do not attribute the entire turn of events to my communication alone. However, I do believe that my shamanic work for this community contributed to the group dynamic.

When it comes to a physical death situation, there is often not a lot we can do for the grieving in this reality. When the grandmother of one of my closest friends was dying of cancer, the only thing I could really offer him in this reality was to be there when he wanted to talk. By that time, we no longer lived a short distance apart and were unable to visit as often as we used to. The telephone became our main connection in this reality.

I made it clear to my friend that my husband and I were always there for him and he was welcome to call or stay with us whenever he needed to. We let him know that we loved him and supported him unconditionally. By that time, he had already lost both his parents and was very close to his grandmother. I made it a point to be the best friend I could be.

In our world, this was the best thing I could do for my friend. Raised Jewish in a mainstream home, he was not open to a shamanic viewpoint. He had become rather nonreligious and, at that time, did not really want a spiritual take on death. He wanted a friend who would listen and be there unconditionally and who would not preach to him about possibilities.

What I could do for him, however, was to journey and work through dreaming for him. Using a variation on the previously described dreaming exercise, I continued to reassure him that we would always be there for him. I made it clear that he always had a safe space to come to and that there would be no judgment of him or his reactions.

Through dreaming and the shamanic journey, I worked with my spirit guides and contacted his spirit guides to determine if there was anything else I could do for him in everyday reality. I asked their help in healing him emotionally. I also used dreaming to connect him with his spirit guides and stepped back to allow them to do their work. I maintained this open connection through this reality and allowed myself to receive their guidance when communicating with my friend.

While we do work shamanically with loved ones or anyone else, it is counterproductive for us to assume the role of the great *Shaman*. This can be damaging not only to the completion of the grieving process but to our personal growth as well as that of the community. We do not want to take control over anyone's handling of a death. We do not want to foster a dependency. Real shamans are not present-day gurus who have a following of groupies hanging on their every word.

A true shaman works for the empowerment of the individual. We find ways for these people to create their own healing. This is one reason the shaman is often referred to as a pathfinder. Empowerment of the individual is often best effected if done subtly and behind the scenes. Calling attention to oneself and looking for glory serves only the ego.

No matter what worldview one holds, the possibility exists for contact from a departed loved one. As I described in an earlier chapter, this contact can open a Gateway to other realities that will not close for some people. This experience has the tendency to either send someone off to the sanitarium or to completely reevaluate her belief system. It is a good possibility that the shaman will be the only one that can truly understand and guide the individual through this experience. How we handle this may mean the difference between medication and a broader awareness of life.

I have known people who were told to go hug a tree or to pray more or to wear a certain type of crystal and all the weird stuff would go away. These were all well-intentioned suggestions. Unfortunately, the people giving this advice had no frame of reference for these experiences. They did their best to help from within their limited experience and knowledge, but this type of advice can create more fear when these suggestions do not work. As a result, many people become even more certain that they are mentally unstable.

Those on a shamanic path should be able to recognize this phenomenon when confronted with it in another person. I do not recommend attempting to prevent anyone from seeking mainstream professional help if they feel it is required, particularly if you are not an experienced shaman and the individual in need was raised in a mainstream society. Even if the individual has begun a course of mainstream therapy, we can assist the process.

While we may need to get into things gradually, starting with the most acceptable topics, we should eventually be able to set their minds at ease and provide them with the tools to get their experiences and their reactions under control. Earlier in this book, I discussed my guidance of a woman who contacted me online for help when she began experiencing significant psychic abilities and paranormal encounters after the death of a family member. This woman was from a small religious community. She had never even heard of many of the things that she experienced. Most of these experiences are fairly common to most of us that walk a shamanic path.

In order to be of any help to this woman, I needed to get a handle on her level of experience and her belief systems. I let her do most of the talking initially. I paid close attention to what she said and how she said it. I began by discussing those generic ideas that we can thank the New Age movement for bringing into the modern collective consciousness. Most of these ideas, like out-of-body experiences, modern physics, and angels are now acceptable, if perhaps a little odd.

Eventually, we approached the subject of shamanism and the potential effects of the death process. By that point, she had gotten used to much of the terminology and had decided for herself that I was not a wacko. She had a measure of trust in me and believed I was committed to helping her. While introducing her to these new concepts, I continued to do a lot of listening, supporting, and encouraging. Whenever possible, I described things in terms that she could appreciate and understand. One of the best things I was able to do was to introduce her to others who had been through the same experience and were productive, accepted members of their communities.

As I said before, this woman has told me that it makes a world of difference to know that she is not alone. She is now connected to teachers, therapists, computer programmers, lawyers, and more, who have all been through similar experiences. Through our group discussions, we were able to make suggestions and offer advice that really worked for her. Best of all, there was no pressure to conform or to perform. We reassured her that each experience is unique to the individual and she had nothing to prove to us.

This woman is still learning to work with these abilities but she no longer fears for her sanity or the well-being of her family. She has accepted the teaching of her spirit guides. With their assistance, she has developed ways to discuss some of this with her family, in terms they can understand, and has contributed greatly to their spiritual expansion. She is eagerly exploring her *self* and other realities.

In functioning as guide and catalyst, rather than allowing my ego to interfere, I have been able to assist this woman in creating her own growth and healing. She does not look to me as teacher or guru, but rather as another being on the path, who was there when she needed me to be. As a result of our working together, she is now able to move along her own path. This is the best possible outcome. Each of us must accept the growth and do the healing on our own. No one can do it for us. In working toward the empowerment of each individual, we are also helping to create a more enlightened, aware reality.

When we encounter someone experiencing a newly opened Gateway, we are not only called to be guides, but to be unconditional supporters and counselors as well. The crumbling of a belief system, particularly one that concerns the very nature of reality (as seen by the individual), can be devastating.

No one likes to give up the security of a long-term worldview, especially when this view is also held by the majority of one's society. This has the potential to put you out there all alone and vulnerable to ridicule and abuse. No one likes to be viewed as different. Even scientists fight to maintain old, comfortable theories. Throughout history, some of the greatest scientific minds were initially ridiculed and outcast by the existing scientific and religious authorities of the time.

Both Copernicus and Galileo, who produced some of the first theories proposing the heliocentric solar system (in which all the planets revolve around the Sun as opposed to the Earth being at the center), were oppressed by the authorities of their time. In 1616, all Copernican books were censored by edict of the Roman Catholic Church. In 1633, Galileo was compelled to renounce his beliefs and was sentenced to life imprisonment. His major books were burned and his sentence was read at every university. Sounds to me like a pretty good deterrent to independent, creative thinking.

These seventeenth-century authorities were reacting to a perceived threat to their reality constructs. From within their limited viewpoints, they could not permit anyone to alter the status quo. Therefore, they were compelled to not only deride any new theories that may threaten their beliefs, but they needed to make an example of any who dared defend the expansion of human awareness. This is a reaction that remains common today.

Individuals whose experience brings about a new awareness of reality can feel terrified, cheated, and angry. They can rebel against all systems that led to their prior misunderstanding or limitations. I see this frequently within the neo-pagan community. People can become very hostile and even vengeful toward the religion or culture of their youth, when they feel their eyes have been opened.

What these individuals fail to recognize is that few of those that indoctrinated them with the old beliefs did so out of a desire to control them with falsehoods or subjugation. The authorities of their youth were working from within a belief system. The vast majority of them believe in the righteousness and truth of their beliefs just as strongly as those who have moved on believe in their new paths. And those old paths honestly work for a large number of people in this incarnation.

Those individuals who are experiencing a breakdown of old reality constructs can also rebel against those who led to their broader awareness. I have witnessed plenty of people who once followed gurus or belonged to meditation groups, or learned in Wiccan covens, but for one reason or another have left these paths out of anger or fear. A few have run away as a result of a frightening experience. Many have reached a comfortable plateau of learning and decided their old teachers are worthless. This latter response reminds me of the relationship between some teenagers and their parents, who suddenly become "stupid" and "mean" once the child reaches a certain age.

Those who react with fear as the result of facing their own shadows or experiencing something that contradicts the world they thought they knew, can become even more hostile to the source of their awakening as those who come to hate their old paths. These teachers, for lack of a better word, represent everything that they prefer not to experience. This reflects the response of the seventeenth-century Vatican to Galileo and Copernicus. Those who represent a threat to the ego's identity cannot be permitted to exist, hence the Inquisition.

183

A significant number of those experiencing an open shamanic Gateway attempt to take refuge in drugs and alcohol. They use these drugs to dull their awareness and avoid the experiences. This does not really work. It may get you to a point where your conscious memory is foggy or absent but it makes the eventuality of the experiences more difficult to integrate. It is also quite possible that certain drugs will propel you into one or more Other levels of reality, possibly with limited control in these realms. The shamanic Call cannot be ignored or drugged away.

In each of these cases described above, we are called to be unconditional supporters, guides, and counselors. It is essential that we maintain a compassionate awareness of the situation without allowing a victim control drama, or an emotional vampire condition, to take over. We work shamanically and follow up whenever possible in everyday reality.

If we become aware of the need for some other type of intervention, it is our responsibility to make recommendations and provide the means for the individual to get the help they need. Again, the role of the omnipotent, omniscient *Shaman* is counterproductive. As pathfinders, we guide those under our care to the correct and most beneficial paths—for them. Whether those paths lead to us or not is irrelevant.

In many cultures it is believed that, once Called to shaman, the spirits will hound you until you either accept the Calling or die. There are many of us who have experienced that death does not end it. In spite of this, there are those who do choose death, believing it to be an easy way out. All this does is eliminate the physical body and drags out the inevitable by separating one from the familiar support systems of this reality.

These individuals must make a choice sooner or later. The shaman works to catalyze the acceptance of the Call through loving guidance and teaching through example. We do these individuals a disservice by enabling their avoidance of what is occurring.

Many people assume that the shaman's responsibility ends with the burial or cremation of the body. Once the ceremonies are over, those of us in the modern world are expected to return to life as usual. The truth is that the role of the shaman with the grieving is just as important, if not more important, after all the set times for grief have ended. We walk a fine line between allowing the individual to work things out for himself, and in assisting him in his healing. The only real way to do this is to continue our personal shamanic work and maintain an objective awareness of the situation. This is all done through a channeling of unconditional love and the empowerment of the individual.

Endnotes

48   Harry Palmer, *Living Deliberately*, p. 104.
49   Harry Palmer is the author of the Avatar materials.
50   From the *ReSurfacing* workbook, Avatar materials, p. 110.

Chapter 8

REINCARNATION

Although most people today are interested in the idea of reincarnation, a relative few have any real belief in it. But beneath the jokes that people tend to make, I believe there lies a desire for it to be true—coupled with a fear that it may be. We want to believe that life goes on. We also want to find some reason for the things that happen in our lives. On the other hand, we would prefer to get away with our misdeeds and there are certain people we don't really want to ever see again, no matter what bodies they occupy.

Most people would prefer to believe that a baby, who is born with a fatal disease that will lead to a painful death in a few short years, is not merely the result of chance or the whims of an unjust deity. It brings some logic to our lives if that child is living something of her own choice, or is reaping the effects of past-life wrongdoing. Without this logic, we are at the mercy of random occurrences and perhaps a deity who is not much more evolved than we are, just more powerful.

Since many of us in the modern world do not hold any real belief in a Hell, we want to know that those people who commit horrible acts receive some kind of payback. We need deeper reasons to live an ethical life. If we are not working toward soul growth or the creation of a better world, than what good does it do to be honest and kind when others, who are not, live the good life?

It is interesting to note that that the percentage of believers in reincarnation increases each year. It would appear that the state of our modern society sends many of us searching for the simple wisdom of our ancestors. These ancient ideas resonate in our hearts and souls, striking a chord of truth. We feel renewed in our attempts to be "good" people and we experience our interconnections with All of Life more readily when we open to the flow of this energy.

Many of our ancestral peoples believed strongly in a life after death. Not only did they believe that we continue in an Afterlife world, but many of them believed that we return to this reality in new bodies. The Welsh druids believed that we continue to reincarnate through the rings of Abred until we eventually reach Gwnvyd, the White Life.[51] Many Saami believe we return to the Saami. These beliefs are not new, just buried under thousands of years of religious and scientific dogma.

The number of individuals who have experienced some form of past life regression, or spontaneous past life memory, is also growing. More and more people are regressing to past lives in an effort to make sense of present relationships and medical conditions. In fact, I have a friend who has achieved a valuable understanding of the difficult relationship between her and her sister through past-life memories. This woman has also obtained an objective view of the situation and a renewed interest in clearing up their problems once and for all.

These two beings have incarnated together many times. The problems have been going on so long that my friend, Kira, has been unable to find an incarnation when the two of them had a good relationship. In this life, her sister is older than Kira by many years. Her sister has hated her since before she was born and has gone about her life making things very difficult for Kira. This sister has always been very jealous of Kira's relationships with their parents, particularly their father.

In the life just prior to this one, Kira has clear memories of being sexually abused by her father in that life. Her present sister was her mother in that incarnation. As the mother, she looked the other way and denied the abuse, while at the same time hating her daughter for stealing her husband's attentions. Kira's sister has clearly carried over those feelings from past lives and continues to act them out without any understanding of where they come from. Kira herself has carried over feelings of abandonment and abuse that she has continued to attract in her current incarnation.

Whether you view this as subconscious symbolism or actual past-life experiences is irrelevant. The point is that Kira has found some meaning in her relationship with her sister. She has achieved some clarity, which makes sense to her and has spurred her to become the peacemaker in their current relationship.

These women are closer now than they have ever been. While they may not be the best of friends, they have managed to find a measure of acceptance and understanding, as well as love for one another. Equilibrium has been restored and those negative bonds of pain and fear are beginning to dissolve.

When we clear and integrate past-life issues, we often receive even more tangible results than simply improved relationships. Many people are working with cellular-memory bodywork and other past-life therapies, particularly regressions, in an effort to improve physical issues that have plagued them for years.

We have a family friend, Richard Ross, who is a brilliant body-centered therapist, as well as a spiritual coach and counselor. He is also the person who introduced my family and I to Avatar several years ago when he was delivering the course. We have all come to value Richard's quiet wisdom and sense of humor.

Richard is a former practitioner of Phoenix Rising Yoga, which consists of a number of visualizations, dialogue, and energy work in conjunction with yogic postures. One of the beautiful aspects of this method of yoga is that the client is physically supported by the therapist in the yogic postures, therefore it is not necessary for a client to have any experience with yoga.

Phoenix Rising practitioners have found that there is usually a deep relaxation when a client is held in a particular posture at "a particular level of stretch."[52] This is obviously a tremendous benefit in and of itself. However, practitioners also find that old memories and emotions may bubble up during a session. The therapist then assists the client in exploring these in order to release them. Richard has found that "while occasionally strong emotions or traumatic memories come up, nothing ever comes up that the client is not ready and able to deal with at that time."[53]

Although Richard is not a past-life therapist, one of his clients spontaneously accessed a past-life near the end of one session with him.[54] At the time, Richard had him in a supported posture called "the fish," in which the client was lying on his back with a pad under him slightly elevating his chest. Richard had one finger resting on the client's breastbone. Suddenly, the client said, "The pain, the pain." Richard realized that he was referring to the spot on his breastbone where Richard had been resting one finger. Obviously something had been activated.

To Richard's relative surprise, the client had gone into trance and was reliving a past life in the 1800s. Apparently, this client had been a Native American in a village that was attacked by the U.S. cavalry. The majority of this man's village had already been killed and he was dying from a gunshot wound to the chest. This client experienced his death in that life then said softly, "I see the white buffalo." After a minute or two of silence, he sat up and asked Richard, "What the hell was that?"

Like many of us, Richard believes that everything occurring at any level of our being, whether mind, body, or spirit, has an impact on our other levels. As he says, "all memories, strong emotions, and life traumas are stored in the body, independent of what may or may not be remembered by the mind." Also like many of us, Richard has firsthand experience of what deep levels of relaxation and the activation of certain body parts can evoke within us.

There are a large number of people who experience physical ailments that originate in a past-life memory stored in the physical body. In most of these cases, the ailments are long-term. These are not necessarily lifelong ailments experienced since birth, because current life experiences, injuries and even puberty can activate these areas, causing the body to re-experience a past-life wound. Often, the medical establishment has no real cure for these ailments. In fact, they may not even be able to determine exactly what the cause is.

Past-life therapies have brought relief and clarity to many individuals who have exhausted more mainstream methods. I had an acquaintance named Kevin, who suffered from severe back problems since he was a young teen. Although the pain improved with exercise, he still needed to remain careful because the smallest miscalculation in movement could put his back out. Doctors could find nothing specifically wrong with him other than a "weakness" in that area.

Kevin finally resorted to past life regression several years ago, as his last hope for any relief. He did not really expect to find anything of value, because he was not entirely sure he believed in reincarnation. However, he was willing to give it a try and did his best to enter into regression with an open mind. What he experienced changed his entire belief system. Through the course of several past-life regressions, Kevin relived his own physical death twice as the result of breaking his back. In one life, he had fallen to his death as a child living in an Anasazi-type cliff-dwelling. He had been playing too close to the edge without paying attention and broke his back on the stones at the base of the cliff. In the other significant life, Kevin had ridden his horse over the side of a gorge in a desperate attempt to escape several men who were chasing him. Both he and the horse died on the way down as they bounced off the side of the gorge. Once more, "Kevin" had broken his back.

What Kevin found to be truly amazing was not only that he had vivid memories of these lives and believed them to be real, but these death experiences also explained his lifelong fear of heights. Ever since he could remember, he had a terrible, irrational fear of heights. This fear was so intense that Kevin was even uncomfortable on escalators and spiral staircases. After the regression sessions were complete and Kevin had integrated these memories, both his fear of heights and his back problems disappeared. When I last heard from him, he had been pain-free for over a year.

To the shaman, a belief in reincarnation is nothing unusual, nor are its effects on the current incarnation. A belief in reincarnation is nothing more than a natural understanding of the cycles of life and the continuity of the soul in its journey through evolution. Much of who we are is due to the path our soul has taken and the experiences we have passed through along the way. It is not unusual to find the current physical body re-creating past-life issues, including one's cause of death. As is true with current issues and blocks, until past-life issues and blocks are cleared, we continue to create and attract situations that give us the opportunity to "dis-create" them.

The path of the shaman is the path of self-knowledge and the release of the bonds of personal history. We walk this path to clear limitations imposed on our limitless beings by the experience of current (and past) incarnations. In order to release one's history, it must be integrated and fully experienced. Only when we have achieved a full understanding of who we are (and why) can we begin to release the bonds of present and previous identities.

Many friends, lovers, and even adversaries today recognize their past-life connections. Sometimes it is just a feeling; sometimes actual memories resurface throughout the course of a relationship. Even those who do not have any substantial memories or feelings of recognition are finding past-life connections through astrology and other divination methods. In many New Age and other metaphysical communities, the past-life connection has become almost cliché. However, it can be a real and powerful influence on one's current relationships. It can also explain seemingly amazing "coincidences."

I met a man several years ago with whom I felt an immediate connection. I was certain I had known him before. Each time I saw Steve, I tried to place his face within my current time frame. It was obvious, though, that we had not met before in this incarnation. Although we each walked a shamanic path, we occasionally worked with a Wiccan coven. When in Circle together, tremendous energy was raised and magical things happened. It seemed our energies were surprisingly compatible for two people who had not worked together previously.

Over the course of our friendship, we had many mutual memories of being druids together in ancient Britain. Some of these memories were spontaneous, as a result of our association; other memories showed up as dreams, which were later confirmed through sharing between us or with other people.

I specifically remember one evening when the Wiccan coven we worked with was to celebrate one of the pagan holidays with a ceremonial Circle. The high priestess was called to work at the last moment and the high priest was ill. Four of us chose to remain and just hang out rather than holding the Circle. Through the course of discussions, Steve and I got on the topic of our druidic memories. We each separately remembered the same leather-bound book and other tools we had used in that past life. Our respective mates were amazed to hear us relate the same stories they had heard previously about the cave where the book was kept and other details. Steve, who was generally very private about his personal magical tools, brought them all out and handed them to me one by one. I could *see* quite vividly his re-creation of some of the tools we had used in that prior life. I could also *see* very clearly his current energies and how he worked. It was obvious we had a psychic connection that extended beyond time.

This is a good example of a past-life connection that occurs within a short period of time. My association with Steve lasted only a couple of years in this life. I was there for him and his girlfriend through some difficult times. Then we all chose to move on and we have not seen Steve or his girlfriend since. It is clear that we came together once more for a specific purpose. Once that purpose was completed, there was no need for a continued relationship.

Many of those we encounter throughout our lives may be "prior" acquaintances with whom we have agreed to cooperate in some way for a specific reason. With these people, we share similar relationships as we do with those spirit guides who enter our lives for a time to bring us necessary energies for one life phase, then disappear once we no longer need them. In truth, we can view all other beings in our lives as spiritual guides. Those we reincarnate with more often tend to be those who love us the most and are dedicated to helping us attain our evolution, even if they do this by incarnating as adversaries. Many of those who continue to return with us, do so within various family relationships.

Many Saami people believe that we tend to reincarnate to the Saami, particularly along family lines. Although there is a naming ritual performed after the child is born, the name is often received by the mother or shaman prior to childbirth. Commonly received during dreaming or journeying, it is frequently clear at that time whether this name is given to indicate the return of an ancestor. When a specific name is not received in this way, the name of a respected ancestor may be chosen for an infant in hopes of attracting that soul to reincarnate, or in an attempt to bring in the qualities possessed by that ancestor.

When a cousin chose to honor his mother's memory by giving his daughter his mother's first name, Elen, as a middle name, he unknowingly named her spirit correctly. He does not adhere to a belief system that would allow for this as a possibility, so we have not attempted to enlighten him. However, it is clear to "our side" of the family that she is indeed his mother returned as a cousin.

My mother was the first to recognize this relative in this young cousin. When "Elen's" parents came for a visit, they brought their new daughter with them. As they handed her to my mother to hold, my mother was struck with the realization. She looked in the girl's eyes and *knew* with absolute certainty, as though the baby had spoken to her. I watched in amazement as my mother sank to the floor, staring at the girl. It is very interesting to note that "Elen's" parents frequently call her by her middle name rather than using her first name.

This belief in reincarnation, to the same people and along family lines, is by no means specific to the Saami. I met a woman at a neo-pagan conference in 1995 whose family was from Jamaica. I was attending a lecture on the Saami by a Norwegian woman, and had brought up some of the beliefs I was raised with. This woman from Jamaica was in the same lecture. She caught up with me later and we were surprised to discover the many similarities in beliefs between our ancestors.

According to Mircea Eliade, the Yukagir people of Northern Asia also believed the dead return to new bodies and live new lives.[55] These people have a specific form of divination used to determine which ancestor had reincarnated in any given child. In ancient times, the bones of shamans were used for this divination. The names of the ancestors were spoken and the relatively heavy bones would become light when the reincarnated ancestor's name was said. The modern Yukagir still recite these names before the infant. However today, the indication of the correct name is when the infant smiles.

I also know a wonderfully psychic Catholic woman who knows beyond a shadow of a doubt that her son is the reincarnation of her own father. For her, this does not conflict with her Catholic belief system. She believes God has blessed her with the return of her beloved father. It would appear that the basic spirituality at the core of most religions emerges through the heart. Like women in shamanic societies often do, she gave her son the same name as her father in an instinctual recognition of his return. Her son is astonishingly similar in mannerisms and attitudes to her departed father.

Most of those who believe in reincarnation, also believe that we tend to return with the same people to work out karmic debts or learn new lessons together. Chris Griscom writes, "we are almost always reenacting the same scenario with the same souls . . . That is how we begin to collect and carry forth our karmic pool of personal players, our karmic pool of extended players, which may encompass the whole global energy . . . "[56] Many people have experienced several lifetimes with the same group of people, as illustrated by Kira's experiences with her sister. The specifics of the relationships will vary from life to life, but the main goal of the group and the recurrent lessons remain the same.

Sometimes we return to balance things out and repay karmic debts. For example, my grandparents had supported and cared for my mother for lifetimes while she went off and did her thing. This time around, one of the things she needed to do was return the favor and restore equilibrium to these relationships. In this life, my mother supported and cared for her parents every step of the way, often putting their needs before her own. She did this not only out of love and respect for who they were in this life, but also because of her understanding that, in doing this, she was restoring a balance of power and support in their relationships. When they passed over, she was satisfied knowing that she had accomplished that particular goal of this lifetime.

We don't need to be karmically indebted to someone to return with them. We may be working on related themes. As Chris Griscom writes, "All the souls that are here on this planet at this time are part of the same collective repertoire and are working on similar themes."[57] No matter what you believe will occur around the millennium, it is clear that everyone on the planet at this time will have many common experiences, both personal and cultural. These are the "similar themes" that we have all chosen to return at this time to be able to experience.

We have come to share in the wars, the economic and political upheavals, the new accessibility of metaphysical ideas, and the changes brought about the Space and Information Ages. There are generational lessons that we can predict with some certainty through astrology. Those who were in their twenties in the 1960s had very different life themes from those who were twenty-something in the 1940s or the 1980s.

By the same token, all those sharing a common environmental or political event are working on comparable issues. Everyone who was incarcerated in a Nazi concentration camp or was a soldier conquering the New World shared a common life theme. I would not be surprised to find those who had been oppressed returning to the majority classes, and vice versa, to gain a more complete experience of these situations and to balance out karmic scales.

This is one reason why I often encourage indigenous peoples, and any who have experienced oppression, to release their reactions to having been victims and become more open to those "non-indigenous" people who are *true* seekers. Not only do we do ourselves, and our children, a disservice by continuing to create our people as victims but our fear and hostility can block the creation of an integrated and more respectful reality.

If one believes in reincarnation, death really isn't goodbye, it's merely a time-out before a change in the relationship. For this reason, during shamanic and other pagan rites of passage, we generally don't say goodbye, but rather "see you later" to the departed. This is because of an understanding of the continuity of the spirit and a belief in reincarnation. We believe we will see each other again in the Afterlife and we are likely to run into one another in a future incarnation, too.

Many very young children have memories of past lives, especially the life immediately preceding this incarnation. An incoming spirit who has not yet been indoctrinated with the limiting beliefs and blocks of our reality is still cognizant of her existence without a body and all of her prior incarnations. Some believe at this stage, we are also aware of potential future lives as well. It is said that some Tibetan lamas, most notably the Dalai Lama, are selected as a result of their incontrovertible memories of prior lives as a certain lamas.

Childhood and infancy nightmares are often related to these memories and to the unfamiliarity of a new body and environment. My son Karl had some real difficulties dealing with past-life issues and fears when he was about a year old. This not only showed up in his astrological chart but I became aware of it through shared dreams with him. He had many astrological transits going on at that time indicating that he was dealing with past-life issues. I was unable to pinpoint the effects of three of these transits. These were seemingly unknown to astrologers, and two of them only occur soon after birth.

Karl and I have our Moons conjunct in Pisces, among other interesting shared astrological aspects. In our case, this manifests as a shared emotional and psychic tie. We instinctively feel what the other feels. This is one of the reasons for our shared dreaming, which has occurred since I was pregnant.

During this time period, I was experiencing nightmares at the same time as Karl. As I rocked him back to sleep, I remembered these nightmares as past-life situations, which were not my lives. I was occasionally also present in these lives, but the memories I was having were not related to my prior incarnations. Through experience and journeying, it became clear that these were Karl's memories.

While Karl was fortunately not overly attached to any noncorporeal old friends, he did have nightmares regarding his inability to communicate through his new body. These issues carried over to his waking hours, as tantrums, crying bouts, and an increased need for physical contact with me. I needed to make a concerted effort to encourage him not to rely on the fact that I usually *knew* what he wanted. Our psychic connection could not be permitted to interfere with his developing abilities to communicate in this reality and with other people.

Of course to some degree, this type of behavior is frequently normal for infants at that age. It can be a challenge with a child who has not yet learned to speak, to determine the exact issues involved, and if the behavior is nothing more than "growing pains." In our situation, I was aware of the additional reasons behind it with my son and was able to take measures to get it under control. I believe that many children, who have been labeled difficult or high-need, have similar issues. Unfortunately many parents are unaware of these psychic influences on their children.

Karl and I worked through this period shamanically through journeying, energy work, and shared dreaming. With our conjunct Moons, it is very easy for me to comfort him just by creating an energy change in my own field while placing a hand on him or holding him in my lap. This is something any adult can do, to some degree, as a result of the psychic openness of children.

I have directed Karl's dreaming, from within and without, to guide him through these memories without getting entangled in them. Through the use of lucid dreaming and creating a sense of peace and safety when he is within my energy field, I have been able to help him face and integrate these memories in the most effective way possible and without trauma. It would benefit no one for me to block these memories, even if I could. Not only would that be an unethical invasion on my child, but these memories would eventually come up. It is quite possible that they would be more difficult to handle later on. I channel unconditionally loving and supportive energy to him for him to use as he feels is most beneficial for him. This is a choice he makes on a spiritual level, where he is unaffected by the fact that his body is a child.

Through our loving support and understanding in all realities, Karl has integrated these memories quite well and is now working on developing a wonderful, if incorrigibly healthy ego. Obviously, his communication skills have rapidly improved along with his increasing abilities to use his physical body. He rarely experiences nightmares any more. When he does, they are usually related to this reality, as is common among toddlers.

By paying attention to things we might normally discount, we can determine if an older child is experiencing past-life memories. It can be productive to pay close attention to things the child may say, such as "I remember that place" when watching television or reading a book. Often their make-believe games will give us clues as to who they were or where they may have lived before.

Children are often very clear dreamers, remembering specific details long after they awaken. Through listening with an accepting ear to their dream stories, we may be able to recognize past-life elements. Children have not yet learned to relegate dream memories to those dark, inaccessible areas of our psyches where we store our "unreal," "illogical" experiences.

It can be beneficial to begin to discuss these dreams and encourage an older child to keep a dream journal. Not only does a journal provide a concrete means for finding clues to past-life issues, but it also encourages the development of personal symbolism and creativity. Many children and adults find resolution to situations that bother them in this reality through paying attention to dream symbols.

The big question today seems not to be *if* we reincarnate, but if we incarnate along linear time lines or have concurrent lives going on at once in parallel worlds, or even within this one reality. These are interesting new developments. As shamans we have found that time is really not an absolute but rather an elastic concept created by consciousness. In journeying though the Middleworld, we are able to travel the space-time continuum at will.

Robert Monroe has posed the question of concurrent lives to his nonphysical friends, who responded that "it is not only possible but does take place frequently." He was given the name and location of a second life he was leading but did not have the "time or courage to verify it . . . " before he died.[58] More than a few psychics and mediums that I have met report being given the same information from their guides.

To the Saami, one's name is an integral part of one's identity. Each name is tied to a particular personality and identity. Traditional Saami do not believe that personality and identity are limited by our perception of time-space. Not only do the ancestor and the newborn who receives his or her name become one, but a newborn can also receive the name of an elderly, but still living relative. In this way, the elderly person and the newborn become one. They are then viewed as two aspects, or two separate lives of the same being. In a sense, this one spirit is recognized as leading two concurrent lives within this reality.

Several years ago, my mother experienced what appeared to be a bleed-through from a concurrent life. For several months, she came face to face with a man who was obviously stalking her. It was obvious by his reaction to seeing my mother that she was not the person he sought. The first time it happened, the man was extremely surprised and confused, as was my mother. The connection was lost and he disappeared.

Several times after that initial breakthrough, she also experienced living as the woman he was really seeking. She experienced this woman's thoughts and body as though they were her own. This experience felt, to my mother, as a split in her being rather than a sharing of another being's body. His appearance in her personal space eventually became so tangible, we were actually concerned for her physical safety. She believes that he succeeded in killing the other "her" and the contacts ended.

If we choose to believe the Many Worlds Interpretation of Quantum Mechanics, it may be quite possible for a future or Otherworldly "me" to have found a way to return and divert my current path from a potential future this person has seen. This would appear to support Robert Monroe's experience of a future "him" intervening in his current life in an attempt to influence the path of worldwide human events.[59] His future self had seen the potential for the human race and the possibilities if we did not realize that potential.

Einstein's special theory of relativity shows that there is no true universal time. You and I may perceive a dog barking and a door opening as occurring at the same time, while we are standing together. However, if one of us changes position, we may experience one of those events as taking place before the other. By changing one's frame of reference, simultaneous events may not appear to be so simultaneous.

Einstein was famous for his thought experiments. He used one of these to illustrate this concept. According to a variety of sources, it went something like this: imagine that you and I are in a room with a light bulb in the exact center. The room is moving and the light bulb is flashing. Someone else is standing outside, watching everything that happens.

When the light bulb flashes, you and I see the walls illuminate, all at the same time since the bulb is in the exact center of the room. However, at that same moment we are also pass the outside observer.

This observer also sees the flash and the light expand out. The difference is that this observer also sees the room in motion. From his perspective, he sees the light in the center as the forward wall moves away from the light and the rear wall moves toward the light. He sees the light hitting the rear wall first.

Our reality does depend on our perspective. This is apparently much more than just a psychological experience. What this boils down to is that our beliefs about the timing of events, really about time itself, vary according to where we are; our observation viewpoint. In light of this, the possibility of concurrent lives may be expanded to include those lives which, to our perception, appear to be in the past or future.

Most pagan belief systems view time and life as a wheel. While life does move in cycles of birth–death–rebirth, this can be taken more literally to indicate a nonscientific interpretation of the lack of an absolute universal time. The space-time continuum does not flow in time, it just *is*, and events are ordered about the continuum. This is not to say that events are predetermined, however. As we have seen, quantum mechanics proves that the mere presence of an observer affects the outcome of events.

Many of us have experienced a manifest Wheel of Life in our shamanic journeys, and other visions. I have been several times to a still-point at the Center of The Wheel around which all of life exists concurrently. In my experience, this is a learning center where we may go between lives or during dreaming/journeying. All I need to do to focus on any particular time is to change my perspective, my "frame of reference" as Einstein put it.

Most of us believe that we reside in a three-dimensional world, and this is certainly how most of us perceive our world. The truth is that our universe is four-dimensional, the fourth dimension being space-time. According to most models of the space-time continuum, time does not flow as we perceive it to. Events are ordered as being separate in time, and cause and effect is reality, however time itself does not move along.

At the subatomic level, our beliefs about a linear time, flowing continually forward become insignificant. Quantum processes don't often seem to care about our beliefs. For example, there is a theory of particle interaction, which shows that during electron-photon scattering, two processes occur simultaneously. In one process, the particles move forward in time; in the other they move backward in time.[60] This would seem to contradict our common sense belief systems.

Several modern physicists have proposed that consciousness itself may be a quantum process. If this is true, then it is certainly reasonable to believe that we may move beyond the experience of linear time simply through expanding our awareness and our "extrasensory" abilities. It is also possible that we are able to shamanically move backward and forward in time, as do the electrons and photons in the above-described experiment.

There are many stories of yogis whose bodies show no effects of aging. When they are ready to pass over, the body simply stops functioning. This can occur well over one hundred years after the body's birth. It is also quite possible to expect that our energy bodies, or journeying souls, are beyond time itself. We, as total beings, may live concurrent lives, or truly be One with All Life deciding what "life" to focus on to obtain the greatest learning at any given time.

However you see it, the point is that many people today either believe, or want to believe, in reincarnation. Possibly millions of people have undergone past-life regressions and come up with something they believe to be real. As Chris Griscom writes, "It doesn't matter if these scenarios are seen as true past lives or as figments of the imagination—because the source of imagination is from our own inner whispering."[61] As long as we gain something from the experience, how we choose to perceive it is unimportant.

When I was ten years old, a family friend took me through a present-life, and then a past-life regression. I remembered three significant lives during that regression. Both present—and past-life—regressions were to have a significant impact on me. I felt as Barbara Hand Clow must have when she wrote, in the preface to *Eye of the Centaur*, "the most meaningful result was the overall integration of my personality . . . opened me to greater happiness, freedom . . ."[62]

One of these lives profoundly influenced my feelings about life and death. I was an old desert nomad, probably Bedouin. I was on my deathbed with my wife beside me. I lay on blankets and pillows in a huge tent and I could hear the wind whipping sand against the sides of the tent. I listened to my sons murmuring outside. I knew my time had come and I said goodbye to my wife. I floated easily out of my body. It was the most peaceful feeling I had ever known. I expanded to include the energy of the universe and felt utterly complete.

I have never feared death and although I have grieved for the times I would no longer spend with someone, I have always been joyful for their transitions. I was fortunate to have been raised in a family that understands our connections to Other worlds and believes in other lives. While this family environment has certainly affected my worldview, I can honestly say that the direct experience of that one life has taken me beyond believing to an experiential understanding of the process.

Shamanically, we can look at other-life issues as part of one's total "shadow side." We do carry over issues and patterns that have affected us in past lives. Very often, these issues continue to affect us in our current lives. On the path to self-knowledge many are discouraged by an inability to determine why they hold certain limitations and fears. Often, they become frustrated by the lack of any discernible origin for these issues in their current lives.

Many of us feel programmed by something beyond our understanding and, therefore, out of our control. Many times these beliefs are the result of behaviors we adopted as children then forgot ever existed as our perspectives changed. However, many of these are bleed-through from other lives. Our spirits hold these memories and often store them in each new body. As these areas are activated, we revert to a very old autopilot, continuing to act out scenarios that our current incarnations never experienced. These can become even more difficult to clear as a result of our beliefs regarding reincarnation.

Whether they are the result of past lives, concurrent lives, future lives, or our own subconscious really makes no difference. The basic issues underlying all of these stories and experiences emerge from somewhere deep within us. During a regression or spontaneous memory, we need to trust that whatever comes up is valid for us and, if accepted and integrated, will lead us to a more balanced, healthy life.

Having guided many people through past-life regressions, my experience has been that whatever comes up is related in some way to other issues that are present in the individual's life at that time. Even those people who could not give up enough control to fully experience the regression and thought they were making it all up, "made-up" scenarios that were extremely useful and pertinent to issues they had been resisting within themselves.

Without getting into hypnosis or hypnotherapy, which I would not recommend anyone practice without sufficient training and practice, I have outlined below a very basic guided meditation and guided shamanic-type journey designed to assist in accessing significant other lives.

It is generally very useful to have the person being guided speak to the "guide" during the regression. This is beneficial both in remembering the regression and in maintaining a witness frame of mind. If for any reason this is not possible or is not desirable, please decide upon a signal to use during the meditation beforehand. Some people say "OK" and some people will use a hand signal. Use whatever feels best to the person being guided. Instruct this person to signal you when each step is completed.

I strongly recommend that the "guide" be prepared to end the session if necessary to avoid trauma. I also suggest that a guide have emergency numbers or contacts for shamanic counselors or professional hypnotherapists available if something difficult comes up. Although these situations are extremely rare, it is always wise to be prepared for anything.

Guided Meditation
Accessing Other Lives

Count down from ten to one. Stop periodically to tell the person: "Take a deep breath. You are getting deeper and deeper. At the count of one, you will be perfectly relaxed and comfortable."

At the count of one say: "One. You are now perfectly relaxed and comfortable. If at any time I need to bring you out of this relaxed state of consciousness, all I need to do is to clap my hands three times. When I clap my hands three times, you will be wide awake, feeling fine, and perfectly safe. (*pause*) When I clap my hands three times, you will be wide awake, feeling fine, and perfectly safe. (*pause*) Take a deep breath and go deeper. When I snap my fingers, you will go to your favorite place of relaxation. This may be a place you have always wanted to go, a place you know and feel safe in, or a place you create in your mind. (*pause*) Go now to your favorite place of relaxation." Snap your fingers once.

Say: "You are completely safe and comfortable and will remain so throughout this meditation. You will remain in control at all times, and can end this meditation whenever you choose."

Say: "You are now standing in the middle of a large bright room. To your left is an open hallway. Enter the hallway and open the first door you see. As you enter the room behind the door, you are greeted by your spirit guides (angels, etc.)."

Pause, then say: "Tell your guides that you are going to observe your other lives. Ask them to be with you, to guide and protect you in your journey. Ask their assistance in accessing lives that have a significant impact on your current life, or lives that have valuable lessons to teach you at this time." (*pause*)

Say: "Turn and leave the room. Your spirit guides are at either side of you as you leave and continue on down the hall. You see doors of all different shapes and colors. When you see a door that seems to interest you, let me know." (*pause and wait for signal*)

If there is no signal within a few seconds, say: "Continue down the hall, looking at each door. When a door interests you, let me know."

If there is no signal soon after this say: "Continue down the hall. Do you see the doors as you pass?" (*pause*)

If there is still no answer, bring them out of trance by clapping your hands three times. If they have fallen asleep, either wake them or let them sleep. It is your choice. Either way, they will be fine.

If they answer, say: "You now see a door that interests you in some way." Continue with normal meditation.

"Enter this door with your spirit guides at your sides. As you pass through the doorway, you see a scene unfold before you. What do you see? (*pause and wait for response)* Describe the scene in detail. *(pause and wait for response)* Do you know what year it is? *(pause and wait for response)* Who are you in this scene? *(pause and wait for response)* What are you doing? *(pause and wait for response)* How do you feel? *(pause and wait for response)* Do you recognize anyone else in this time? *(pause and wait for response)* Do you understand what is significant about this life? *(pause and wait for response)* Ask your guides for any help or clarification you need." Continue guiding and questioning according to what feels right to you.

When it appears nothing more can be gained from this life say: "Release this life and all involved. Thank your spirit guides for their guidance and support. Leave this scene and return to the hallway."

Say: "When you see a door that seems to call to you, let me know." *(pause and wait for signal)* Continue with above meditation through a few more doors until the person feels ready to return.

Say: "Follow the hallway back to your favorite place of relaxation. *(pause and wait for signal)* If you feel you need assistance grounding or integrating these memories, ask your spirit guides for their help." *(pause and wait for signal)*

"Thank them again for their continuing guidance and support in your life. Let me know when you are ready to return."

Count up from one to ten. Stop periodically to say: "At the count of ten, you will be wide awake, feeling fine, and perfectly safe. You will remember everything and you will feel completely comfortable with these memories."

At the count of ten, say: "You are wide awake. You feel fine and are perfectly safe. You remember everything. These memories feel comfortable and you understand the significance of these lives. These memories will continue to integrate into your consciousness."

A personal journal can be invaluable in understanding and integrating these memories. In order to keep the memory clear, it is generally recommended that the regression be recorded immediately afterwards. Many people have found that after a period of time, elements of different regressions, dreams, or journeys will begin to fit together like the pieces of a puzzle.

Semi-Guided Lowerworld Journey
Accessing Other Lives
....

To be read while drumming, or with a shamanic drumming tape in the background.

Say: "Find an opening in the ground that feels familiar to you, perhaps a hole, an entrance into a tree down to the roots, or a freshwater spring. If you cannot find a natural opening, imagine something that will carry you below the surface of the Earth, such as an elevator, a burrowing animal, or a subway."*(pause)*

Pick up the tempo of your drumming and say, "Enter this opening and feel yourself moving down below the surface of the Earth, deeper and deeper. *(pause)* Pay attention to the hole or tunnel you are in. Is it dark or light? How is the temperature? Is there anything unusual about it?" *(long pause)*

Say: "Soon you see an opening up ahead of you." Slow your drumming and say: "You emerge into a new world. *(pause)* What do you see here? Take some time and look around. *(pause)* Now stop and call to your spirit guides. *(pause)* Greet them as they approach. *(pause)* Ask their help in accessing significant other lives that may have valuable lessons or issues for you at this time in your life. *(long pause)* Ask them to accompany you on your journey to see your other lives." *(pause)*

Say: "Now you notice a path that seems interesting. *(pause)* Follow this path with your guides. *(pause)* What do you see as you walk? *(pause)*Soon you notice a smaller path off to one side. Take this path to see a scene from one of your other lives. *(long pause)* What do you see? *(pause)* Who are you in this life? *(pause)* Do you recognize anyone else? *(pause)* Do you understand what is significant about this life? *(pause)* Ask your spirit guides for any help or clarification you need." Continue guiding and questioning according to what feels right to you.

When it appears nothing more can be gained from this life say: "Release this life and all involved. Thank your spirit guides for their guidance and support. Leave this life and return to the main path."

Say: "As you walk, you see another side trail. Follow this trail to another of your significant lives." Continue guiding and questioning according to what feels right to you.

Continue exploring these paths to other lives until the person feels ready to return.

Say: "Follow the main path back to the opening to the above world. *(pause)* If you feel you need assistance grounding or integrating these memories, ask your spirit guides for their help. *(pause)* Thank them again for their continuing guidance and support in your life. Let me know when you are ready to return."*(pause)*

Pick up the tempo of your drumming and say: "You are now following the hole or tunnel back up to the surface. *(very long pause)* When the drum beats three times then three times again, you will have returned to the here and now with full memory of the journey. These memories will continue to integrate into your consciousness and your guides will continue to be with you in this reality."

Beat drum three times twice and stop.

What I find equally interesting regarding past lives is something I briefly discussed earlier in this book. Many people have discovered that they (as a future incarnation) have been their own spirit guides. Robert Monroe writes of how he finally came to the realization that he was the one who met himself after the death of previous incarnations and how he guided himself out of this reality.[63]

In one situation, he describes answering a call for help from a young warrior who had died in a battle. As he watched, the warrior died and then attempted to return to the fight, not realizing he was dead. Monroe realized that he had been to this same battle twice before. Not only was he the young warrior he helped on that warrior's journey after death, he was also Robert Monroe who had been shown this scene before as explanation and as a healing for a physical pain he experienced in his present life. Furthermore, he was the one who had taken him as Robert Monroe to see that life.[64]

Ancestors play a large part in shamanism, both traditional and modern. The ancestors are frequently those who Call us to the shamanic path. They are also often some of our best teachers. In several cultures, it is the ancestors and other spirits who are responsible for the training of a new shaman.

Many of us have experienced one or more previous lives as an ancestor. My great-aunt would tell me stories of another Kristin many years ago in Saamiland (Lapland) because she felt I was that ancestor. Although I have not yet investigated that particular possibility, I did experience a spontaneous memory of a past-life incarnation as a male Saami who told me he was an ancestor of mine.

My great aunt introduced me to this male ancestor-incarnation shortly after she died. She told me that she had been the last of those who could continue to teach me about our family in this reality. Now, she said, I must learn from the ancestors and spirits alone.

This was an ancestor who had a strong desire to assist me in my spiritual growth and my learning about that part of my heritage. Since that time, he has taught me a great deal and has guided me to others in this reality who have helped me to better understand my Saami ancestors.

As both shamans and science have shown, time is elastic, at least on a spiritual or quantum level. When we move into an expanded awareness beyond the limitations of our third-dimensional perception, our psychic and shamanic experiences do not seem so fantastic. And for me, in this identity occupying this point in space-time, the belief that we are more than just this one life, and that there is some reason to all this, is a preferred reality.

Endnotes

51   Philip Carr-Gomm, e-mail discussion.
52   Richard Ross, e-mail discussion.
53   Ibid.
54   Ibid.
55   Eliade, *Shamanism: Archaic Techniques of Ecstasy*, p. 246.
56   Griscom, *Ecstasy is a New Frequency*, p. 50.
57   Ibid., p. 50.
58   Monroe, *Far Journeys*, p. 270.
59   Monroe, *Ultimate Journey*, pp. 197–199.
60   Capra, *The Tao of Physics*, p. 183.
61   Griscom, *Ecstasy is a New Frequency*, p. 50.
62   Clow, *Eye of the Centaur*, p. 26.
63   Monroe, *Ultimate Journey*, throughout chapter 9, pp. 105–124.
64   Ibid., pp. 110–116.

Chapter 9

DEATH AND PETS

The animals that share our lives are considered family members by many. In *Circle Network News*, there is a section for announcements of births, deaths, and other transitions. People write many of the obituaries in *Circle* about the passing of their animals. Their passing can affect us just as deeply as the passing of a beloved human. The animals we associate with sometimes need assistance in their passing. It is for this reason that I chose to include this chapter.

Many modern shamans have performed deathwalks for pets or other animals. I have not only Walked pets to the Other side, but I also assist any animals I see in need. I work for animals on the side of the road, deer on car roofs during hunting season, and those who gave their lives so that we might have a hot dog at a baseball game. Certainly not all animals need our assistance, just as all humans do not, but I feel it is important to make the offer and do what I can if my offer is accepted.

Indigenous peoples honored the spirits of the animals they needed to kill for food and other essential items. They respected the fact that these "relations" filled a vital place for us in the cycle of life. These animals were our brothers and sisters as well as our teachers and guides. We all shared the need for food and sustenance in the planetary life cycle. It was understood and honored that we may also become a meal for one of them someday. Even if we did not, our ashes would become one with the ashes of all our relations and continue to create life on this planet.

Many indigenous peoples held special rituals in gratitude for the life an animal gave to the people. My Saami ancestors held a three-day festival honoring the sacred Bear after such a kill. Immediately after the kill, the Bear would be tied to the sled with birch branches and then tapped with these branches. It was a Saami belief that the life force contained in these branches could be conferred to another being through tapping or physical contact. In this way, the Saami hunters gave the Bear a supplement or substitute in thanks for the body they had taken and a boost to the next life for the Bear.

During this three-day festival, all Bear meat must be completely consumed. Specific parts of the body of the Bear were preserved and buried in honor, so that the Bear might be use them in the next life. The People used all of the other body parts for clothing, tools, and other necessities. Even the blood was used: for ritual and purification. Nothing was wasted; everything was honored.

While my husband and I usually give thanks for all our blessings including the food we eat, we offer a special prayer when eating meat. The following is this special prayer:

> *Great Spirit,*
> *We thank you for the gift of this food.*
> *We send blessings of peace, love and release to all*
> *whose bodies and energies went into bringing us this nourishment.*
> *We honor you in our enjoyment and utilization of this meal.*
> *May it bring us health and joy,*
> *reminding us of our interconnections with All That Is.*
> *As we receive, so do we give back*
> *And give thanks for this gift in the Cycle of Life.*[65]

In modern society, many of us have adopted the belief that animals are lower forms of life deserving of little to no respect. Many people feel that animals were put on this Earth for us to use and discard as we choose. They are not sentient beings; they are commodities.

As one who walks a shamanic path, my entire Being screams out at the close-minded, egocentric injustice of this attitude. I have had many teachers who were in animal form, both in this reality and in Others. I have been told by some of my animal allies that they are aspects of me and that we are One.

I have seen an amusing bumper sticker on some cars that reads something like, "The more people I know, the more I like my dog." While this is not necessarily true for me, I do wonder how we as a species can be so blind to the true beauty and brotherhood inherent in other lifeforms on this planet. We have allowed our sciences to severely limit our beings and our experience of life. If we can't measure it, it doesn't exist. If it can't speak, it must be stupid. And of course, if it can't create weapons of mass destruction, it is certainly a lower life form.

207

Even if one chooses to believe that we have no equals on this planet, it should be obvious to most that a dying pet is very similar to a dying or very ill child. In life, they are much like our children. Many of us feel the same protective, gentle love for them and they depend on us for just about everything. They look to us as examples, friends, and occasionally, guardians. And just like a child who is ill, all they know is that it hurts and they want "Mommy" or "Daddy" to comfort and help them.

Call it "bleeding-heart liberalism" if you wish, but we owe it to these beings who rely on us and trust us implicitly, and to ourselves, to be worthy of that trust. We are not stronger or better if we turn our backs on an animal in need. We are weak and disrespectful of all Life. We need to look deep within ourselves to find that being of wonder that our animals see in us. Even more, we need to be strong enough to allow that being to emerge.

Animals, whether in the wild or as a domesticated pet, function mainly on an emotional and instinctual level. They *feel* the innocence and the value within us. Empathic individuals occasionally report being flooded with emotion once an animal realizes they can understand them. Our pets tend to instantly feel what we are feeling. They can, and do, react to the emotional atmosphere of their environments.

Ever since I was a child, my dogs have reacted the instant I became emotionally upset. On occasion, the dogs have known before I was aware of my feelings. Before I could say or do anything, each of these animals was aware of my emotional state. Although they all responded in their own ways depending on the emotion I experienced, it was clear to everyone in our family what the cause of their behavior was. On a purely emotional level, each of these animals felt and experienced what I was feeling, as if it was his or her own emotion.

The authors of *Dr. Pitcairn's Natural Health for Cats and Dogs,* confirm in their book that our feelings affect the well-being of our pets.[66] Our pets, they write, will absorb any feelings in the home, even if those feelings are unrelated to the pet. These emotions can aggravate a pet's existing health problems, and can even create behavioral or nervous health conditions. Finally, even veterinarians acknowledge the impact of stress and emotional health on animals.

Many shamans have found that animals often act as filters for our emotions and illnesses. They will soak up the emotions in their environment, returning the love and support while holding onto any destructive emotions. Most of the time, animals are able to instinctively ground these energies so they do no harm to anyone.

However, problems frequently arise when these emotions are too intense or too consistent in the animal's environment. Some animals will continue to screen out negative emotions for their humans to the point that the animal's physical body can no longer handle the influx of destructive energies. In certain situations, the emotions can be so damaging or so consistently strong, that a person or family will seem to go through pets like water.

For example, I knew a family who had been having extreme emotional difficulties, both within the family and with most of their friends. Relationships were falling apart and fingers were pointing in all directions. These individuals were unaware that they continued to attract the same destructive situations. Although it was within their power to alter these patterns, they did not recognize this. As a result, they all felt victimized. No one wanted to live together and hostile emotions were at an all-time high when their pets began to die off. Although everyone was upset when another animal passed over, no one stopped to look at potential psychic causes because each animal's physical cause of death was different. Now, in addition to the public issues plaguing this family, the fact that their pets continued to die created an additional emotional element in the chaotic mix that was their experience of life at that time. By the time a year had passed, all of their dogs, cats, and one of their birds were gone.

As an objective witness to the situation, it was clear to me what was going on. Unfortunately at that time, all I could do was to be objectively supportive to the family in this reality and offer my assistance to the animals as they passed over. Some of them just could not take the intensity of the emotions projected by their people. Others felt that they could better serve their family from the Other side, where their physical bodies would not limit them.

Since our animals are so open to us on an empathic and frequently telepathic level, it is very important that we be careful what we project when we are with them. Although we all know personal issues should be taken care of, we get lazy or we just don't want to face it *right now*. Few of us realize how these issues that we allow to continue affect those around us, particularly pets and small children.

When communicating with animals, it is equally important that our actions are not in conflict with our hearts. Like children, animals instinctively know when we are not being honest. For example, there is no way for me to hide the fact that we are going to the vet from my dog, Aiko. Even if I block that image and focus on something completely different, all it takes is one small slip of my attention and she's got it. She also instantly picks up on my feelings of dishonesty in trying to hide where we are going and my regrets that she finds these visits so traumatic. It is far better to just be honest from the start and focus, instead, on the long hike we will take after we leave the vet.

The most effective way for us to communicate with animals is by using what a friend of mine refers to as picto-empathic language. All this means is that we psychically send a picture or feeling along with a verbal communication. In this way, we are clear on all levels of our communication what we wish to convey to them.

When I ask Aiko if she wants to go for a walk, I visualize where we will be walking and I feel excited to go. I rarely need to consciously focus on this, since it is already in my mind when I make the decision take her with me. She usually starts jumping around before I even open my mouth to ask. Of course, this can be annoying when she is not invited, but catches the image and wants to come anyway. She can be a bit of a telepathic bully at times.

Similarly when you are telling an animal to do something, you hold and send the appropriate picture and feeling. While we rarely order our pets about on whim, it is essential that they listen to us on occasion. When crossing a busy highway or when confronted by a hostile dog off the leash, it is imperative for all of us that Aiko do what I tell her. It is at times like this that I project a steel wall of command, if my first request is disregarded. This lets Aiko know that the situation is serious and I need her cooperation to get us all through it safely.

This clarity of communication can be vital when an animal is sick or dying. In this way, we can be very clear in our offers and efforts to heal them. We are also more psychically open to them and can receive their messages more clearly. Not only are we able to comfort them more effectively but when difficult decisions need to be made, we can explain the situation and ask for their input.

Several years ago, our dog Misty was suffering from hip dysplasia and bone cancer. As a family, we discussed the option of hip replacement surgery, which was still experimental for dogs and could only be performed some 2,000 miles away. We were desperate, but we wanted to be sure Misty had every opportunity for healing, no matter what the cost to us.

No one even wanted to mention euthanasia but I felt it should be an option. I knew that the cancer in her bones was spreading and that the long trip and surgery was likely to be extremely stressful for her. I wondered if it was fair to put her through all that knowing that she had only a short time left with us. We were also not entirely sure she would make it through the surgery. I opened psychically to Misty and let her know how we felt. I allowed her to feel, directly through me, how much we loved her and how we did not want to lose her. I explained the medical situation and the options as best I could for her level of understanding. Then I asked what *she* wanted. Misty was in extreme pain and could not even stand alone to go to relieve herself. She did not want to be shipped off for surgery and she knew her time was limited. She did not want to be alone. She wanted to die with us. I made the difficult phone call and was by her side throughout the whole euthanasia procedure.

Euthanasia can be an impossible decision for some people to make. It can be difficult to know what the "right" choice is. This is a highly individual choice and should not be rushed into. Although generally, we do not want to disrupt the natural death process, just the fact that these animals are domesticated, vaccinated, and live in our homes, alters their own natural responses to the death transition.

In the wild, most animals will separate themselves from others, knowing their end is near. They will go off somewhere to die in peace. Domesticated pets not only rely on us for just about everything, but they have few opportunities to isolate themselves and await their deaths. Since we have become surrogate parents to our pets, we must accept the fact that there may be times when they need us to make life and death decisions for them as well.

When faced with it, I make this choice based on a number of factors. The main variables are the extent of suffering and the time frame involved. Our family is more than willing to do whatever it takes to care for an animal at home, just as we would for any family member. However, when an animal is suffering greatly for an extended period of time, euthanasia becomes an option.

When our dog Ram was dying, I held him in my arms for an entire day, working with stones and energy to dull his pain and help him pass over easily. Several times he stopped breathing or convulsed but he came right back. Ram felt it was necessary to hang on until my father could get home. This was very important to him—not to leave without saying goodbye to *his* human.

By the time my father arrived, Ram was unable to make the final leap out-of-body on his own. The majority of his spirit had passed over already and he only retained enough energy to keep his body going. We decided it was not right to make him endure obvious pain and difficulty of breathing when he was ready to go. By the end of the day, we felt it was time to end his suffering and release him.

Often we are so attached to the animal or so afraid of death ourselves, we can't bear to make such a critical choice. Many people can be so upset by the necessity of such a choice that they are unable to be present for the procedure. Obviously, we need to be honest and clear with ourselves and with our pets. If we either cannot be supportive or cannot keep our emotions under control, or if we believe we are doing something wrong by physically assisting a death in this way, we probably should stay away.

On the other hand by staying away, we are denying these beings our comfort and strength when they need it most. I do not say this to make anyone feel guilty for an inability to handle this situation, nor should you fear that your animal friend is doomed to be stuck between realities because you were not there for him. Like any relationship, this is a sharing of two beings' individualities. However, unlike many strictly human relationships, it is a true sharing.

Our animal companions understand at a deep level what we are capable of at any given time. They have shared our lives by choice for various reasons. Whatever the reasons, they have specific lessons to teach us. They have things to learn from us as well. Often, an animal will choose death as their final gift and lesson for us. We need to view this as an opportunity for growth. One's ability to immediately climb out from under heavy emotions is not nearly as important as how the experience is used.

When we can grow through the death of a loved one, we honor them in a very important way. We do not hide behind our memories of them and use that loss as an excuse to escape from the world. We elevate them to a higher level by accepting this gift and using it as they would have wanted. We become stronger, more enlightened beings as a result. In this way, they can move on to their next worlds with the knowledge that this life brought spiritual growth to another.

The shaman can be invaluable in such a situation. A shaman can assist an "owner" with the release of guilt and attachments. We can often help this person gain enough emotional control to be there for her pet, even if that control only lasts as long as the procedure does. Afterward, whether this person was at the procedure or not, a shaman can guide her through her emotions into healing.

By putting our responses in terms of the individual worldview, we can most effectively direct this healing to pet "owners." We open to spirit guidance in order to channel the necessary energies to those in need. We encourage the release of grief. In much the same way we do during a human death, we can facilitate goodbyes, pass on messages, and help to create healing rites of passage.

Grief regarding the death of an animal is an issue that has been well covered in some books on animal care. Those loved ones, that have lost an animal friend, need the same assistance and guidance as those who have lost a beloved human. We give them their privacy, while alternately encouraging them to share their feelings. Rather than allowing them to dwell on the loss, we direct their thoughts to happy memories, to honoring the lessons they learned in that relationship, and the knowledge that their friend has moved on to a new life.

The death of an animal can be even more difficult for the humans who grieve for this loss because society is generally less understanding of these feelings. Many people are told to go get another animal, as if an animal companion were just another possession to be replaced like a broken car. When a beloved animal dies, our grief can be dismissed and even ridiculed by our communities. There is an equally great need for a support system after the death of a pet as there is after the death of a human. Even if this support is just one other person who can listen with compassion and empathize with our feelings, it can be vital to one's ability to move through this grief. Although the percentage remains relatively small, there are more and more people falling in love with their pets. A good place to go for support may be your local pet shop, or animal specialty store. Many vets today are willing to speak with people or refer them to a support system.

I have found that some people will use animal companions as buffers for their own lives, both during life and after the animal's death. These people are frequently unable to release an animal's ashes or personal belongings for years after the death. They use these items and their unresolved feelings to prevent any deep attachments with other people or animals. Although they may adopt another animal, the bond they shared with the departed pet just is not there with the new animal. These people are also often incapable of reaching a decision regarding the release of the animal's belongings or ashes. Even after messages from the departed pets have been clearly received, the acceptance of these wishes is often blocked. In situations such as this, forcing the issue is not recommended. Before any burial, scattering, or release of personal items is possible, the deeper issues that are responsible for the block must be addressed. These are often issues related to a fear of getting too close and being hurt by another.

A shaman or other counselor can be necessary in guiding these individuals past these issues. This entails facing a deeply repressed and feared aspect of the shadow. To do this effectively requires a considerable amount of courage as well as a willingness to be vulnerable to oneself. It may also require one or more soul-retrieval processes before any significant progress can be made.

What is not usually discussed, in literature or in conversations, is the effect of grief on a pet. When an animal loses someone close to them, most people just assume the animal will go on as usual. This could not be further from the truth. Not only can animals suffer extreme grief and loneliness when their favorite human dies; they also react to the loss of other humans and other animals. As highly emotional beings, a death in their family can affect them deeply.

We see a minor recognition of this in bittersweet commercials where a dog will sit at the bus stop all day waiting for his little boy to return from the first day of school. Not many people realize that this dog does not know whether his boy is ever coming back. We think, "Oh, isn't that sweet" but rarely do we attempt to help an animal through a difficult time like this. When the primary caregiver or favorite human passes over, many animals will choose to die, too. Some go immediately before or after the death of their human, and some will refuse to eat, slip into depression, and just waste away.

When it became necessary for my grandfather to move from his home to an assisted-living respite center, his cat, Tommy, became very depressed. During the four years since my step-grandmother's death, Grandpa and Tommy had become extremely close. Although we all visited Tommy frequently, while my grandfather was in the respite home, and my mother was at my grandfather's house every day feeding and spending time with Tommy, he went downhill very quickly.

He went from a playful, affectionate fat cat to a skinny, lethargic cat that tended to isolate himself more often than not. He seemed to be waiting for the right time to hide and die. While he permitted my mother to comb his hair (which he once loved) and hold him on occasion, he had lost his spark for life. He *felt* sad and hopeless.

Tommy seemed to *know* when my grandfather had his stroke. Afterwards, he became even more sullen, refusing to eat. His coat had lost its shine and he was more listless than ever. Tommy eventually died a few days before my grandfather did. He wanted to be with his human on the Other side.

Much to the consternation of the other side of the family, we had Tommy buried with my grandfather inside the foot of his coffin. We believed it was the right thing to do. They had been constant companions, supporting and comforting each other through some very difficult and lonely years. Tommy obviously left his body in response to my grandfather's impending departure. We all felt it was important that their bodies be permitted to remain together. We *felt* it was what they wanted us to do.

Sometimes there is not much we can do for a grieving animal in this reality. We can be there to care for them physically and to give them love if they allow it, but we cannot make them get over their grief. We cannot force them to play or connect with us, or even to go on living. What we can do, however, is attempt to reach them shamanically.

We can use the shamanic journey specifically to connect with the animal in need. We can find out on a shamanic level what, if anything, we can do for them in this reality. Bear in mind that they may respond that they do not want us to do anything for them. This is a request that we must honor. It is important to be prepared for whatever they may ask. There have been animals that have requested euthanasia. It is best to decide what you are, or are not, willing to do and make that very clear to them up front.

We can also establish psychic connections between the animal and her departed loved one. Sometimes, this is the most useful thing we can do. Even though animals tend to be more open to Other realities and energies than most humans, grief and fear may prevent them from establishing this connection for themselves.

Often once this link is made, there is a radical change in the animal's attitude. They are then able to continue to receive the love and support of the departed loved one. As a result, they no longer feel abandoned and alone. Knowing that a loved one has not really left us can make it easier for anyone to go on living and establish bonds with others in this reality.

Rites of passage for departed animals are just as instrumental as rites for humans are, in allowing those who are grieving to begin to heal. The rituals for animals tend to be simpler, but they are no less profound. Also, just like our own ceremonies, they will vary according to the animal and the loved ones. Both rituals and deathwalks for a pet commonly reflect the beliefs of owner, or shaman.

Many people will invoke the deities they associate with animals or they will call on their own personal guides when performing a death ritual for an animal. In this way, we use our personal and cultural symbolism to invoke the most beneficial beings for our departed animal friends. Occasionally, who we invoke is not who shows up. We must learn to trust our intuition and our perception. Our higher selves, or the guides of the animal, may be letting us know that they have taken care of it. The energy we called upon may not be what is required in that particular situation.

We may find ourselves calling upon beings or images we know little about but suddenly spring to mind as we speak. Trust that you are receiving what is necessary. And then there are the times when we really experience the presence of exactly who we intended to call all along. This can be an awesome encounter with truly magnificent beings.

My friend West Hardin assisted his partner's cat Clara in her passing and, in doing so, had an unforgettable experience of an ancient goddess. When Clara died in his arms, West called upon Bast, the Egyptian cat goddess. Bast is the deity that he associates with cats and their Afterlife. He felt certain this would be the being to call upon to guide Clara beyond her physical life. As West asked Bast to come and take Clara back into Her pride, he felt Her presence enter the room. He felt surrounded by the warmth and love of Bast, then he saw Her take Clara and leave our reality.

This is interesting because many of those who assist animals in death report the presence of a larger Being manifesting as that type of animal. Bast is often depicted as a cat or as a woman with a cat's head. Some believe this larger being is the archetypal animal that embodies the energies of that species; the personification of the group soul. Others believe this is the easiest way for our minds to comprehend the reality of what occurs. If it works for you and the animal in need, it makes no difference what you believe.

I had a similar initial experience with a cat. A huge feline presence visited our home the night before our family cat Karma passed over. My mother and I first felt it outside just before it passed through our front door. This presence stationed itself in the corner by the door for the remainder of the night. Its energy was intense. It was quite obviously feline, to our *sight* and *feeling*. I asked if it was Bast, although it did not feel female, and was told that Bast is a part of It. That is all It would say to me. It was there for Karma, not me.

Karma was very old and had been ill for some time. Her kidneys had finally failed and we made the decision to have her euthanized, with her permission. Karma sat on my mother's couch watching this *big cat* with huge eyes. Finally she went over to it and slept there until morning.

When we brought her home from the veterinarian's office, Karma was buried near our dog Misty, on my parents' land. The *big cat* was nowhere to be *felt*. Although Karma was a true hunter, or maybe because of this, we felt a strong pull to put feathers on her grave and I was inspired to sing "Fly like an eagle, fly so high, circling the universe, on wings of pure light," during her death rite.[67] We all felt that she flew out of there into the next realm.

As family members, our animals deserve to have their own memorial services or funerals. This is a time for us to honor them and to say goodbye. It can be a safe forum from which to tell them how much they mean to us and to release their spirits lovingly. I would suggest keeping with whatever religion or tradition you or your family follows. Loosely base the service on a human ritual but simplify it. If you prefer to have a structured ritual prepared, decide ahead of time what you want to do and say. Write it all down.

Sometimes the act of recording a ritual for future reference is beneficial for those individuals who get very emotional. It is also a wonderful memory and can provide the basic format for future rituals. In preparing the ritual ahead of time in writing, there will not be additional pressure to remember or to do things "right." There is no shame in reading a ritual. What is important is the intent and energy put into it, not how it looks to someone else.

During rites of passage, my family normally keeps things very simple. During or immediately after death, we send the departed a flood of love and release them. We direct spiritual healing, if it is needed. When we lived on five acres of woodlands, the body of the departed animal was buried on the family land, usually in their favorite spot. The graves were surrounded with a circle of rocks.

Sometimes a crystal or other stone is charged with energy and placed in the grave with the body. Our dog, Ram, was buried along with the chrysocolla used in healing him. Not only does this keep the object of healing with an animal's body but it also returns the stone to the Earth for clearing.

Now that my family members and I live in a city, we will need to create new burial methods. There are a number of options for pet owners available, from cremation to pet cemeteries. This is something that should be discussed with the pet and other family members before making a decision.

In my family, we usually smudge the area and all attending, then we take turns speaking our prayers. We thank the animal for sharing our lives, for teaching, for playing, and for loving us each step of the way. Often I will drum, sometimes we will sing, and I offer a deathwalk immediately after the ritual.

Guiding an owner in creating their own rituals for a departed pet can be extremely rewarding for all involved. I am continually amazed at the creative and intuitive elements that are included, even by those who seemingly have no interest in "such things." Our love for these beings crosses all barriers, and in bypassing our rational minds, allows us to instinctively channel our own healing into these rituals. This is important no matter who the rite is for. To follow a preset ceremony that holds no personal meaning does nothing except possibly appease a cultural feeling of "should." To simplify and personalize speaks to our souls and catalyzes release and healing.

One issue I must address here is the fact that while rites of passage are beneficial for both the living and the departed, we do not hold up the passage of the spirit by not immediately performing these rituals. Some people have expressed surprise when they discover that a departed animal has reincarnated years later when they are still carrying around the animal's ashes. Others fear that their inability to make a decision is somehow impairing the ability of the departed to move on. This is not necessarily true.

Our departed animal companions may choose to hang around us to better serve our spiritual progress and healing from beyond the Veil. This is a choice they make and a gift to both of us. They are not bound to our world for lack of a ritual or due to our resistance. While it is certainly true that they feel our resistance and this may

216

make their decision more difficult, we cannot forever bind any departed spirit to us by refusing our own healing or by ignoring rites of passage.

Having addressed that common fear, I can now turn to the details of rites of passage. In order to facilitate the creation of these rites for an animal, I have outlined three simple, nondenominational ceremonies below. Keep in mind that these are outlines only. Please feel free to alter, or to add, whatever you feel is meaningful and applicable.

Animal Burial Ritual

Using incense, smudge, or a drum, purify the area and charge it with healing energy. If this animal disliked fire or smoke, omit those elements.

Once the grave has been dug, place some flowers or herbs in the base. You might choose to use forget-me-nots, roses, or other flowers you associate with everlasting love. Some beneficial herbs are sandalwood for its high spiritual energies, or sage (*Salvia* spp.) for its association with immortality, healing, and protection. Then place the body on top of these, and cover it with a few more of the flowers or herbs.

If you have chosen to place personal items, crystals, or other stones in the grave, now is the time to charge them (if this has not already been done) with energy and place them in with the body.

Call upon the Spirits of the six directions and the Creator to join with you in this ceremony. Ask that they bless your work. Request guidance, that your every action may honor them.

Call upon the spirit of the departed to join with you. Let him know the reason for this ceremony and make it clear that you honor him through it.

Offer a prayer, such as: "Through this ceremony, we commend the body of our beloved _____ to the Earth as we entrust his spirit to the Creator. We gather here to honor his memory and to send him our blessings for a joyous reunion with All of Life."

The leader directs the gathering in a special prayer or song at this point. I would only recommend that this focus on the continuity of life and love as well as celebrate life, freedom, and rebirth.

If one person has been designated to replace the earth in the grave, do so now. Alternatively, you may choose to take turns each placing a shovelful of earth in the grave. However you choose to organize this, make each step a sacred one.

With each consecutive shovelful, offer a prayer to the Earth who receives this body, to the being who is now on his way to a new life, and to the Great Spirit who will receive his spirit. Continue to offer prayers for peace, love, release, and anything else you choose, until the grave is full.

Holding hands and forming a circle, if you can, sit or stand around the grave. Allow yourself to feel every emotion you experience. Feel comfortable expressing these emotions as an offering of honesty and respect for this departed animal.

Go around the circle and take turns offering prayers, good wishes, stories, jokes, and whatever you feel. Continue this until all present feel some sense of release.

Offer one final prayer: "Although we grieve for the times we will no longer share in this world, we rejoice in your freedom. We are grateful for the sharing of our lives during your time here in this world. Your memories and gifts live on within each of us as we freely release you to your next world. We send you heartfelt blessings of peace, love, and joy. We say not goodbye, but farewell until we meet again."

Animal Memorial Service

Also excellent for use as part of an ashes-scattering after a cremation (if you know that this animal disliked smudge or smoke, omit those elements unless this ceremony takes place at least a month after the animal's death).

Prepare the area with any flowers or decorations you prefer. Set up a simple altar with a photo of the departed in the center, surrounded by personal effects and items symbolizing the Earth and Great Spirit.

Using incense, smudge, or a drum, purify the area. Charge it with healing and loving energy.

Set up a central altar on a blanket inside or outside—at the animal's favorite spot. Place a picture of the animal in the center and surround it with items that were special to this animal or items that are symbolic of this animal's favorite things, places, and people. Also on this blanket, have a bowl of earth. As is true with the human rite, the earth is our Earth Mother to whom this animal's body has returned.

Clear those attending with your drum or smudge as they enter. The ritual leader should explain the symbolism of the altar and other decorations to those attending. Allow everyone some time to look over the altar and get comfortable.

Sit or stand in a circle. The leader states the purpose for this ritual and invites the spirit of the animal to join in. Any other deities or spirits you wish to invite should be called at this time.

Go around the circle, speaking your prayers for this animal; share stories and feelings about your time together or your grief. Everyone should be made comfortable to say what they feel. Go around the circle at least three times, until everyone feels some sense of release and closure.

Conclude with specific prayers and blessings of release, peace, and love. Allow everyone time to let this animal know how honored they were to have shared this life, how grateful they are for the blessings of that relationship, and how much they will always love that animal. Encourage everyone present to release their ties to this animal so that she or he may easily move on to the next world.

Some families will choose to honor this animal's memory by giving a home to another animal in need. If this is the case, let the departed animal know that this is what you have chosen to do and ask for his or her blessing in this. Promise to honor and love the new animal as family, yet make it clear that no one will ever replace this departed animal in your hearts.

Finish up by doing something that may have been special to this animal. If this animal loved to hike in a particular place, go there for a walk; if this animal tended to be a couch potato, lie around all day. Be aware during this time of the possibility that this animal may decide to be with you.

Scattering an Animal's Ashes after Cremation Ceremony

Purify the area where the ashes will be scattered and all ritual items using any of the three purification ceremonies from chapter three. If this animal disliked smoke or fire, do not use smudge or incense unless this ceremony takes place at least one month after the death.

Set up a central altar on a table or a blanket. Place the container of ashes in the center along with a picture of the departed. Surround this with objects that were special to this animal, perhaps photos of a favorite place, food and water bowls, a blanket, etc.

Clear those attending with your smudge or drum as they enter. The ceremony leader should explain the symbolism of the altar and other decorations to those attending. Allow everyone some time to familiarize themselves with the room and altar.

Sit or stand in a circle. The leader should then invite everyone to hold hands and center for a moment. It may help to count down from ten to one.

Call upon the Spirits of the six directions and the Creator to join with you in this ceremony. Ask that they bless your work. Request guidance, that your every action may honor them.

Call upon the spirit of the departed to join with you. Let her know the reason for this ceremony and make it clear that you honor her through it.

"Through this ceremony, we release the ashes of our departed _____ . We commend your body and spirit to the Creator. May you once again become One with All That Is, in body and spirit. We gather here to honor your memory and send you our blessings for a joyous journey."

The leader directs the gathering in a special prayer or song at this point. I would only recommend that this focus on the continuity of life and love as well as celebrate life, freedom, and rebirth.

Holding the ashes, stand in the center of this circle. Have everyone go around the circle and speak their prayers for the departed. See these prayers enter the ashes. If you are aware of the departed there at the time, see these prayers flying directly to her.

If you need to travel to the specific area for scattering, do so now. If possible, have everyone follow you to this place. You may choose to sing or walk in silence. As her ashes fall to the Earth and are carried away on the wind, have all attending release her to her next world. Visualize letting go of the cords binding her to each of you and send your unconditional love for her out with her ashes.

"Your ashes have been released to the directions and to the Great Spirit. You are now free to move on to your next realm. Although we grieve for the times we will no longer share in this world, we rejoice in your freedom. We are grateful for the sharing of our lives during your time here in this world. Your memories and gifts live on within each of us as we freely release you to your next world. We send you heartfelt blessings of peace, love, and joy. We say not goodbye, but farewell until we meet again."

Allow everyone time to experience the ceremony and their feelings. They may wish to sit in silence for a while. Arrange to meet at a predetermined location for a meal. This allows any energy or grief to be grounded more easily and provides a supportive atmosphere for all concerned.

We need to be patient with animals in transition. It is equally important to continuously channel unconditional love to them. These are beings, just like us, who are about to take a huge step, beyond the physical life and the surroundings that they know so well. Imagine yourself in the animal's position, if you need help finding consistent compassion. Contemplate how you would feel, or how a child would feel, if faced with the possibility of entering that big Unknown alone.

Few animals remember past lives or the state between lives, while they reside in a physical body. Although they communicate and perceive differently than we do, they are subject to the same physical laws and limitations of this reality as we are. Even though our animals are frequently aware of noncorporeal beings, few can recall what to expect for themselves beyond physical life. They see noncorporeal life forms as just another being, not as a probable next step for them. They just don't normally think that way.

Above all, we need to be honest with the animals in our lives and with ourselves. As I discussed before, they know when we are holding back. While they may not understand what we are hiding, the fact that we are not being completely truthful can be stressful and frightening for them. Dishonesty can also block our own abilities to receive communication from the animal or from spirit guidance. In addition, it can interfere with successful grieving and release of attachments on both sides.

Again, I feel it is important to stress the fact that if an animal should choose to die in spite of all our attempts to heal the body, this should not be labeled as bad. It is no reflection on us or on our abilities and it is vital that we be supportive of this choice. As is true with humans, this is a choice that animals make, usually on a higher, more expansive level of being. If they choose to go, we respond by doing whatever is necessary to create an easy, loving death. Then we remain available if the animal needs guidance after physical death.

The deathwalk for an animal is very similar to that of a human, although it does appear that animals travel to different Lands of the Dead. Whether this is a function of our perceptive abilities and interpretations or not, is unknown. In my personal experience, most animals pass through the Veil and join others of their kind in a similar world.

Several years ago, I was saddened to see two dead dogs lying on the side of a busy Connecticut highway on my way to work. They both had collars on and were obviously someone's pets. It was also clear to me that they had been hit by a vehicle on the highway. I was powerfully aware of the spirits of these animals desperately seeking someone to help them get home. I allowed them into the back seat of my car and we pulled off to the side of the road.

During a simultaneous deathwalk for both dogs, my consciousness was split as I watched two very similar deathwalks occur. Each animal went to the same neighborhood but different houses. Apparently they were in the habit of slipping their leads and going off on adventures together before returning home.

These dogs found their worried families wondering why they had not yet returned home. I channeled peaceful, comforting energy to them as they became disturbed by the fact that their humans were not aware of them. I explained the situation to them, using feeling and image only. At that point and particularly with animals, words are far too limiting to be of any use.

They each spent a short time with family before I gently guided them past this, letting them know they could return whenever they chose to. I felt the usual tension of the Veil, as though passing through the surface of water. Once past the Veil, they were met by other dogs. A young human boy briefly greeted one of the dogs, but he faded quickly, smiling and waving as he went. I will not venture an opinion as to who this boy may have been. These two dogs stayed together as they ran and played with the other dogs. As they moved deeper into this reality, I felt the Veil close before me and I went on my way, late to work.

It is important to note that our work is not always complete once the journeying is done. It is not enough to handle a deathwalk or channel some good energy someone's way, while ignoring or avoiding any work that may need doing in this reality. In the above situation, it would have been very easy for me to let it go after the deathwalk.

However, there were two families frantically wondering where their pets were; and two bodies, deserving of proper burial, lying on the side of a highway. Since I had not been able to reach their bodies physically with rush hour traffic around me, it was necessary for me to call the State Police. It was also important that I follow up to be sure that their bodies had been retrieved and their families had been notified. The fact that the departed is animal rather than human should not affect our assuming this type of responsibility. Imagine if you would want to know whether that was your dog or cat, or your spouse or child.

Wild animals, in particular, tend not to be met by humanoid beings when they die. My spirit guides have told me that this is because wild animals have little experience with humans and have not learned to trust and depend on us as domesticated animals have. Wild animals are either greeted by a large personification of the species soul, or they enter a world similar to ours where they continue a type of parallel life for a short while before moving on.

Sometimes I will experience a humanoid deity form acknowledging the death-walk and receiving a wild animal, but it appears that the departed themselves are rarely aware of these beings. It is also quite possible that I interpret these beings as humanoid as a result of my own beliefs and conditioning.

Several years ago, my husband and I came upon a female white-tailed deer who was left paralyzed in the middle of a dark country road after having been hit by a vehicle. We stopped to see if she could be healed and to drag her off the road. She was sitting up and wide awake but her back had been broken. She was in no pain but it was clear she could not be physically healed. We channeled love and comfort to her, assuring her we would return soon. Then we went to call the police for assistance. By the time we got back to her, the police had already shot her and moved her off into the brush.

After they left, we held a simple honoring for her and I entered the shamanic trance to see if she needed my assistance. She was disoriented and afraid but she allowed me to lead her deeper into the forest. As we approached the Veil, the Gates opened. She continued in without a second look at me and joined a herd of other deer. It was as natural as breathing for her, although I am not certain whether she understood she was no longer in a physical body. At that point, it didn't matter. As the deer passed through the tension of the Veil, I saw a man and a woman at the

Gate. They felt very peaceful and loving yet very strong. They nodded to me as if to say "It is done" and the Gates closed behind them.

This experience illustrates my point regarding the humanoid beings acknowledging the deathwalk and the parallel world of others of the same species. This deer was utterly unaware of the man and woman who nodded to me and appeared to be Gatekeepers. She moved on quite normally to continue the life she was familiar with. The presence of a physical body was irrelevant, as were the Gatekeepers.

My feeling concerning these Gatekeepers varies with the deathwalk. Sometimes I get a clear impression of them as similar to Celtic deities of the Wilds. Other times, I get the feeling that they are much greater than my experience of them and that they are allowing me this perception as thanks for my assistance to the departed. In either case, they are certainly multidimensional beings encompassing far more than the symbol they present to me.

People have often called upon their own departed loved ones to watch over a departed pet. This is particularly true when the loved one knew the animal, or even lived in the same home with them. In this way, we instinctively invoke the continuing energy created in our relationships with our animals in this reality.

Just as we tend to carry our beliefs beyond physical life, so do our pets. They have lived their lives being cared for by their humans. They have come to believe that a human will always care for them. In calling upon a loved one, we are providing a human, usually one known to them, to continue to care for them on the Other side. Often the act of guiding and caring for another being shakes a spirit free of personal limitations. As they assist the newly departed, they create their own ability to take their next step, if they were previously stuck somewhere. This is also why so many pet animals will be greeted by a humanoid being after death. This is a comforting, familiar image for them. Domestic pets are often more easily willing to trust a human than another animal.

My mother created an interesting situation when she called on my departed grandmother to take our dog Misty after Misty's death. After some arguing that where my grandmother currently resided was not the place for a dog, my grandmother agreed to take her. Several months later, when my mother went looking for Misty to be sure she was all right, she found her with my grandmother and a family friend. They were walking around a holographic ring with a large number of other people in what appeared to be some type of learning phase between lives. This ring reminded my mother of the rings around Saturn.

My mother was not allowed to talk to Misty. She was told, in no uncertain terms, to leave Misty alone. The family friend said that they had assumed the responsibility and that Misty was learning quickly. My mother's presence was no longer required nor, apparently, was it welcome. It would appear that this was an uncommon occurrence that worked out all right.

Many people believe the spirits of departed pets remain with them in spirit for a period of time after death. Sometimes, these animals appear years after their physical deaths. In *Far Journeys*, Robert Monroe described his surprise at finding three beloved family cats sitting and observing him as he left his body.[68] Each of these cats had passed over within three years of this time. They had obviously chosen to stick around and keep an eye on their loved ones.

Some people believe that departed pets have protected them or saved them from certain disaster. I have a friend who frequently hears her childhood dog running through the house. To be honest, I have heard him myself. She swears that he appeared to her when she was driving one day. She instantly swerved to avoid him, since he appeared to be standing in the middle of the road before her oncoming car. Within seconds after she swerved, a drunk driver plowed into a stop sign just ahead of where she stopped. No one else in the car saw a dog. This woman is absolutely certain that she would have been killed or seriously injured by that drunk driver, if her childhood dog had not warned her and forced her to avoid the accident.

This is not surprising considering that many pets, especially dogs, assume responsibility for the protection of the pack while in this reality. A change in status from physical to spirit often does not deter these animals from their chosen role in defending those they love. After a lifetime of caring for them, many of these animals will choose to remain with us, returning the favor, until we pass from the physical as well. Talk about unconditional love and loyalty.

It is also not uncommon for our pets to let us know that they are all right and have made the transition successfully. As is true with humans, just because an animal has successfully passed into the Otherworld does not mean they will never return. It is quite common for animals and people to pop in to see how things are going or to let you know how they are doing. Those energetic bonds we share go a long way in maintaining communication beyond this reality. And as my friend discovered while driving that day, our pets can show up when you are in greatest need.

After burying our dog Misty on my parents' land, my parents, my husband, and I were sitting at the dining room table. Suddenly, all of us heard her characteristic bark—in this reality. It was nothing like a psychic *hearing*. It was clear that a dog outside had just barked exactly like Misty. My father flew out the door to check on her and be sure there were no other dogs around. There was no one for miles. Misty had just found a way to say goodbye.

In *Dr. Pitcairn's Natural Health for Cats and Dogs*, the authors describe the appearance of a cat, watching them, as they finished burying their beloved kitten, Miracle.[69]

Miracle had only been with them a short time, having been adopted from an animal shelter where the book's author, a veterinarian, had already saved her life twice. For a week, they nursed and comforted her. They discussed euthanasia but felt it would be somehow wrong for Miracle.

The Pitcairns write eloquently of Miracle's last night and of finding her body in the morning. Then they describe how they took her to a place they felt was "right" for her and buried her. As they finished covering her body with earth, they heard a rustling in the leaves. They looked up to find a cat watching them.

Although I was obviously not present, it appears to me that *someone* found a way to let them know that Miracle had successfully made the transition. They were given the realization that life and love does continue after physical life. Perhaps, this was Miracle's way of thanking them for their love and kindness at the time when she so desperately needed it most. In any event, these authors were reminded of our interconnections with All Life and the continuity of Spirit.

Often our pets find more subtle ways to communicate with us from beyond this life, through dreaming for example. Many people dream of recently departed pets. Unfortunately, this is often viewed as wishful thinking, or the subconscious attempting to deal with grief. In reality, it is more often an honest communication from a loved one who was recently in animal form in our reality. For our own healing and growth, we need to accept these messages and honor the love that prompted them. They are a special gift.

Those methods for communication with the departed described in previous chapters are equally as effective with animals. In truth, these methods are often easier with animals due to their relative lack of blocks and limiting beliefs both in physical life and beyond. Both dreaming and journeying work exceptionally well with animals that have passed over. The exercises in this book for contacting spirit guides and the deathwalk exercise can both be adapted to contact departed pets or anyone else.

Those energy cords that bind us to other humans we have relationships with, also bind us to the animals we love. In the case of animals, it is most commonly a heart chakra attachment. Not only do animals tend to relate on a mainly emotional level, but their unconditional love for us activates and opens our hearts. In a society that frowns on overt emotions and softness, many of us need animals to break through the blocks we have created within our hearts.

Animals have a way of reminding us who we are deep within. We are free to be open and childlike with them without fear of ridicule or rejection. Animals do not judge us by our clothes or our jobs or our stuff, all they care about is protecting and loving us, and how we treat them. The more love we lavish on them, the more we feel and the more love we receive. They are often our lifelines; our connections to unconditional love and Spirit. Human relationships can gain much through observing the way pets interact with their people.

I experienced a very interesting deathwalk with a man who pestered me for two nights in September, 1997. He didn't want any spiritual guidance and was not interested in contacting his spirit guides, but he would not leave me alone. By the second night, I had enough. I wrapped him into my energy body and swept him down to the Lowerworld to see if he might change his mind about staying in our reality.

We ended up in a place where he was greeted by many people he knew. They were all very happy to see him and he rather coolly said hello to each of them. As I went to leave, I had a strong feeling that this was not complete. I heard "This is not far enough," so I grabbed him and we went down a nearby hole.

A short time later, we popped into a sunny meadow. As soon as we emerged, a large dog leaped at the man. I turned to see the man as much younger, approximately in his early twenties. His face was beaming as he embraced this dog. I suddenly *knew* that this was his beloved dog that had passed over many years ago. The man had never gotten over the loss. I watched as they ran and played happily together. Just before I turned to leave, the man looked at me and quickly smiled a "thank you" before tumbling into the grass with his dog. I have not seen him since.

This situation beautifully illustrates just how attached we can become to these animals that share our lives. They really do tug at our heartstrings. These animals are our friends, our children, our protectors, and our teachers. They embody the natural world, our suppressed wildness, and our spirit guides. In several religions, it is believed that we can reincarnate between forms on earth.

Robert Monroe writes of an encounter with an animal at an entry point between lives. This being was just about to enter human form for the first time. This being appeared to be smaller than him and was quite surprised to have "qualified" for the human incarnation. This small spirit said that the being had never been human but had studied them for a long time. "I've lived with them, they've fed and loved me . . . and now I . . . I'm going to be human." The being was very excited to go on and be a "good one."[70]

In *Animal Talk*, Penelope Smith writes that she has found animals who previously incarnated as human, and humans that were once animals. She goes on to say that some of our present pets are really guardians or allies, wanting only to serve us in any way they can. These pets and people may have incarnated together before in human relationships or the present pets may have been looking after their people from other realities as spirit guides.[71] So the next time you think your animal friend is almost human, you may be closer to the truth than you realize.

Keep in mind that these beings, who are currently in animal bodies, love us unconditionally. This is a tremendous gift that should not be taken lightly. In our relationships with the animals we love, we can also use Death to our advantage as an ally or advisor. When we treat every encounter with them in this life, as though it were our last encounter with them, we honor ourselves as well as our pets. This allows everyone to enter the next World without regret, satisfied that we have loved and lived with honor.

Let us honor these special beings, both in life and in their rites of passage. Allow yourself to feel and to speak from your heart during ceremonies and in any communication. They don't care if your grammar is correct or even if it makes logical sense. They *feel* what you mean, just like they always have. Experience your feelings of sadness and loss, but rejoice in their freedom. And in the end, return their gift of unconditional love as you release them.

Endnotes

65 First published in *Circle Network News*, summer 1997 issue.
66 Pitcairn & Pitcairn, *Dr. Pitcairn's Natural Health for Cats and Dogs*, pp. 104–107.
67 Popular neo-pagan song, often sung at festivals; author unknown.
68 Monroe, *Far Journeys*, p. 268.
69 Pitcairn & Pitcairn, *Dr. Pitcairn's Natural Health for Cats and Dogs*, pp. 134–135.
70 Monroe, *Far Journeys*, p. 138.
71 Smith, *Animal Talk: Interspecies Telepathic Communication*, p. 92.

Chapter 10

IN PARTING

Throughout the course of this life, we experience many births and deaths. These are not always physical changes, but each represents the ending of one chapter of our lives and the beginning of a new adventure. These deaths may manifest as a move, a graduation, a change in a relationship, or a personal transformation, but all contribute to our growth and development as spiritual beings.

The death of the physical body is just another change in status, a graduation if you will. When we have accomplished what we chose to do during this incarnation, we move on. We graduate from that particular lesson plan. In leaving our bodies behind, we free ourselves of the limitations of this reality. We merge with the Oneness of the multiverse and journey to our respective next steps in our energy forms. This viewpoint is not limited to those on a shamanic path but seems to have gradually become once more part of our collective consciousness.

Our departed loved ones are not gone from us. They have moved, in a sense. We may no longer be able to interact with them on a purely physical level, but we can still communicate with them and, in most shamanic cultures, they are understood to have the ability to continue to affect our reality. They can become our guides and guardians, as well as our children and grandchildren when they choose to reincarnate.

Many people believe that the years surrounding the millennium are likely to be times of upheaval and change. Many of these people expect great numbers of deaths during this period of transformation, due to Earth changes and possibly wars. They point to the ending of the Mayan calendar, the Hopi prophecies, and the writings of Nostradamus. If these prophecies and beliefs do come true, then the need for an understanding and acceptance of death will be even greater in the coming years. There will also be a tremendous need for anyone able to guide and assist others through the transition, on both sides of the Veil.

Even if this is nothing more than millennium fever, it is a fact that as modern society gains more in progress, we lose in our spirituality and our emotional well-being. We see this manifest in our unhealthy relationships, abandoned children, increasing crimes, and the unbelievable dichotomy between rich and poor. Every minute people die feeling afraid and alone because they have no support and no idea what to expect once their bodies cease to live.

In our reality, people experience wars, epidemics, and natural disasters that all result in large numbers of beings leaving this existence together. Most of these people lost their respect for death long ago. Yet, they fear death because it is no longer acknowledged as a natural part of life; it has become the Big Unknown.

In truth, death is not unknown to us. We have all been there before and we will each experience it again. Our conscious minds have merely forgotten. When we reincarnate, we become subject to the limitations of this reality and our own beliefs. These limitations create an effective filter to the limitless knowing we all experience beyond the physical realm. It is for this reason that so few of us remember our dreams. We have allowed our rational minds to take full control as we have become more modernized and more civilized.

As modern society has evolved, we have divorced ourselves from as many natural cycles as possible. We insulate ourselves in climate-controlled cars and buildings. Women no longer menstruate with moon cycles because of artificial lighting, ingested hormones, and our own beliefs that these cycles are somehow inferior or shameful. Many of us love to watch nature shows and subscribe to magazines like *National Geographic,* but a relative few have ever really experienced a one-on-one relationship with deep wilderness.

I do not say this to place judgments. It is a fact. And the further we get from our *wildness* and our spirituality, the more we feel that something is missing in our lives. We need to cram in as many vacations and as much *stuff* as possible before death, because this may be our one and only chance. And we desperately hope that these things will satisfy that feeling of loss in our centers.

Modern people work hard, play hard, and shop hard in a fruitless attempt to fill that hole we all seem to feel. That place within us that recognizes our loss of the experience of our interconnections with all of life. We get that good job or that nice house and soon after, it just isn't enough. We need *more!* We buy hairplugs, makeup, and new clothes to try to cheat old age. And in the end, we fear and resist death to the point that some of us are willing to live connected to machines in a hospital bed forever, just so we won't have to face that Big Unknown.

Although modern science is beginning to discover what shamans and mystics have experienced for millennia, historically, science has been very mechanistic. We have been indoctrinated for generations that nothing is real unless it is tangible and can be reproduced in the laboratory. A large number of us believe (or fear) that we are nothing more than our bodies. When our bodies die, we just end. We cease to exist.

Youth has become the ideal in most of our societies. Both males and females are given physical role models that are rarely the norm for our society. In a futile attempt to live up to these images, we have developed eating disorders and dangerously low self-esteem. While these men and women are beautiful, they are not alone. We are all beautiful and sacred in our own right, whether we match the current societal image of perfection or not.

Too many of us ship off our elderly to nursing homes and call them once a year. We rob and beat them and laugh at their feeble bodies and failing minds. We lay them off or force them to retire early to make room for college graduates with new ideas. They are old and, therefore, no longer of value.

Most indigenous peoples, and all those who truly walk a shamanic path, understand the beauty and power inherent in aging. Elders are honored and respected for their life experience and their personal wisdom. A lifetime of experience is at least as valuable as a college degree. This is the difference between *knowledge* and *wisdom*.

The power of the Winter of Life is revered by all. Those nearing death are cared for and prepared to meet their passing with strength and ease. Their closeness to the Other side is a sacred gift to the community, as they are more easily able to vision for their people. Death, as a natural transition as wonderful as birth, is handled with love, honor, and respect.

Our cultural denial and fear of death also manifests in our reactions to the sick in our societies. We fear them. Often, we don't even want to see them. How many people have been fired from jobs or abandoned by friends as the result of HIV? These people don't even need to have full-blown AIDS to be outcast. We avoid germs to the extent that everything seems to antibacterial today, even toothbrushes. What we are missing is an understanding of balance in all things.

Although we all have our own cultural and personal beliefs regarding death and dying, both modern and traditional deathwalkers share methods and experiences that correlate with others across the globe. We have all walked the Roads of the Dead to guide both animals and humans to the next World. We all work to create healing for those in transition and among those who remain in this reality. This healing may take the form of rituals, physical and energetic healings, or counseling and guidance.

Since an increasing number of modern people are moving away from religion and spirituality, rites of passage have been largely forgotten. They are no longer the sacred markings of passage into another life phase. The death ritual is the last vestige of this ceremonial marking of life's great changes. Unfortunately, even this ritual has become a hollow social event rather than a catalyst for healing and release. Often it becomes either a burden or an effective means of repression for loved ones. There is a real need in our culture for honest ceremonies that speak to our souls. Once we permit our egos to take a break from their continual self-protection, we can allow ourselves to grieve successfully.

Those walking a shamanic path use the shamanic journey and altered states of consciousness in many ways. We work to connect with guides, work in dreaming, and remain open to universal wisdom so that we may be of greatest service to our communities. What was once the realm of a select few who received the shamanic Call is now available, at least in part, to all of us.

Many indigenous cultures believed that everyone had the ability to journey and this was most often done through dreaming. Today, not only are we more aware of our dreams and their significance, but an increasing number of us are learning to consciously use the shamanic journey for our own personal evolution. With the advent of the millennium, our collective consciousness does appear to be quickening.

In the last few decades, our world has become a much smaller place. As a result, we now have access to spiritual philosophies and disciplines that once existed only in the outside world. This is one experience we can thank the Age of Technology for. We are becoming One People and as a result, many of us feel a change occurring in the energy of our reality.

We have expanded, whether we planned to or not. The media and cyberspace has broadened our horizons and exposed us to ideas and cultures very different from our own. There has been an integration of many different paths in the consciousness of millions of people. These different paths each hold a piece of the puzzle for the individual. As they begin to gel in one's being, and the seeds of enlightenment take root, the individual jumps up an evolutionary step or two.

I understand this expansion as just that: a matter of evolution. According to Professor Catterall of Syracuse University, the brain forms new connections between neurons during any kind of learning.[72] Over time, these connections become more defined and change their strength depending on the need for each. It is my opinion that we access our shamanic and psychic abilities through generally unused neural pathways. The more we use them, the stronger they become.

This would also explain why these abilities tend to run in families. I believe we are genetically passing on these abilities to our children. With each generation, we produce more children with easier access to these abilities and less indoctrinated limiting beliefs. However, the fact that more and more adults are seeking ways to develop their own innate access to these pathways is contributing to the quickening of our collective unconscious.

Eventually, we will approach a critical mass and the "Hundredth Monkey" phenomenon will occur. This is a term coined by Ken Keyes, Jr., in his book of the same name, in which he discovered that once enough monkeys on an island had learned a specific new behavior, overnight all of the monkeys exhibited that behavior. Perhaps, this is the big change that will occur through the millennium. Enough people will have reactivated these pathways and we will experience a new civilization.

It is interesting to note that modern shamans are our friends, our neighbors, our lawyers, and our plumbers. Whether they name themselves as shamans or not, they work within our communities to channel healing to us and to support us in our personal and cultural evolution. These are individuals who are consciously focusing the necessary energy to bolster a cultural change in consciousness. Very often, they cross cultural boundaries and incorporate modern metaphysical philosophies in their efforts to live an honorable life. In recent years, more shamans are turning to modern science in an effort to reach those with limiting belief systems.

Through modern science we have learned that reality is not what it appears. Our three-dimensional perception limits our ability to truly comprehend our four-dimensional reality. I believe it is quite possible that as we reactivate psychic and shamanic pathways, our perceptive abilities will also increase. We experience life through the filter of this perception, which is further limited by our beliefs. We interpret our experiences based upon the symbolism of language and the images we have available to us.

Even our power animals and other spiritual guides are not merely that manifestation we experience them to be. What we perceive is a symbol, interpreted by us and translated into consciousness so that we may better comprehend their lessons for us. In reality, they are multidimensional beings and an embodiment of multiversal energies beyond our human understanding.

234

Recently, modern science has begun to discover physical evidence that confirms many of the experiences of mystics and shamans throughout time and across the globe. As I delve deeper into quantum weirdness (albeit as a nonphysicist), I am struck by the recent theories of wormholes. I am enthralled at theories that propose that black holes may transport energy-matter from our reality to other realities and that quasars (or white holes) may work opposite of this theorized black hole transport and bring energy-matter into our reality from other realities. The Many Worlds Interpretations of Quantum Mechanics intrigue me, as they seem to be bordering on the shamanic knowledge of parallel lives and Other worlds.

In these theories, I see modern scientific interpretations of the shamanic journey into other Worlds through openings in the sky and tunnels below the earth. I also see hope for the future of our overly technological society. Computers are wonderful inventions; in fact I use one daily. I also benefit from many other technological advances of our time. But I envision a preferred reality for all the world's children.

Someday, I expect to see a more holistic school of modern mathematics and physics that will explain in "rational" terms what mystics and shamans have been doing for millennia. I pray for a balanced society of technology and spirituality. It is time for a healthy equilibrium between God and Goddess. My dream for our children (and our own future selves) is a world that recognizes the sacredness inherent in all things and our interconnections with all our relations. And I wonder how we will all feel about death then.

As Chris Griscom writes, "Death is only a passage, a surrendering, which guides us forth into the expansion, into that expanding swirl which is our true self without encumberment."[73] A friend recently wrote of her discussions with two scientists at the Lawrence Berkeley Laboratory. They were discussing how an energy fragment smaller than an electron races frantically around in an attempt to reintegrate with the whole.

Many of us see this as an apt analogy to the incarnation situation. As we choose to incarnate, we become more defined, more limited. We live our lives evolving and learning in an attempt to reintegrate that whole we forgot about when we incarnated. Death then becomes our successful return to complete integration with the totality of the multiverse and ourselves. We release the necessary limitations of a physical body and expand to include All That Is.

I can also see this as an equally apt analogy to modern society. We truly have become separated from the Whole. From the development of the ego in our toddler years, we are forever frantically racing around blindly in an attempt to reconnect. We just don't remember, or don't choose to recognize, what it is we are trying to reconnect with. Once we are able to reintegrate our total selves, including our shadows, we spontaneously reconnect with All Life. And then we find peace.

235

We also find peace once death is no longer viewed as a frightening unknown. When we accept death as a natural part of life and a mere transition through which we gain rather than lose, we can begin to work with Death as an ally. Death is as powerful a transformation as birth. It is the ultimate shamanic initiation. We each experience a complete physical and spiritual transition as we become a more complete being. Once we leave or enter a new incarnation, we have embarked upon an incredible new adventure.

We cannot return to the way things were, just as an adult cannot return to age three. But we do not lose our loves nor do we lose our memories. We know we will be together soon enough in a form beyond the physical and we may yet be together in a physical reality again. And that is all right, because we are exploring both new and familiar realms. We'll take a trip and catch up with loved ones later.

With this understanding, Death automatically becomes an ally. We may need to remind ourselves of this occasionally when life trips us up, but for the most part, we view our lives and our loved ones with expanded, wiser eyes. We see this life from the much broader perspective of our total spiritual existence, which is without beginning and without end. Each life is a unique and beautiful patchwork in the complete quilt of our experience. And our loved ones are the brilliant "points of light" that sustain and invigorate our souls.

Some people might think that the realization that this life is not all there is might lead to a lack of concern; an "oh well, I'll get it next time" attitude. Quite the contrary, we recognize that what we leave unfinished, we really do get all over again. We have renewed incentive to live our Earthwalk with honor and respect. We do this, not out of guilt or to satisfy some human authority or a vengeful god, but to contribute to our personal and collective spiritual evolution. So, we live each day with an understanding that it may be our last.

Many people may find it depressing or frightening to consider each day as though it may be your last. I find my life is wonderfully happy and satisfying when each choice is made as though it were my last choice. I have no regrets; no guilt. Those I care about know without question they are loved. Whether I choose to pack a day full or lie on the couch, I choose according to my heart. Even days where I have a list of "must-dos," I experience the beauty in that day. Each being I meet is respected as my relation and potential teacher. I know that if I die tomorrow, I have lived an honorable life and have brought love and, hopefully, growth to those around me through my example.

Death can be a powerful ally if used to empower yourself with courage and love. When we can meet our deaths with honor and the knowledge that our lives were lived wisely and honestly, perhaps our societies will also come into balance and respect.

When we renew our ties to the rest of Life and universal energies, we *recognize* that we are integral parts of the Oneness permeating the multiverse. We remember that we do not really die, we just change. And to be honest, change really is the only constant there is. To remain the same is to limit our own growth.

We are the caterpillars who become butterflies. When we emerge, our forms have changed and we are able to experience a world of things we never could as caterpillars, but we are the same beings. Should the caterpillar fear the chrysalis or its emergence from the safety of that chrysalis? Certainly not; it is a natural part of the caterpillar's life cycle. To attempt to avoid this would be limiting its glory, both as caterpillar and butterfly.

When we attempt to cheat or deny death, we dishonor ourselves as limitless creators of and participants in our realities. We fear the butterfly within us all. We also dishonor that Great Spirit which created us and continues to support us lovingly until we return. To fly may take courage, but what wonderful rewards for taking the leap!

Blessed Journeys.

Endnotes

72 Simon Catterall, *The Mind and Machine Module* Web site.
73 Chris Griscom, *Ecstasy is a New Frequency*, p. 155.

APPENDIX: CONTACTS

The Monroe Institute
62 Roberts Mountain Road
Faber, VA, 22938
Telephone: (804) 361-1252
E-mail: MonroeInst@aol.com
Web site: www.monroeinstitute.org

The Avatar Course
Star's Edge International
237 N. Westmonte Dr.
Altamonte Springs, FL 32714
Telephone: (407) 788-3090
E-mail: avatar@avatarhq.com
Web site: www.starsedge.com

Richard Ross
Telephone: (208) 853-2980
E-mail: Coachwiz@richardross.com

Silva International (The Silva Method courses)
P.O. Box 2249
Laredo, TX 78044
Telephone: (956) 722-6391
E-mail: silvamethod@silvaintl.com
Web site: www.silvaintl.com

Kundalini Yoga and Pranayama:
Sikh Dharma/The 3HO Foundation,
International Secretariat,
P.O. Box 351149
Los Angeles, CA 90035
Telephone: (310) 552-3416/557-8414

Foundation for Shamanic Studies
P.O. Box 1939
Mill Valley, CA 94942
Telephone: (415) 380-8282
Web site: www.shamanism.org

Maureen B. Roberts, Ph.D.
Telephone: (Australia) 61 8 8362 0980
E-mail: nathair@camtech.net.au

To receive a catalog of publication and workshops by Penelope Smith, contact
Pegasus Publications: P.O. Box 1060, Point Reyes, CA 94956, (415) 663-1247

REFERENCES

Ahlback, Tore, ed. *Saami Religion*. Abo, Finland: The Donner Institute for Research in Religious and Cultural History. 1987.

Ajaya, Ph.D., Swami. *Psychotherapy East and West: A Unifying Paradigm*. Honesdale, PA: The Himalayan International Institute of Yoga Science and Philosophy of the USA. 1983.

Andrews, Ted. *Animal-Speak*. St. Paul, MN: Llewellyn Publications. 1996.

Brennan, Barbara. *Hands of Light*. New York, NY: Bantam Books. 1987.

Campbell, Joseph. *The Power of Myth*. New York, NY: Doubleday. 1988.

Capra, Fritjof. *The Tao of Physics*. Boston, MA: Shambhala Publications, Inc. 1991.

Catterall, Simon. *The Mind and Machine Module*. Syracuse, NY: Syracuse University, www.suhep.phy.syr.edu/courses/CCD_NEW/mind. 1997.

Castenada, Carlos. *The Power of Silence: Further Lessons of Don Juan*. New York, NY: Simon & Schuster. 1987.

———. *Journey to Ixtlan*. Harmondsworth, Middlesex, England: Penguin Books Ltd. 1974.

———. *The Fire From Within*. New York, NY: Simon & Schuster. 1984.

Chappell, Miken, ed. *Avatar Journal*. Fall 1997 issue, inside cover. Altamonte Springs, FL: Star's Edge International. 1997.

Clow, Barbara Hand. *Eye of the Centaur*. Santa Fe, NM: Bear & Company Publishing. 1986.

Collinder, Bjorn. *The Lapps*. Princeton, NJ: Princeton University Press for the American Scandinavian Foundation. 1949.

Conway, D. J. *By Oak, Ash, & Thorn*. St. Paul, MN: Llewellyn Publications. 1995.

REFERENCES

Davies, Paul and Gribbin, John. *The Matter Myth*. New York, NY:
Simon & Schuster/Touchstone. 1992.

Eliade, Mircea. *Archaic Techniques of Ecstasy*. Princeton, NJ: Princeton University Press,
Bollingen Foundation. 1964.

Farrar, Stewart. *Writer on a Broomstick*. draft for Starwood workshop. 1995.

Griscom, Chris. *Ecstasy is a New Frequency*. Santa Fe, NM: Bear & Company. 1987.

Grof, Stanislav. *Beyond the Brain: Birth, Death, and Transcendence in Psychotherapy*. Albany,
NY: State University of New York Press. 1985.

Harner, Michael. *Way of the Shaman*. New York, NY: HarperCollins Publishers. 1980.

Jung, Carl G. *Man and His Symbols*. Chicago, IL: Ferguson Publishing Company. 1968.

Keyes, Jr., Ken, *The Hundredth Monkey*. Koos Bay, OR: Vision Books. 1982.

Mails, Thomas E. *Secret Native American Pathways*. Tulsa, OK: Council Oak Books. 1993.

Monroe, Robert A. *Ultimate Journey*. New York, NY: Doubleday. 1994.

———. *Far Journeys*. New York, NY: Doubleday. 1985.

Palmer, Harry. *Living Deliberately*. Altamonte Springs, FL: Star's Edge
International. 1994.

———. *ReSurfacing*. Altamonte Springs, FL: Star's Edge International. 1994.

Pitcairn D.V.M., Ph.D., Richard and Pitcairn, Susan Hubble. *Dr. Pitcairn's Complete Guide
to Natural Health for Cats and Dogs*. Emmaus, PA: Rodale Press, Inc. 1982.

Rama, Swami, Rudolph Ballantine, M.D., and Alan Hymes, M.D. *Science of Breath*. Honesdale, PA: The Himalayan International Institute of Yoga
Science and Philosophy of the USA. 1979.

Roberts, Dr. Maureen B. *Soul-Making and Soul-Retrieval: Creative Bridges Between Shamanism and Depth Psychology*. (work-in-progress, 1998.)

Rydving, Hakan. *The End of Drum Time*. Uppsala, Sweden: Uppsala University. 1995.

Sanchez, Victor. *The Teachings of Don Carlos*. Santa Fe, NM: Bear & Company Publishing.
1995.

Singh, Ravi. *Kundalini Yoga for Strength, Success, & Spirit*. New York, NY: White Lion
Press. 1991.

Smith, Penelope. *Animal Talk: Interspecies Telepathic Communication*. Point Reyes, CA:
Pegasus Publications. 1989, third edition.

Wheeler, John A. "Foreword" in *The Anthropological Principle* by John D. Barrow and Frank
J. Tipler. (Oxford, UK: Clarendon Press, 1986), p. vii.

Wolf, Fred Alan. *Parallel Universes*. New York, NY: Simon & Schuster. 1988.

240

INDEX

245

Animal-Speak

The Spiritual & Magical Powers of Creatures Great & Small

Ted Andrews

The animal world has much to teach us. Some are experts at survival and adaptation, some never get cancer, some embody strength and courage while others exude playfulness. Animals remind us of the potential we can unfold, but before we can learn from them, we must first be able to speak with them.

In this book, myth and fact are combined in a manner that will teach you how to speak and understand the language of the animals in your life. *Animal-Speak* helps you meet and work with animals as totems and spirits—by learning the language of their behaviors within the physical world. It provides techniques for reading signs and omens in nature so you can open to higher perceptions and even prophecy. It reveals the hidden, mythical and realistic roles of 45 animals, 60 birds, 8 insects, and 6 reptiles.

Animals will become a part of you, revealing to you the majesty and divine in all life. They will restore your childlike wonder of the world and strengthen your belief in magic, dreams, and possibilities.

0–87542–028–1, 400 pp., 7 x 10, illus., photos, softcover $17.95

By Oak, Ash, & Thorn

Modern Celtic Shamanism

D. J. Conway

Many spiritual seekers are interested in shamanism because it is a spiritual path that can be followed in conjunction with any religion or other spiritual belief without conflict. Shamanism has not only been practiced by Native American and African cultures—for centuries, it was practiced by the Europeans, including the Celts.

By Oak, Ash, & Thorn presents a workable, modern form of Celtic shamanism that will help anyone raise his or her spiritual awareness. Here, in simple, practical terms, you will learn to follow specific exercises and apply techniques that will develop your spiritual awareness and ties with the natural world: shape-shifting, divination by the Celtic Ogham alphabet, Celtic shamanic tools, traveling to and using magick in the three realms of the Celtic otherworlds, empowering the self, journeying through meditation and more.

Shamanism begins as a personal revelation and inner healing, then evolves into a striving to bring balance and healing into the Earth itself. This book will ensure that Celtic shamanism will take its place among the spiritual practices that help us lead fuller lives.

1–56718–166-X, 288 pp., 6 x 9, illus., softcover $14.95

To order, call 1-800-THE MOON
Prices subject to change without notice